T0306144

FINANCIALIZATION AND THE FUTURE OF THE AMERICAN ECONOMY

Financialization is a set of processes which has led to a financially driven and commodified economy with rising inequality, tax avoidance, and a lack of investment in the physical and social infrastructure. Given the influence of money politics, and the secular increase in the burden of debt, financialization has produced a deeply flawed economic system which mainstream economists are unable to address. This book discusses the causes and costs of financial crises, how financialization produces inequality and instability, and the patterns of value extraction it enables. It draws on key theoretical traditions, most prominently the writing of Marx, Keynes, and Minsky that illuminate much that is ignored and rejected in mainstream theorizing, including by many who identify as Keynesians. After decades of low interest rates and years of quantitative easing (QE), keeping borrowing costs near zero, many borrowers – households, businesses, banks, shadow banks, and governments – will not be able to finance their debt at the higher interest rates initiated by central banks to address inflation. The resulting stagflation will be global, producing a severe downturn that may be postponed through still greater debt creation but not avoided by conventional means. The book also explores the ways that standard financial criteria contribute to the climate emergency and the manner in which the commodification of nature proceeds from the desire to create new, marketable derivative products. It concludes with a discussion of what needs to be done to move away from a harmful regime of accumulation premised on financialization and to adopt a far better one. This book is essential reading for anyone interested in the causes and consequences of financialization and its impact on the economy.

William K. Tabb is Professor Emeritus of Economics Queens College and of Economics, Political Science and Sociology at the Graduate Center of the City University of New York.

FINANCIALIZATION AND THE FUTURE OF THE AMERICAN ECONOMY

William K. Tabb

Routledge
Taylor & Francis Group

LONDON AND NEW YORK

Designed cover image: Image taken by the author, their own photo

First published 2024
by Routledge
4 Park Square, Milton Park, Abingdon, Oxon OX14 4RN

and by Routledge
605 Third Avenue, New York, NY 10158

Routledge is an imprint of the Taylor & Francis Group, an informa business

British Library Cataloguing-in-Publication Data
A catalogue record for this book is available from the British Library

ISBN: 978-1-032-47247-8 (hbk)
ISBN: 978-1-032-47246-1 (pbk)
ISBN: 978-1-003-38524-0 (ebk)

DOI: 10.4324/9781003385240

Typeset in Bembo
by Apex CoVantage, LLC

CONTENTS

1

INTRODUCTION

The financial sector extracts economic surplus produced in other parts of the economy. Its growth has increased inequalities in income, wealth, and political influence, and its tools of analysis and criteria for investment have imposed devastating damage on the planet. Such concerns are central to this study, as are the costs of the Great Recession, which vastly exceed the capacity of the financial institutions that crashed the economy to make reparations, had they been asked to do so. Rather, they were rescued by the Federal Reserve even as working people suffered as collateral damage from the events that had transpired. The theoretical discussion of the causes of financial crises analyzed here differs significantly from many other available accounts. It extends beyond the challenges that financial crises present for governments and central banks, and beyond the stabilizing efforts that are the topic of most studies, which do not delve into the cost of the finance accumulation regime that has been promoted by the Federal Reserve. This study focuses on the U.S. but also considers the impact of decisions by the Fed on the economies of other nations.

We begin our inquiry with a question that was asked at the London School of Economics (LSE) in 2008 by the Queen of England for the light it sheds on the understanding of economists regarding financial economics in the real world. The Queen famously wanted to know about the Global Financial Crisis: "If these things were so large, how come everyone missed them?" Explaining the origins of the crisis, Professor Luis Garicano, director of research at the management department of the LSE, told the Queen, "At every stage, someone was relying on somebody else and everyone thought they were doing the right thing" (Greenhill 2008). His observation was accurate to be sure, though hardly much of an answer – but then economists generally have not done well in responding to this question.

On a tour of the Bank of England four years later, Her Majesty received an unsolicited comment as she stopped at the gold vault. Sujit Kapadia, one of the Bank's

DOI: 10.4324/9781003385240-1

top financial policy experts, interrupted the Queen to say he would like to answer the question she had first posed at the LSE. "Oh," she said, slightly taken aback. He told the Queen that financial crises are "a bit like earthquakes and flu pandemics in being rare and difficult to predict" (Neate 2012). However, perhaps to follow on Kapadia's analogies, while their exact timing cannot be predicted, indicators do precede their occurrence, tremors before an earthquake, not feeling one's best before it is clear that flu has arrived. As to being rare, this is a question of perspective. Financial crises are familiar events to economic historians (Kindleberger and Aliber 2005).

Former Fed Governor Tom Hoenig had warned about the consequences of asset bubbles for a decade before the Great Recession occurred (Leonard 2022). Others also had reason to foresee the coming crisis (Fullbrook 2010; Dyer 2021). As to the earlier answer the Queen had received at the LSE: if "everyone relies on everybody else and in doing so thinks they are doing the right thing," it would be well for economists to understand *why* everyone doing the same thing for too long can offer a prediction of a coming crisis. In Chapter 6, "The Mainline Tradition and Endogenous Cycles," the explanations given by Marx, Keynes, Minsky, and others will be offered to explain that in financial markets "everyone doing the right thing" often fails and leads to financial crises.

On June 17, 2009, the British Academy convened a group of prominent academics, journalists, politicians, along with past and present civil servants for a roundtable discussion to provide an authoritative response to the Queen. The chairman, Professor Peter Hennessy, explained that a purpose of the forum was to offer the basis for an "unofficial command paper" that attempted to answer her question. Hennessy and Professor Tim Beasley signed a letter addressed to Her Majesty which summarized the views raised in their discussions. It noted that "some of the best mathematical minds" were involved in risk management but that "they frequently lost sight of the bigger picture." The writers concluded on behalf of the assembled notables that

> failure to foresee the timing, extent and severity of the crisis and to head it off, while it had many causes, was principally a failure of the collective imagination of many bright people, both in this country and internationally, to understand the risks to the system as a whole.
>
> *(2009)*

The collective imagination must do better. And the ways in which we can both understand the bigger picture and change that picture will be discussed.

Another group of U.K. economists wrote to the Queen that, while agreeing with many of the points made by the academy, they found the letter to be inadequate because it failed to acknowledge deficiencies in the training and culture of economists. While recognizing that models and techniques "are important," they argued that given the complexity of the global economy, what is needed "is a broader range of models and techniques governed by a far greater respect for substance, and much more attention to historical, institutional, psychological, and other highly relevant factors." The Besley and Hennessy letter overlooked "the part that many leading economists have had in turning economics into a discipline that is detached from the real world, and in promoting unrealistic assumptions that have helped to sustain an uncritical view of how markets operate" (Hodgson 2009). These responses form the underlying assumptions for the present study, which rejects what has been the "be all and end all" criteria for economists: market efficiency. It is the economists' favoring market allocation with minimal regulation as "efficient" that has led to crises caused by "mistakes" that are better understood as risk-taking with other people's money to such a dangerous extent that financial collapse becomes inevitable. The failure to see whose interest is guiding decision-making is a problem that extends beyond choices made by financiers, to those taken by government officials and functionaries of political parties.

During the 2008 crisis, senior members of the investment bank community defended the simpler "nobody could have known" story. When the Global Financial Crisis broke in August 2007, David Viniar, the CFO of Goldman Sachs, declared that his institution had experienced "25 standard deviation" events several days in a row. As John Kay writes of Viniar's comment, "anyone with a knowledge of statistics knows that the occurrence of several '25 standard-deviation events' within a short time is impossible. What he meant to say was that the company's risk models failed to describe what had happened" (2015:100). We shall explore why such risk models are deeply problematic when it comes to predicting discontinuous events in the economy.

The next financial crisis, which followed a little over a decade later, was almost universally attributed to the onslaught of Covid-19 and its economic impact. The usual explanations for the crisis and the resulting inflation referred to the consequences of the pandemic on the labor force and supply chains as well as the impact of the war in Ukraine. However, it is helpful to contemplate a counter-history, one in which a financial crisis would have occurred without these contingent events as a result of the changed structure of the debt-dependent global political economy. The crisis threatened greater risk in a financial system in which deregulation and the continued low-interest policy of central bankers had allowed the overextension of credit in a slow-growth economy, a pyramiding of fictitious capital that would not have found a counterpart in the real returns necessary to repay or continue to finance the debt overhang. Even as growth slowed, global debt had risen at twice the rate of the global Gross Domestic Product (GDP). Investment notably involved financial assets rather than an increase in the output of goods and non-financial services.

After the new global downturn, Britain was back in the headlines and a new question was being asked in the U.S. Federal Reserve researchers and administration officials were questioning experts as to whether a market meltdown of the kind that had recently befallen the U.K. "could happen here." The not very reassuring answer was that it probably could, even though it did not appear imminent. "While the shock was British-specific, the violent reaction has caused economists around the world to wonder if the situation was a canary in a coal mine as signs of financial stress surface around the globe" (Smialek, Tangersley, and Rennison 2022). There was a lot of worry in the markets and for good reason, as will be argued here.

Debt levels had risen remarkably in the 21st century, and not only in the U.S. Since the only strategy the Federal Reserve and other central banks had to confront a financial collapse was the creation of still more debt in the system, there had become a question of how long this can continue, especially in the face of the extreme inflation the world was experiencing. To fight inflation central banks needed to raise interest rates, which could bring on a sharp economic downturn. To prevent this central banks would have to buy more financial assets and so provide liquidity to markets. Could this be done convincingly, especially by weaker economies? Would there be blowback from failure in the many weakened emerging market economies impacting the U.S.? Even for the U.S., was it sensible to save a financial system that had long been growing in parasitic form on the rest of the economy? Soon, bank failures in the U.S. itself forced the Fed to guarantee deposits in excess of the FDIC's $250,000 ceiling to avoid contagion. This too put pressure on central banks in other nations, even as it sent shivers of fear through the American banking system. The weaknesses of the financial system and its regulation became overwhelmingly obvious.

As the Federal Reserve raised interest rates in 2022 and 2023 to counter inflation and financial weakness became widespread, the International Monetary Fund's global economic outlook and financial stability reports warned of "stresses and vulnerabilities" and the World Bank's chief economist Intermit Gill declared "A lost decade could be in the making for the world economy" (Rappeport 2023). When this crisis came to pass, there would have been a great many premonitions of its arrival.

What is widely termed "financialization," a concept to be defined and discussed in the following chapter, has produced problems in many areas in addition to the basic one of growth and stability, leading to a number of questions: How does it affect the broader economy? What determines financial fluctuations and shocks? What impact does the modern financial system have on the rest of us? Can governments make financial crises less frequent and less disruptive?

This book provides answers to these and other issues prompted by the centrality of financialization in the current stage of capitalist development. It suggests that given the secular increase of debt in the American economy and internationally, the contemporary high inflation that so worries central bankers, leading them to raise interest rates to an extent that threatens a new downturn on the heels of the last, should be understood as a structural crisis of the system that puts them in a very difficult position. They cannot responsibly follow the lead of Paul Volcker and raise interest rates until the inflation is beaten; the amount of debt in the system is so great that such a tactic will lead to widespread defaults, bankruptcies, and economic devastation beyond the damage that was done fighting stagflation in the 1970s when debt was at a far more modest level. This debt trap may be the most consequential cost of the decades of the financialization of the American (and international) economy.

An Uncertain New Economic Era

"We don't have a sense of the final destination," chief economist of the International Monetary Fund Olivier Blanchard announced at the time of the 2008 crisis. "Where we end I really don't have much of a clue. . . . We don't have a clue of what financial stability actually means," he declared (Porter 2013). It should be added that we do not know because the "end" is open, subject to contingent events and choices effected by the policy makers, the financial community, and the people. How causation is understood, how blame is allocated, and what alternatives are taken seriously in public debate will determine whether the system continues to be prone to costly crises.

"The long era of low inflation, suppressed volatility and easy financial conditions is ending," stated Mark Carney (2015), a former head of the Bank of England, describing the global economy. In his view, "It is being replaced by more challenging macro dynamics in which supply shocks are as important as demand shocks." Fed chair Powell, responding to a question he was asked in early 2022, argued that "[f]or the last quarter century, we've had a perfect storm of disinflationary forces." He agreed that "the old regime" had been disrupted by the Covid pandemic and that the shift to higher interest rates by the Federal Reserve (a response to the inflation unleashed by supply chain problems and the Russian invasion of Ukraine) was generating "untold" economic uncertainty. "As we come out the other side of that, the question is: What will be the nature of that economy?" he asked, expressing the indeterminacy that characterized the new period (Smialek 2022). The "other side" turned out to be further away than those who stressed the presumed temporary nature of the crisis had thought.

Inflation would persist, with the presumed only possible cure of higher interest rates available to central banks inviting pain for the majority in both the core and peripheries of the world system. Also, the impacts of global warming are no longer in some distant future. Moreover, the responsibility of those who have financed, and continue to finance, the misuse of the planet's resources must be acknowledged and confronted. The expectation of large numbers of climate migrants, along with the worry of renewed Covid episodes as new variants come into existence, should not be allowed to supplant the high risk of a financially driven, deeply flawed economic system. Concern over rising inequality, tax avoidance, the lack of investment in physical and social infrastructure, the influence of money politics, and the burden of debt are other areas of concern requiring discussion.

The models that have prevailed among mainstream economists do not provide satisfactory answers even as the need to reflect on the system of 21st-century capitalism *tout court* has become more urgent. Such concerns are apparent at business schools that had embraced the teaching of the maximization of shareholder value measured by quarterly returns but which now also teach both maximizing stakeholder value and ESG (environmental, social, and governance) priorities. "After decades of emphasis on financial markets and shareholder returns, business schools are trying to take on deeper philosophical problems – including, maybe, tentative questions about the means and ends of capitalism itself," Molly Worthen (2022) writes; she recognizes that while society requires managers "who can grapple with uncertainty and operate in a culture divided over basic questions of justice and human flourishing, most business schools still emphasize specialized skills and quantitative methods, the seductive simplicity of economic and social scientific models."

Faced with criticism of their actions and finding themselves pressured to take political stands by customers and staff, corporate leaders have been forced to enter the public arena in new roles to an extent they find uncomfortable, especially as conservative elected officials have attacked "woke" capitalists for responding to pressure to take stands on racism, the right to abortion, and the environmental crisis. Recognizing the need for a background knowledge in the relevant branches of history, political science, and sociology, corporate leaders understand that the best and the brightest of a more idealistic generation seek a personally fulfilling place in society, desiring to be engaged in jobs that allow them to work for the values they believe to be important.

There is also the wish to avoid the embarrassment that comes when clueless executives show public ignorance and contempt for ESG matters. Hence business schools teach courses, as does the Harvard Business School, on "Reimagining Capitalism." This is because trust in capitalism and big business is weak. Anat Admati (2017), a professor at the Stanford University Business School, cites a Gallup poll revealing that only twenty-five percent of respondents expressed "a lot" or "a great deal" of confidence in big business; half said big business has excessive influence on society; low trust was especially evident among young people. In the pages of the *Harvard Business Review*, Admati (2019) stresses that the loss of faith in capitalism "goes hand in hand with the decline of trust in governments and in democracy." For this reason, she argues that "before consigning society's issues to big business, we must ask *why* governments appear dysfunctional and *why* politicians are not taking action." Part of the answer, she maintains,

> is that standard capitalistic success metrics, routinely taught in business schools, such as high stock prices, can create incentives to weaken or bypass governments. to achieve business objectives managers may do what they can to avoid taxes, lure capable individuals from the public sector, and lobby for outsized subsidies.
>
> *(2019)*

The financial crashes attributed to the behavior of the financial sector, the growing economic insecurity for most people, and the evidence of extreme income and wealth inequality have had political consequences. "Now that the evidence is in, is it any wonder that trust in elites and confidence in democracy have plummeted?"

Joseph Stiglitz (2019) asks. Responding to his rhetorical question he told an interviewer, "Nowhere was this intolerance greater than in macroeconomics, where the prevailing models ruled out the possibility of a crisis like the one we experienced in 2008. When the impossible happened, it was treated as if it were a 500-year flood – a freak occurrence that no model could have predicted." But models do exist that predict such occurrences, if not their precise timing. Crises are not like a 500-year flood; rather they are endemic to capitalism, caused by speculative excess then followed by the collapse of asset prices that have grown to unrealistic levels.

Government in the era of global neoliberalism involves and enables – indeed encourages – a regime of accumulation that engenders asset bubbles and their collapse. Economic crises addressed by taxpayer bailouts to restore profitability to the financial sector have provoked public concern, raising the question of what the impact of the central bank's response would be to the inflation that gripped the world from 2021 with its successive increases in interest rates. Would it allow for a soft landing, reducing inflation without causing a recession? Many at the time doubted it. William Dudley, the former president of the Federal Reserve Bank of New York and senior research scholar at the Center for Economic Policy Studies at Princeton University, was not alone when he offered the view that "a hard landing is virtually inevitable" (2022). Such a new crisis, perhaps of stagflation, invited political as well as economic impacts. During recent decades, critics within the profession have grown more insistent in pointing to the consequences of slower growth and stagnant working-class well-being in their questioning of the premises upon which a still-dominant macroeconomics has been built. Political observers suggested the rise of the hard right was to be an outgrowth of such economic failure.

The focus here is narrower, even as it illuminates a major failing of mainstream economics and of macroeconomics in particular (Batra 2020; Mitchell, Wray, and Watts 2019). The economic and political dominance of finance has reduced competition, leading to price increases in excess of the costs of inputs while slowing growth and increasing the share of profits in GDP. (In the U.S., after-tax corporate profits as a percentage of GDP rose from five percent in 1990 to over ten percent in 2021.) At the same time problems developed in the economy: secular stagnation, the extent of international financial weakness, the ways that globalization and financial deregulation facilitate tax avoidance and evasion, and the significance of extensive buybacks by companies of their own stock all pointed to problems to which that policy makers and regulators were not attending. The increases in interest rates engineered by the Federal Reserve devalued the holding of bonds that made up a large part of bank portfolios, throwing a number of banks into collapse as worried depositors withdrew their funds. These are all weighty factors that must be taken into account when evaluating a growth model heavily dependent on financialization without proper regulation.

Financialization is closely linked to a rapid increase in inequality, as discussed in Chapter 4, "Inequality and Financialization." The focus is not on a moral condemnation of the dramatic and continuing escalation of income, wealth, and political inequality but rather on its consequences for the economy. Inequality increases the funds available for asset speculation and elevates asset prices, which together produce still greater inequality. This process has been supported by actions of the Federal Reserve, which has developed a strategy of combating financial crises by increasing market liquidity through bond buying, including of toxic assets, to prevent a collapse. Such a policy greatly expands the balance sheet of central banks, a course of action that is difficult to reverse without damaging consequences, even when monetary policy turns to fighting inflation. As a result, the Federal Reserve takes control over the allocation of capital from the market and in so doing supports the survival of so-called zombie corporations, as is explained. The chapter also considers how accounting and legal conventions favor financial risk-taking, including the manner in which international capital mobility has harmed poor nations and emerging market economies, thereby further increasing global inequality.

Chapter 5, "Value Extraction and Financing Monopoly Power," explains how financial firms appropriate the surplus created in other sectors of the economy and how financial investments made with borrowed funds raise stock prices, expand ownership claims, and substitute debt for equity in mergers and acquisitions. Such factors mean that many corporations have become part of massive portfolios of companies bought and sold by controlling firms, which exist as legal entities in order to raise money to buy, restructure, and sell them. The increased concentration and centralization of capital that have resulted impact suppliers, small retailers, workers, and consumers, generally reducing their well-being.

Chapter 6, "The Mainline Tradition and Endogenous Cycles," rejects the macroeconomic theories that regard economic crises as a consequence of factors external to the economy. Heterodox explanations for endogenous business cycles, from those offered by Karl Marx to John Maynard Keynes and later political economists, recognize the growth of fictitious capital and the consequences of unfulfilled expectations to be central to business cycles – and to the collapse of the credit system (unless rescued by government intervention). Hyman Minsky and other heterodox economists articulate the understanding that modern capitalism is a money economy in which liquidity cannot be guaranteed and the animal spirits of investors matter. The chapter calls attention to the wide-ranging ideas of Keynes, discussing why many of them were rejected in the U.S. after World War II when the so-called Keynesian-neoclassical synthesis became dominant.

Chapter 7, "Inflation in the Contemporary Conjuncture," discusses the dramatic turn the economy has taken as a result of exogenous events. In this, it provides a sharp contrast to the preceding chapter, which explains how the internal workings of speculative finance create crises. It suggests that if the Covid pandemic and the war in Ukraine had not occurred it is likely financial markets would have produced a new crisis; however, the focus is on the slow response by the Federal Reserve to what it thought was temporary inflation, followed with a lag by its turnaround to raising interest rates quickly and dramatically out of fear of a wage-price spiral if expectations of inflation became entrenched in the public's thinking. The high cost of this response for the American economy and for other countries is explored. It is argued that there is an alternative strategy for confronting the inflation.

Chapter 8, "Finance and the Environmental Crisis," investigates the role of the limited horizons which the financial sector brings to investment decisions and how such a strategy contributes to increased global warming, which threatens all living things – and even the financial sector, with those profiting from carbon-based fuels and their use striving to make as much income as they can before being prevented from doing so. As awareness has grown of what the world is facing, important voices among central bankers and the regulatory community demand that corporations transparently identify and communicate to investors the hazards that climate change threatens for their firm and the firm for the environment, along with what actions the company is taking to address them. The extent of corporate greenwashing is explored, since an unwillingness to relinquish profit opportunities provides a major impediment to forthrightly addressing the climate emergency. It concludes with a reflection on transformative proposals on current offer.

The last chapter, "Making the Future: Beyond Financialization," examines the contemporary situation, reviewing measures that can replace the growth of self-expanding financialization as an accumulation strategy. Forecasts based on historical data reveal that increases in the debt-to-GDP ratio amplify the likelihood of financial crises. Consequently, interest has grown in debt reduction to prevent a future economic catastrophe, even as there is considerable evidence that it may be too late to avoid a deep downturn under existing conditions with the overly conservative policy measures currently being taken. The chapter considers the desirability not only of re-regulation but of a comprehensive role for government in guiding the direction for growth. It offers guideposts for action, calling for a care economy, a Green New Deal along with a discussion of the desirability of extending the parameters of economic calculation in a return to the foundational commitment of political economy in moral philosophy. It concludes with a critique of the profession's outdated assumptions and suggests how economists may more effectively contribute to building a new social structure of accumulation, one that promotes a future for Americans and for others sharing a planet that is currently threatened by a financial order dangerously out of control.

References

Admati, Anat R. 2017. "A Skeptical View of Financialized Corporate Governance." *Journal of Economic Perspectives*, 3(13).

Admati, Anat R. 2019. "How Business Schools Can Help Restore Trust in Capitalism." *Harvard Business Review*, September 3.

Batra, Ravi. 2020. *Common Sense Macroeconomics*. World Scientific.

Carney, Mark. 2015. "Breaking the Tragedy of the Horizon – Climate Change and Financial Stability." *Speech given at Lloyd's of London*, September 29. https://www.bis.org/review/r151009a.pdf.

Dyer, Nat. 2021. "Susan Strange Saw the Financial Crisis Coming, Your Majesty": The Case for the LSE's Great Global Political Economist." *Real-World Economics Review*, 98.

Fullbrook, Edward. 2010. "Keen, Roubini, and Baker Win Revere Award for Economics." *Real World Economics Review Blog*, May 13.

Greenhill, Sam. 2008. "'It's Awful - Why Did Nobody See It Coming?': The Queen Gives Her Verdict on Global Credit Crunch." *Daily Mail*, November 5.

Hodgson, Geoffrey M. 2009. In Response: Our Letter to the Queen. https://www.geoffreymhodgson.uk/letter-to-the-queen.

Kay, John. 2015. *Other People's Money: The Real Business of Finance*. PublicAffairs.

Kindleberger, Charles P. and Robert Aliber. 2005. *Manias, Panics and Crashes: A History of Financial Crises*. Palgrave Macmillan.

Leonard, Christopher. 2022. *The Lords of Easy Money: How the Federal Reserve Broke the American Economy*. Simon & Schuster.

Mitchell, William, L. Randall Wray and Martin Watts. 2019. *Macroeconomics*. Red Globe Press, Macmillan International.

Neate, Rupert. 2012. "Queen Finally Finds Out Why No One Saw the Financial Crisis Coming." *Guardian*, December 13.

Porter, Eduardo. 2013. "Economists Agree: Solutions Are Elusive." *New York Times*, April 23.

Rappeport, Alan. 2023. "World Bank Warns of Global 'Lost Decade'." *New York Times*, March 28.

Smialek, Jeanna. 2022. "Fed Official Didn't Reveal Full Extent of Trading." *New York Times*, January 7.

Smialek, Jeanna, Jim Tangersley and Joe Rennison. 2022. "Could a Bust Like Britain's Hit the U.S.?" *New York Times*, October 20.

Stiglitz, Joseph E. 2019. "The End of Neoliberalism and the Rebirth of History." *Project Syndicate*, November 4.

Worthen, Molly. 2022. "Can Business Schools Really Reimagine Capitalism?" *New York Times*, May 5.

2

FINANCIALIZATION, ITS CONTEMPORARY SETTING, AND SIGNIFICANCE

Jeremy Rudd, a senior researcher at the Federal Reserve, has offered a critique of conventional macroeconomics, indeed of mainstream economics *tout court*. When his challenging essay appeared in the Fed's own Finance and Economics Discussion Series in 2021, his views received wide notice. As he wrote, "everyone knows" that "[a]ggregate production functions (and aggregate measures of the capital stock) provide a good way to characterize the economy's supply side"; that "The theory of household choice provides a solid justification for downward-sloping market demand curves"; and that "Over a sufficiently long span – specifically, one that allows necessary price adjustments to be made – the economy will return to a state of full market clearing" (2021). However, he found these assumptions in no way reflective of the real-world economy. Nor are they, as has been convincingly argued by other insiders for some time (Buiter 2009). Still, it appears that "everyone" does not know that what continues to be taught across much of the macroeconomic curriculum is of little value to policy makers in the actually existing economy.

Greater humility has developed in a profession that had been unable to offer satisfactory responses to the question of what has caused the serious downturns that have afflicted the U.S. in the 21st century: the tech bubble debacle at its onset, the subprime mortgage bubble and its disastrous collapse in 2008, and the recession coinciding with the Covid-19 pandemic from 2020. In each case, policy makers and regulators missed what was occurring in the economy to produce these sharp downturns. And they failed to recognize that the crises were a product of financial deregulation. The impacts should have been evident after the collapse of the savings and loan (S&L) banks in the decade from the mid-1980s to the mid-1990s. But even as estimates of the S&L bailout reached $1.4 trillion over forty years, the public was "curiously subdued" (Shaw 2019). Through this trauma the Fed's promise to do what was necessary to preserve the financial system (after the S&P 500 Index lost ten

DOI: 10.4324/9781003385240-2

percent of its value in the week ending October 16, 1987, and an additional twenty percent the following Monday) heralded the onset of what became more than three decades of liquidity, debt, and asset inflation, which exposed the American economy to frequent financial crises (Nygaard 2020; Popularis 2022). The subsequent downturns reveal a pattern of financial fragility and painful consequences that have had a profound impact on the public's quotient of discontent and consequently on American politics. Economists have gotten better, in retrospect, at understanding finance in more critical terms. The macroeconomic pattern that continues should be difficult to ignore, even as its reality has to a large extent been obscured in public debate by the impacts of the Covid pandemic and the war in Europe.

Economists have been slow to revise their thinking regarding the macroeconomics of economic breakdowns. Neil Irwin writes of Rudd's intervention that

> In effect many of the key ideas underlying economic policy during the Great Moderation – the period of relatively steady growth and low inflation from the mid-1980s to 2007 that also seems to be a high-water mark for economists' overconfidence – increasingly look to be at best incomplete, and at worst wrong.
> *(2021)*

They are only accepted, Rudd himself suggests, because the economy is a complicated system "that is inherently difficult to understand, so propositions like these" – the "arrant nonsense" in question – "are all that saves us from intellectual nihilism" (2021). With the unexpectedly high subsequent inflation, dispute over its causes and what the Fed should do increased as basic debates over economic theory grew intense and disparate, with fervently held opinions often clashing.

Some prominent economists acknowledged mainstream macroeconomics to be deficient, characterizing it as only in its scientific infancy. Adam Posen, president of the Peterson Institute for International Economics, writes that macroeconomics

> behaves like we're doing physics after the quantum revolution, that we really understand at a fundamental level the forces around us. We're really at the level of Galileo and Copernicus . . . just figuring out the basics of how the universe works. It requires more humility and acceptance that not everything fits into one model yet.
> *(Irwin 2021)*

Rudd's essay was more pessimistic even as it offered a critique of what Thomas Kuhn termed "normal science," the conventional wisdom of the profession. While yet to be formalized into anything as grand as the rejection of the Ptolemaic system by the Copernican Revolution (featured in Kuhn's classic work), the broad intellectual upheaval occurring in economics announces the same type of scientific revolution of which Kuhn wrote, one produced by the challenges offered by a more convincing paradigm than the one that had previously dominated (Kuhn 1962).

Of course, economists are not being asked to determine how the universe works – although this may be the hubristic presumption of some of them. The most prominent case in point is the influential Becker and Posner (2009). The argument here, in Kuhnian terms, is that it is not a question of further developing the existing model, but rather of departing from it and providing a better one. Kuhn found that the issue involves the resistance of the accredited authorities of the science in question who, committed to the old way of thinking, refuse to entertain new explanations. This is the problem; it is why change typically originates in the work of younger scholars. However, the failures of mainstream theory have been increasingly recognized by many in the profession through the decades of hegemony of global neoliberalism; a number of commentators, many now prominent scholars who have made what are acknowledged to be important contributions throughout their careers, are outspoken in their critique of the questionable givens that continue to be accepted by the mainstream of the profession.

With regard to economics as a discipline, there are signs that a paradigm change is underway. While references will be made to such a Kuhnian revolution, it is not possible to do this broad topic justice here, given the focus on financialization, although comments reflective of this larger transformation will be made throughout this study, especially in the concluding chapter. Any reference to a Kuhnian scientific revolution must be deployed with care, however, as much of the work of the reformation of economics should include the contributions of ignored, dismissed, forgotten, or repressed perspectives from the discipline's past that are relevant to the present. It will be suggested that some of these ideas usefully challenge conventional views of market psychology and monetary policy. The necessary scientific revolution in economics may have aspects of a counterrevolution.

Economies Evolve and Change

Since its beginning in the moral philosophy of the 18th-century political economy, a contest has existed in economics between what have been termed "the mainstream" and "the mainline" traditions of the discipline (Tabb 1999). The difference lies in the assumptions regarding how the world works and what they choose to regard as givens that economists adopt before they undertake research. The mainstream tradition focuses on the allocation of scarce resources among various and competing ends (Robbins 1932). It describes a market that is believed to assure that supply and demand reach an equilibrium at a competitive price, thus at a price that is fair to willing buyers and willing sellers. It does recognize that those not involved in a transaction or business decision may nonetheless be impacted, but it considers such occurrences to be "externalities," marginal to the general optimality of markets. The cost of such a presumption has grown clearer. It is important to acknowledge that bias in terms of fostering and protecting financial institutions is also a political choice, one involving redistribution from the society to the financial institutions, their owners, and their top executives.

The mainline tradition recognizes the evolution of economies over time and the importance for markets of the power generated by political and legal interventions, institutional change, and discrimination based on ascriptive characteristics. It understands that collective action problems are extensive and best not regarded as externalities; in fact, they need to be addressed actively by government, overruling private, profit-oriented agents and institutions, being necessary to achieve what may be defined as social efficiency, the effective use of resources to meet the goal of an inclusive, sustainable economy.

The data that economists choose to stress and how they interpret them are hardly innocent of what Joseph Schumpeter has termed "their pre-analytic vision" (Schumpeter 1954: 41). This pre-analytic cognitive act on the part of economists surely cannot be ignored in a project such as this one. It forms the root of disagreements among experts. Economists have increasingly recognized that fiscal and monetary policies are themselves political in nature. For example, inflation reflects spending and saving patterns that are influenced by political choices; it is therefore fundamentally a political phenomenon (Coppola 2021).

Economists in the mainline tradition are often called heterodox, to distinguish them from the mainstream orthodox. For the purposes of this study, Thomas Palley's view is accepted that heterodox economics

> interprets financialization through the lens of political economy, whereby the economy constitutes a political economic system in which politics and political interests are intrinsic and inescapably present. The economy is a contested terrain and its structure is constructed by dominant interests.
>
> *(2021)*

He explains that mainstream economics

> resists recognizing the inevitable politically constructed nature of both the economy and policy. Consequently, mainstream economics struggles with the essence of political economy, and that shows up in the absence of a construct akin to financialized neoliberal capitalism.
>
> *(2021)*

That is to say, the very project of the present study is absent from the dominant mainstream conversation, even as it exists in a lively discourse at the margins of the profession (Jo, Chester, and D'Ippoliti 2017).

Among Marxists one of the key aspects of financialization is the rise of financial securities as a dominant form of property, a form of fictitious capital – fictitious "not because they are not real or the income they provide is an illusion" but because they "are not really capital"; rather, they represent a contractual claim on future income that is ultimately produced with capital. In other words, they cannot be understood without a consideration of financialization in relation to the class struggle on a global scale (Kaldor 2022).

The Metastasizing of Finance

John Maynard Keynes famously wrote the oft-quoted:

> Speculators may do no harm as bubbles on a steady stream of enterprise. But the position is serious when enterprise becomes the bubble on a whirlpool of speculation. When the capital development of a country becomes a by-product of the activities of a casino, the job is likely to be ill-done.
>
> *(1936: 80)*

While highly profitable to some, the "job" that financialization has done in the era of global neoliberalism has cost the economy – and the society at large – a great deal.

In recent decades, money centers have grown both in absolute size and in proportion to their national economies. As Servaas Storm argues, "[o]urs is, without a doubt, the age of finance – of the supremacy of financial actors, institutions, markets and motives in the global capitalist economy" (Storm 2018: 303). Numerous factors have created this reality: the confluence of a supportive ideology (neoliberalism); historical circumstance (the stagflation of the 1970s); the development of sophisticated mathematical tools for valuing financial assets; and the revolution in information technology, which lowered the cost and increased the speed of financial transactions, allowing for quick profits on miniscule price differentials. The finance, insurance, and real estate (FIRE) sector accounted for forty percent of domestic corporate profits in the U.S. by 2007, on the eve of the system-jolting Great Recession (as it is called in the U.S.) or the Global Financial Crisis (as it is termed elsewhere).

Financialization describes an expansion in the size and importance of the financial sector relative to the overall economy, one characterized by "the increasing role of financial motives, financial markets, financial actors and financial institutions in the operation of the domestic and international economies," in Gerald Epstein's telling (Epstein 2006: 3). Mike Konczal and Nell Abernathy add a political dimension, defining financialization as "the growth of the financial sector, its increased power over the real economy, the explosion in the power of wealth, and the reduction of all of society to the realm of finance" (Konczal and Abernathy 2015: 4). Lenore Palladino stresses corporate financialization, "the increasing share of profits earned from *financial activity* and the increasing *flow of profits to shareholders*" (Palladino 2018: 4). She understands corporate financialization as the mechanism for such a capture, specifically through the domination of financial activities within firms.

Luis Carlos Bresser-Pereira explains that his use of the term "financialization" "will be understood as a distorted financial arrangement based on the creation of artificial financial wealth – that is, financial wealth disconnected from real wealth or from the production of goods and services. Neoliberalism, in its turn," he maintains, "should not be understood merely as radical economic liberalism but also as an ideology that is hostile to the poor, to workers, and to the welfare state" (Bresser-Pereira 2010: 500). A great number of other definitions of financialization exist at different levels of analysis (Mader, Mertens, and van der Zwan 2020), but these frame the discussion here.

There are various methods of measuring the importance of financialization, each with strong and weak aspects (Karwowski, Shabani, and Stockhammer 2020). Marwil Dávila-Fernández and Lionello Punzo (2022) select employment. They describe a positive, long-term relationship between the share of financial employment and more equal income distribution and demonstrate the evolution of the proportion of financial assets to corporate total assets over the sixty years prior to 2020. In the 1980s, their data are divided into two periods. As they argue, it is in this decade that "there is a clear structural break." They also identify a positive, long-term relationship between the share of financial employment and income inequality, as well as between financial assets and income inequality. Looking at the key trends in sectoral employment, Dávila-Fernández and Punzo find that around seventy percent of the reduction in industrial employment corresponds to a rise in the share of financial and business service employment. They conclude that in this sense, financialization "can be seen as a mirror to deindustrialization." They also find a correspondence between the latter and the rise of income inequality in the U.S. (2022: 196 and 203–4; for a more extensive discussion of the relationship between financialization and GDP see Assa 2016; and between financialization and inequality, Godechot 2020).

Remzi Baris Tercioglu demonstrates that by considering expenditures on financial, healthcare, and professional business services, which rose disproportionately between 1947 and 2017 as intermediate consumption (that is, necessary but not final consumption, for reasons he argues), it is clear that the usual measure of well-being exaggerates the presumed improvement for the average household. This reclassification allows him to compare the widely used national income and products accounts, which he labels the conventional measures, with his own estimates, which he terms "alternative measures." The dissimilarities between the two reveal rapidly rising costs of intermediate consumption, a deeper slowdown in growth from 1973, and a more moderate rise in consumption share after 1980, along with a sharper decline in the ratio of labor share (defined as compensation to employees) to GDP from 1985 to 2015. These differences are substantial. His conclusion is that the cost of basic requirement spending has increased (including the extractions of finance), reducing the standard of living for the working class by adding to the cost of basic provisioning (Tercioglu 2021).

Compatible with the significance of such a calculation is the view that neoliberalism "seeks to shift how human beings exist in the world, to change how we relate to each other and what we expect from life. Over time, we move from considering ourselves mutually responsible beings with a shared fate to isolated atoms liable solely for our own lives," Lynn Parramore (2022) argues. "Gradually, we shift from empowered citizens to people destined for servitude to arbitrary economic powers that [lie] well beyond our reach or understanding. Our humanity fades . . . in an invisible global economy ruled somehow by an invisible fist." In more familiar specifics, "neoliberals dedicated themselves to protecting unrestricted global trade, crushing labor unions, deregulating business, and usurping government's role in providing for the common good with privatization and austerity."

Such a judgment would not be amiss in a profession guided by the moral philosophy found in the work of Adam Smith who wrote not only the book that economists cite if few have read, *The Wealth of Nations* (1776), but found in greater detail in a second important Adam Smith contribution, *The Theory of Moral Sentiments* published in 1759. There he established the groundwork for the desirability of a market economy to be embedded in a moral society (Tabb 1999: chapter 3). The opening words of *Sentiments* state: "How selfish soever man may be supposed, there are evidently some principles in his nature, which interest him in the fortune of others, and render their happiness necessary to him, though he derives nothing from it except the pleasure of seeing it." Later in Part I he tells the reader that "to restrain our selfish, and to indulge our benevolent affections, constitutes the perfection of human nature" (Smith 2002 [1759]: 11 and 30).

With increasing frequency, if usually without attribution to the father of economics, advocates and practitioners of progressive policy argue that a sense of morality must guide our programmatic suggestions, which should derive from our capacity to empathize directly and indirectly with other people, and that efficiency and competition should not be the be-all and end-all of economics. This understanding features prominently in the treatment here.

The ways in which finance impacts the larger economy and appropriates profit by its interventions and which categories of institutions and individuals benefit are both prominent aspects of ongoing investigations of financialization (Jayadev, Mason, and Schröder 2018). It is certainly the case that since the 1970s, American corporations have increasingly derived profits from financial activities. The important issue raised by the data concerns why profitability from the traditional production of goods and services made in the U.S. has not attracted greater investment. In fact, the rate of profit from such production has not recovered from the waning days of the National Keynesian era, when a profit squeeze was responsible for slowing economic growth (Kotz 2019). The new reality has involved disinvestment from production of goods and non-financial services; making money from money through asset speculation and forcing down real compensation, accompanied by speedups for workers have become prominent, all sustained by the greater power of capital in an era of trade union decline.

What must be explained, as Paul Sweezy argued, is how and why financial capital, "once cut loose from its original role as a modest helper of a real economy of production to meet human needs, inevitably becomes speculative capital geared solely to its own self-expansion." He wrote of his realization that in "earlier times no one ever dreamed that speculative capital, a phenomenon as old as capitalism itself, could grow to dominate a national economy, let alone the whole world. But it has" (Sweezy 1994). Decades after Sweezy's insight, there has been an acceleration of leveraged buyouts by private equity and hedge funds relying on borrowed money to purchase control of large companies. This has been accompanied by greater pricing power in the now more substantially concentrated industries of the economy. As income has stagnated, the indebtedness of working-class families has become a more important source of bank and other financial firms profitability.

Financialization has not only redistributed income upward and increased inequality; it has also slowed growth. The phenomena are related (Stockhammer 2004). Barry Cynamon and Steven Fazzari demonstrate that even before the Covid outbreak, output may have been running ten percent below the demand-led path that would have prevailed had the distribution of income between the bottom ninety-five percent of Americans and the top five percent been at levels consistent with what they were in the 1960s and 1970s (2015: 179–180). Business analysts have recognized this as well (Cynamon and Fazzari 2015). In a report to investors, S&P Capital IQ contends that "Higher levels of income inequality increase political pressures, discouraging trade, investment, and hiring." Inequality is simply not good for the economy, the firm's analysts insist. "Our review of the data, as well as a wealth of research on this matter, leads us to conclude that the current level of income inequality in the U.S. is dampening GDP growth" (Cynamon and Fazzari 2015).

That rising asset values are not correlated with growth or productivity prompts questions about "basic economic policy assumptions and their theoretical foundations," as Julius Krein argues. Rather, different policy approaches are "required to achieve these distinct objectives," and "the larger relationship between capitalism and development will need to be rethought" (McKinsey and Company 2021). The data support such concerns. In a 2021 report, the McKinsey Global Institute explained that the tripling of global net worth mainly reflected valuation gains in asset prices. The growth of what the analysts termed "investment in productive assets that drive our economies," on the other hand, has been disappointing, even with government subsidization of consumer spending. A key finding of their report is that across ten countries that account for about sixty percent of global GDP (Australia, Canada, China, France, Germany, Japan, Mexico, Sweden, the U.K., and the U.S.), the historic link between the growth of net worth and the growth of GDP no longer holds. The researchers found that while economic growth "has been tepid" over the past two decades in advanced economies, balance sheets and net worth "that have long tracked it [growth] have tripled in size" (McKinsey and Company 2021).

Thus, divergence is caused by the dramatic rise in financialization – not, as might be expected, by the growing digitization of the economy, as some have suggested. While an important increase has occurred in the value of intellectual property, McKinsey focuses on "a glut of savings [that] has struggled to find investments offering sufficient economic returns and lasting value to investors." It is not that intangible assets (intellectual property like R&D and software) are not playing an increasingly important role in today's economy with their high expected return (McKinsey predicts twenty-four percent, the highest rate among produced asset categories), but that intangibles represent only four percent of total net worth.

Asset values in 2020 were nearly fifty percent higher relative to income than the long-run average. For every one dollar in new net investment over the past twenty years, overall liabilities grew by almost four dollars, of which about two dollars involved debt. Dividing the global balance sheet into three components – the real economy balance sheet, the financial balance sheet, and the financial sector balance sheet – the McKinsey researchers found that each amounted to roughly $500 trillion. What they term "the real economy" balance sheet comprised $520 trillion in real assets (such as machinery and equipment, infrastructure, buildings, natural resources, and intellectual property). In the financialized economy, the balance sheet of households, corporations, and governments amounts to $510 trillion in financial assets: stocks, bonds, pension funds, and cash and deposit. Financial institutions create and intermediate another $510 trillion in financial assets and liabilities. This tripart division allows for a better understanding of what net worth consists.

Financial assets represent wealth to sectors, institutions, households, and countries, but on the consolidated global balance sheet they do not increase net worth, nor do financial liabilities subtract from it. This is because financial corporations, designated as the intermediators of wealth, "mirror the assets and liabilities in other sectors" (Woetzel, Mischke, Madgavkar, Windhagen, Smit, Birshan, Kemeny, and Anderson 2021). That is, they hold financial assets: mortgages, public and corporate bonds, and equities, and they owe deposits, bonds, and pension assets, mostly to households.

What does this tell us? There are different ways to interpret the expansion of balance sheets and net worth relative to GDP. But it is useful to see that "what is essentially double counting invites a paradigm shift that could precede from the possible reversion to the historical mean, softly or abruptly" of the real economy balance sheet, as the McKinsey economists suggest. They argue that "[n]ot only is the sustainability of the expanded balance sheet in question; so too is its desirability, given some of the drivers and potential consequences of the expansion." While this is certainly correct, the focus of their alternative, investing in innovation while pulling back on the dangers of financialization (a term they do not use), requires the redirection of investment to the real sector by government.

Two things are required. The first is the use of policy to reduce the pressure of what is a very large superbubble. The second calls for a decisive reliance on fiscal policy to spend on what is necessary to reduce global warming while expanding needed public goods as an alternative (and sustainable) growth path to replace financialization as the engine of growth. It will be demonstrated that the heterodox tradition both provides an explanation for the financial collapse that is implicitly premised in the conclusion to the McKinsey study and goes beyond its proposals for what is to be done.

Revisiting the Function of Banks and Finance

Governor of the Bank of England and Chairman of the Financial Stability Board Mark Carney (2014) was not alone in believing that "financial capitalism is not an end in itself, [but] a means to promote investment, innovation, growth and prosperity." He assumed that banking is fundamentally about intermediation, about connecting borrowers and savers in the real economy. But he worried that "when bankers become detached from end-users, their only reward becomes money." This seemed wrong to him: "Purely financial compensation ignores the non-pecuniary rewards to employment, such as the satisfaction from helping a client or colleague succeed" (2014). Such satisfaction, a survey of financial world participant behavior suggests, is not uppermost in the minds of the financial wizards who judge success by how much money they make; consequently, they are not infrequently caught perpetuating socially costly schemes (Natarajan and Robinson 2019).

In contrast to Carney's view in 2014, the most obvious aspect of financialization involves a dramatic change in the dominant business of banks. They have become part of a speculative network, one involving excessive risk-taking. Banks are themselves large borrowers from non-depositor sources. Rather than lubricating the economy by mediating between savers and those needing to fund productive investment, they have become focused on securitizing credit-card borrowing, collateralizing home mortgages, and since 2008 generating other, similar debt obligation products. This transformation of finance in the neoliberal era has created new products to facilitate the capture of financial rents from changes in the prices of securities, often financed through the overnight repo market. Such practices allow speculating with money borrowed short term and regularly rolled over by lenders – funds that finance not only the buying and selling of financial products but, as will be discussed, the buying and selling of companies.

One can certainly agree with Andrew Haldane that the maximum efficient scale of banking as traditionally understood, or the current style of banking if it were carried out without the huge government guarantees against loss and implicit subsidies, could be relatively modest and that the cost of great size comes with the inability of top management to evaluate risk as the size of the financial institution has grown, engorged by new subsidiaries. Of the bank mergers and acquisitions which had taken place by that time, Haldane, then chief economist and executive director of monetary analysis and statistics at the Bank of England, spoke at a conference in 2010; he asserted that the majority of the merged firm under-perform the market in the subsequent period. He suggested that the most likely cause was articulated by Austin Robinson in the 1930s:

> Man's mind and man's memory is essentially a limited factor. . . . Every increase in size beyond a point must involve a lengthening of the chain of authority . . . at some point the increasing costs of co-ordination must exceed the declining economies.
> *(1934)*

In support of such thinking, he remarked that when Lehman Brothers failed, it had almost one million open derivatives contracts. Haldane reckoned that whatever the technology budget available, "it is questionable whether any man's mind or memory could cope with such complexity" (Haldane 2010).

The largest single increase ever recorded in financial services output occurred in the fourth quarter of 2008, coinciding with the Lehman bankruptcy and the near collapse of other major banks. At the time Lehman was a 164-year-old firm and the fourth largest U.S. investment bank. Although its bankruptcy initiated the Global Financial Crisis, it was allowed to collapse because it was obviously badly run, deserved to fail, and provided no real services to the economy that were not available from others. It would not be missed, and it would serve as an example. But investors knew that Lehman's bankruptcy threatened the financial institutions that owned its bonds; the risky business of Lehman was interconnected with much of Wall Street, and its demise would bring down others, as Washington policy makers soon saw as well.

It was not too big to fail. Rather it was too complex to be allowed to fail. Lehman had relied on the overnight financial market; when it could not meet its obligations, lenders panicked. The decision to let it go undermined the confidence in the entire financial system. If the deposit taking and lending to final borrowers for mortgages and business loans had remained separate, the financial conglomerates might have been allowed to fail. Indeed, if the separation had remained and the implicit protection had not been extended, few of the derivative products would have made sense to buyers. Separating trading from taking deposits would shrink finance and save the cost of the bailouts. But in the short run this would have to wait. Given the interdependencies, U.S. regulators cast about for some other entity or entities to take over Lehman, once again promising they would prevent a reoccurrence. Barclays ended up buying the U.S. operations of Lehman Brothers the day after it filed for bankruptcy, while Nomura purchased the firm's Asian and European operations.

Deregulation and the incentives of bank officials have changed the nature of banking over the past half century. In the 1970s the products that banks could offer were limited, as was their price. "It was almost like a public utility. There were no exotic securities such as credit derivatives to deliver exorbitant profits that put the whole economy at risk. Globally, fixed exchange rates and capital controls meant that bankers could not make bets against currencies and entire economies (Kuttner 2018: 102). By the second decade of the new century, however, it was clear that financial institutions "legally manipulated markets in plain sight by pushing their own share prices up with cheap money availed to them by the central bank that is supposed to regulate them," as a former Goldman Sachs managing director explained (Prins 2017). The regulators allowed, indeed encouraged, such behavior.

There were few economies to scale even as there was market power to be achieved. A study at the end of the 20th century showed that efficient banks appeared to operate with assets of less, perhaps much less, than $100 billion, and that putting the matter conservatively, "there is no strong evidence of increased bank efficiency after a merger or acquisition," according to a conclusion based on a survey of over 100 studies (Berger and Humphrey 1997). By 2008, 145 banks globally had assets worth above $100 billion, with most of them being universal banks combining multiple business activities. Taken together these institutions account for eighty-five percent of the assets of the world's top 1,000 banks. The U.S. government's long-term approval – indeed, often encouragement – of mergers between the mega banks and traditional smaller and midsized banks followed the Depository Institutions Deregulation and Monetary Control Act of 1980 and subsequent permissive enforcement practices with regard to mergers. It was the largest banks that accounted for the financial sector quadrupling its borrowing relative to the real economy between 1978 and 2007, with profits rising by 800 percent adjusted for inflation between 1980 and 2005 (compared to a profit growth of 250 percent for the non-financial sector).

Elected officials were major deregulators. Legislative deregulation, which had begun during the Carter administration, continued under President Reagan, who signed the Garn-St. Germain Act that deregulated S&L – which soon went into crisis, dragging the U.S. into the first of the financial crises it was to experience from the end of the 20th century. In 1994 under Bill Clinton, the Riegel-Neal Act had reinterpreted the Depression era Glass-Steagall Act, further allowing commercial banks to gain more of their revenues from activities that had previously been in the provenance of investment banks. In 1999, Glass-Steagall was replaced by the Gramm-Leach-Bliley Act, which allowed mega-mergers in finance, permitting a further step in what was a movement to deregulate banking. It authorized a single institution to act as a bank, a securities firm, and an insurance company. Its adoption further demonstrated the culture of risk-taking in finance that was gaining Washington's imprimatur. The Commodities Futures Modernization Act of 2000 exempted financial derivatives such as mortgaged-backed securities from regulation. The appeal of derivatives is that they presumably distribute risk to those most willing to take it on, allowing others to buy insurance against risk. "Actually," writes John Kay, "[i]ts purpose was not to spread risk more effectively by passing it to those better equipped to handle it, but [to] dump it on those who understood less about it. Risks were not more, but less, effectively managed as a result of the transfer" (Kay 2015: 69). The impact of the growth of derivatives was soon felt in the Great Recession of 2008.

In 1987 Alan Greenspan, an Ayn Rand disciple, was appointed by Ronald Reagan to head the Federal Reserve. The following year, Greenspan allowed Travelers Group and Citicorp to merge, forming Citigroup Inc., which would become the largest financial services company in the world. The Glass-Steagall Act of 1933 had prevented commercial banks from owning brokerage firms and insurance units, but the companies asserted at the time that they were taking a chance because they expected those laws to change in the near future. New York Republican Alfonse D'Amato, chairman of the Senate Banking Committee, noted that most legal obstacles to the Citigroup merger had already been eliminated (Schultz 1998). This was de facto true. In 1989, Greenspan allowed JPMorgan & Company, a commercial bank, to underwrite a corporate bond issue, which was understood by many as a violation of the Banking Act of 1933 that separated commercial banking from investment banking. Greenspan had served on the board of directors of JPMorgan & Company for a decade, but it may be that ideological loyalties more than ties to a former employer were responsible for his action.

"The Maestro," as Greenspan was called by Bob Woodward in a flattering biography (2000) that celebrated his presumed virtuosity in guiding the American economy through years of prosperity, stepped down in 2006, thus avoiding the embarrassment of presiding over the Great Recession that his policy choices had done so much to bring about. Unsurprisingly, his reputation has suffered from the fall in esteem. A 1999 cover of *Time* magazine hailed the actions of the trio (Greenspan, Robert Rubin, and Lawrence Summers) dubbing them the "Committee to Save the World." The inexperienced President Barack Obama had simply renewed the remit of such men as key White House economic policy makers. The media and the economics fraternity were slow to accept that they had been misled by such presumed geniuses. Had she been elected, there is little doubt that Hillary Clinton would have favored such advisers as well. It was not until the 2008 global financial crisis that the path these men had set regulators upon was seen to have been dangerous indeed.

Even as they increased the risks they were taking with other people's money, bankers pushed politicians for more deregulation. It is probably relevant to think of Lehman's failure in September 2008 as the result of banker hubris in a context of inadequate regulation. That the company could violate realistic margins of safety and get away with doing so, earning huge profits in the process, was the norm of the era, hardly the exception. One can certainly agree that Haldane's critique of the limits of thinking regarding regulation was realistic. Looking at the usual "solutions," he submitted that "it is possible that no amount of capital or liquidity may ever be quite enough," and that profit incentives may place risk "one step beyond regulation. That means banking reform may need to look beyond regulation to the underlying structure of finance if we are not to risk another sparrow toppling the dominos" (Haldane 2010). Banking regulators also need to look further than attempting to fix finance; they needed to repurpose the financial resources of the nation. This is a major political struggle of the sort the U.S. has not experienced since the 1930s. The failure of the Silicon Valley Bank and others, both those that collapsed and the many more that were threatened by the lack of close regulation in the context of rising interest rates engineered by the Fed, brought into question the wisdom of the Fed and its chairman, who had not opposed the disastrous deregulation of middle-sized banks in 2018.

At the time that finance and the larger economy were deregulating, inequality was rising, incomes stagnating, and insecurity growing as a result of macroeconomic policy choices. Even as the country was experiencing a slow recovery, the Budget Control Act of 2011, designed to reduce spending, was passed with bipartisan support. Reading from the Republican hymnbook, President Obama said that it failed to make a serious down payment on the "deficit reduction we need" (Appelbaum 2011). Austerity was the order of the day. The resulting slow growth contributed to the election of Donald Trump in 2016, as did Obama's strong advocacy of the corporate-backed Trans-Pacific Partnership, which was understood by working-class voters to hurt American labor while helping American financiers penetrate the region more substantially.

The Federal Reserve consistently played a major role in the deregulation process. It reduced bank capital requirements, weakened bank stress testing, and lessened the obligations of banks to provide resolution planning in the event of bankruptcy. In 2020, as in 2008, the Fed policy encouraged larger financial institutions to take over smaller ones. Firm turnover of industry leaders declined significantly, with those at the top able to increase their advantage through mergers and acquisitions (Philippon 2019). When the Fed grew worried about a possible downturn as it raised interest rates, it made its stress tests more rigorous. In 2022 while all thirty-three of the largest lenders passed, JPMorgan Chase and Citigroup were told to increase their high-quality capital to protect against possible losses. Jamie Dimon, Chief Executive Officer (CEO) of JPMorgan, declared of the tests, "It's a terrible way to run a financial system." He complained it would force banks to reduce mortgage lending to poor people (Saharan and Reyes 2022). But this could be avoided by raising the percentage of capital banks held in relation to their assets by raising new capital and retaining more of their profits. The Fed was not forcing banks to reduce their lending to the low-income people or anyone else. Rather, the insistent change by the Fed was so that banks would be less likely to fail. However, the new caution meant many would-be borrowers were denied loans, slowing the economy.

When President Biden nominated three candidates to fill vacancies on the Federal Reserve Board of Governors who favored such an alternative, Republicans predictably complained about their views, particularly those of Sarah Bloom Raskin, the nominee for vice-chair of supervision. She had expressed concern about the effects of climate change on financial stability as well as the risks posed by shadow banking, cryptocurrencies, and cyber security. Stiff resistance by Republicans and some conservative Democrats in the evenly balanced Senate prevented her approval, as had been the case for others nominated by President Biden for important regulatory posts (Ackerman 2022).

Conservatives claimed that such appointments would "politicize bank supervision." Rana Foroohar argues rather than the notion of "politicizing" the Fed ignores

> the fact that it has for several decades been increasingly political, in the sense that central bankers have, by choice and by force, become the chief economic actors in the country. From Alan Greenspan onwards, the Fed has successfully used low interest rates to bolster asset prices and stretch out the business cycle
>
> *(2022)*

As argued here, this "stretching out" the structural change of the economy has increased the danger created by a financialized growth regime that remains poorly understood.

Securitization

In the 21st century, banks have borrowed hundreds of billions of dollars short term on the wholesale money market from institutional investors, corporations, and other banks with excess funds. Most of this money is re-lent overnight, with the debt almost invariably rolled over and the borrowing renewed for another night for as long as the borrower desires the loan. This is routine unless and until there is reason for creditors to fear that the borrower's assets have decreased in value or might do so. Then the rollovers immediately cease and repayment is demanded. Banks thereupon sell assets for whatever they can in order to cover their obligations. Since these assets can involve financial promises that are rapidly decreasing in value (because so many others similarly desperate to meet their own commitments put their own assets on the market), the worth of the remaining assets falls still further. This was essentially what happened in the financial crisis of 2008, when asset values plummeted and overnight funds stopped being available to banks at affordable rates or indeed at any price – until the Federal Reserve stepped in and protected them (Haltenhof, Lee, and Stebunovs 2014; Buera and Nicolini 2014).

The bubble that collapsed in 2008 was a consequence of mortgage originators finding subprime borrowers who were often unqualified, collecting upfront fees for their work. The mortgages were bundled and sold as derivatives. The collateralized debt obligations (CDOs) were then marketed to investors throughout the world. Securitization allowed traditional banks to provide the financial system with the "raw materials" necessary for the manufacture of CDOs and other complex, structured financial products, most of which were allotted triple-A ratings. Those who wished insurance against loss could purchase credit default swaps (CDSs) from a seller such as Lehman Brothers or Bear Sterns. When sentiment shifted, these greatly overextended pillars of Wall Street were allowed to fail by the Fed and the Treasury. As mentioned earlier, a crisis loomed as other sellers, likewise unable to make good on the legal agreement they had contracted, were threatened with a similar fate, thus imperiling the entire financial system.

Because the securitization of debt makes immediate sales on future claims to income possible, the short term dominates with much "investment" involving speculative trades. Loans, repackaged in tranches reflecting their perceived risk, are then sold to buyers, who believe they understand that risk. Insurance against loss can also be bought at a price, although in a downturn these guarantees may not be realized without government bailouts of the guarantors. Such complex financial instruments – tradable assets with large debt components – produce unprecedented leverage. In the financial sector, the assets of one institution are mostly the liabilities of other financial establishments. With their extensive distribution across borders and markets, they require the Fed to bail out foreign as well as U.S. institutions and investors as a consequence of such interdependencies and thus of the extent to which they threaten the stability of national banking systems. New norms therefore prevail in the neoliberal era that contrast with the post-World War II years, when a far different model dominated banking and finance (Jomo 2020: 106).

It is understood that the collapse of the value of such swaps and of the collateralized mortgage obligations was central to the 2008 crisis (Adrian and Song Shin 2010; Tymoigne 2009). But it was unlike the program that the U.S.-led International Monetary Fund (IMF) had imposed on the Latin American debtors in the

1980s and Asian debtor countries in the 1990s. Those included the closure of local banks for which purchasing money center derivatives had proven so disastrous. American policy involved bailing out its own financial institutions, treating them generously after a brief flirtation with permitting two leading institutions to fail, and recognizing the obvious damage of the contagion that would result.

Whether or not the mortgages that were at the base of this financial crisis would be paid was not of concern to those who had originated them, nor was it of interest to those who had packaged and sold them; both groups profited up front. The incentive to sell derivatives to those seeking higher returns has not changed. Instead, other forms of collateralizing future income streams have emerged. The risk-taking has likewise continued, with investors still seeking higher returns on low-rated or unrated financial products. The rescue of speculators and institutions by the government created prospects of greater moral hazard as investors became increasingly aggressive in their pursuit of returns; they accepted elevated levels of risk, willing to purchase illiquid securities that could not be easily resold – except to the government – believing the Fed would of course purchase them to prevent the collapse of the asset market.

Central banks allowed, indeed enabled, the use of collateralized debt as the preferred vehicle for expanding liquidity in order to boost the growth of the economy based on asset appreciation. What has been termed "securitized banking," the combination of securitization plus repo (repurchase agreement) finance, which was integral to the 2008 Great Recession collapse, revealed a U.S. banking system effectively insolvent for the first time since the Great Depression (Gorton and Metrick 2012). Because the Fed and the European Central Bank bought mortgage-backed securities in 2008, shadow banking was in effect authorized to further expand the creation and use of asset-backed securities as collateral in the overnight repo market, thus creating even greater liquidity. This was in fact the goal of the central banks seeking to avoid economic contraction (Braun and Gabor 2020).

The Federal Reserve protected the banks by accepting their assets as collateral at far above their current market value and giving them as much money as they needed through the QE program, which involved the purchase of bonds to provide a large amount of new money in order to deal with the inability of banks to reduce interest rates further once the zero-bound had been reached. It is a way of pushing real interest rates down below zero in the hope of stimulating investment and job creation. In this it mostly failed, even as it succeeded in maintaining the value of financial assets, favoring those who held such assets, thus preventing a painful crash of the financial system. The short-run imperative dominated. "Nothing matters but liquidity," asserted Michael Hartnett, a chief investment strategist at Bank of America Global Research, in a research note describing what he termed the "nihilistic" bull market of 2020 (Fox 2020).

The Fed had been forced by the logic of this overriding goal of protecting the financial system to expand its tool set; as a result, it became an agent of fiscal policy (even as this was not clear to most observers). Karen Petrou (2021) makes the important point that the manner in which the Fed has executed policy since 2008 has had a direct fiscal impact by virtue of the effects of market valuation, credit allocation, debt monetization, and new money creation. Its expanded role makes the distinction between monetary and fiscal policy far less distinct than in the past.

While few economists predicted meaningful growth as a result of QE, investors were betting that slow growth would lead the Fed to continue buying bonds, which would bolster stock prices. Below-investment-grade junk bonds sold well, even from companies that, being unable to borrow before the Fed policy announcement, could then do so even if they did not have a viable business plan (Banerjee and Hofmann 2018). The amount of liquidity created by the Fed and the spending by the government after the 2020 financial crisis were far greater than in 2008, with economic and political consequences to be discussed.

This policy changed in 2021–2022 when inflation rose to worrying levels. But before the Fed moved to raise interest rates, to reduce its bond purchases and then to sell down their holdings, American corporations had taken advantage of historically low interest rates to engorge themselves on debt. After the pandemic led to the sharpest economic downturn in history, the Fed made it possible for businesses to assume even more debt. "During a standard recession, and that would include the global financial crisis as well, you would expect to see corporate debt as a percentage of G.D.P. begin to come down," asserted Paul Ashworth, Chief U.S. Economist at the consulting firm Capital Economics (Phillips 2020). However, it went up. It increased yet again after the advent of the economic crisis in 2020. As a matter of policy, economic crises have been accompanied by significant increases in the money supply to avoid bankruptcy and economic collapse. This, as shall be discussed, creates problems for the future.

While the extent and sources of increased inequality require a separate chapter, it is useful to note that global wealth in terms of net worth more than tripled from 2000 to 2020 (to $510 trillion). Much of this money was invested in the purchase of safe U.S. Treasury bonds. The supply of such bonds increased dramatically, from three trillion dollars to twenty-three trillion dollars over these years as America's national debt rose from fifty-five percent of its GDP to over 120 percent. The demand for bonds rose faster so that the interest rate, adjusted for inflation in early 2022, was a negative half percent. Investors paid the U.S. government to hold their money. This should have been a troubling indicator.

By 2019, fifty-one percent of all outstanding investment-grade bonds were rated BBB (the lowest level to qualify for that status), an increase from thirty-nine percent before the crisis of the Great Recession (Çelik, Demirtaş, and Isaksson 2020). This is significant because for asset managers who run pension funds, mutual funds, and insurance companies, if a company were to lose its BBB ratings, its bonds would have to be sold, dumped on the market. In a downturn, below investment grade (widely called junk bonds) lack for buyers and the many zombie companies are unable to raise funds to remain in business. This leads the Federal Reserve to prop up the market to ward off a downturn widespread bankruptcies might cause.

By 2021, the debt levels of households, companies, and sovereigns were at historic highs relative to output. The debt levels did not seem a problem because of the low interest rates (which fell globally over these years from a high of twelve percent to near zero percent before the subsequent inflation led to their rise again). What was termed the "savings glut" made low-cost funds available to borrowers. In the recent ten-year period, corporate debt increased by sixty percent in advanced economies relative to its level in 2008. While wealth in the global system had accelerated so substantially, some of those who followed such matters were not worried since the "huge debt boom is, mechanically, the flip side of the surge in gross savings and the multiplication of financial wealth experienced in recent decades" (Boone, Fels, Jordà, Schularick, and Taylor 2022). The accuracy of this judgment depended on valuations of the assets impacted by the Fed's fighting inflation by dramatically increasing interest rates. The situation was soon judged to be quite serious due to a confluence of overpriced major asset classes – stocks, bonds, real estate, and commodities – all having reached bubble price levels before declining precipitously. Jeremy Grantham, often described as a legendary investor, suggested that if valuations across all of these asset classes "return to even two-thirds of the way back to historical norms, total wealth losses will be on the order of \$35 trillion in the U.S. alone" (Lee 2022). The decline could be even greater if what he termed the fourth "superbubble" of the past century were to collapse. (Its predecessors were 1929, 2000, and 2008.)

Bankers increasingly transgress in numerous ways, with regulators and legislators weakening regulations to accommodate them. Lowering capital requirements and easing stress tests allow greater dividend payments and stock buybacks, with the consequences to be experienced during the next financial crisis (Smialek, Eavis, and Flitter 2019). While taxpayers took major losses in the decade from 2009, the largest banks more than doubled their profits (Armstrong and Noonan 2020) – profits that were mistakenly understood as a measure of the contribution that finance had made to the economy.

Not the Only Cockroach in the Kitchen

The profit-making of banks has been produced not only by higher fees and interest costs on credit card balances for retail customers but in some cases by illegal extractions. Wells Fargo has been a clear repeat violator. The corrupt leadership of its CEO John Stumpf led to his resignation in disgrace. Not long before his downfall he had been celebrated as *American Banker's* "banker of the Year" (in 2013) for the way he had increased the profits and the scale of operation of his fiefdom. In 2016, it was learned that employees of the bank, on pain of being fired if they did not meet quotas, had opened two million false accounts. Stumpf blamed the employees, "a few bad apples." The bank fired 5,000 low-level employees for these fraudulent tactics (practices that had been demanded by the bank's top leadership). A number of those dismissed were whistleblowers who had called unwanted attention to the dishonest practices of higher-ups, presuming they would be stopped. The bank policy, however, was to terminate those who objected to the demands for malfeasance (as later confirmed by human resource personnel).

Such hypocrisy and criminality formed a core part of the bank's business model. Tellers had to meet with managers every day to explain, for example, why they did not convince customers to open separate accounts for Christmas, for school, for their children's birthdays, for saving for a rainy day, for shopping, and for other purposes, accounts that the customer did not need. The quotas were reported to be insanely high, not achievable except by lying and fraud. Yet Stumpf insisted to the *Wall Street Journal* that there was no incentive "to do bad things." At the same time, he was promoting to employees the slogan "eight is great" – that every bank customer should have a total of eight Wells Fargo accounts, cards, and loans. Sworn testimony from former employees detailed how they were instructed to target college students opening their first bank accounts and older adults with memory problems – those who could most easily be duped (Cowley 2017).

A year after the original scandal in 2016, Wells Fargo, still the country's third largest bank as measured by assets, acknowledged that an outside investigation had uncovered nearly seventy percent more potentially unauthorized accounts than originally revealed. Such venality suggested that yet more similarly dishonest dealings would be disclosed, as indeed they were. Wells overcharged customers at its wealth management business and cheated in a wide range of other areas, employing for instance outright fraud in car loans; the bank had added duplicate insurance policies along with their auto loans to over half a million customers (Gray 2018). Additional lawsuits accused the bank of overcharging small businesses for processing credit card transactions. The bank paid a record $100 million in penalties to the Consumer Financial Protection Bureau for these transgressions. Yet the fines, penalties, and refunds comprised but a small fraction of the eleven billion dollars it had earned in the first six months of 2017 alone (Gara 2017).

Carrie Tolstedt, the Wells executive in charge of community banking who had led this effort, quickly retired in the face of the bad publicity, taking with her tens of millions of dollars in reward for the success of her strategies. Tolstedt's bonuses were defined as performance pay and so tax deductible for the bank. Mr. Stumpf, who fared poorly under Elizabeth Warren's withering questioning at a Senate hearing, also retired with a generous golden parachute. Nobody went to jail or was even charged. The bank paid a fine, one of a number it rendered for offenses, for instance overcharging hundreds of thousands of homeowners for appraisals ordered after their homes went into default. Expenses such as these were simply listed as "other fees" or "other charges" by the bank so customers did not understand what they were paying for – or that the charges were illegal. The idea that the bank's board of directors was ignorant of such schemes is believable only to the credulous. As Dennis Kelleher, the CEO of Better Markets, which advocates for stricter financial regulation told *Barron's*, "You're looking at an incredibly pervasive, longstanding, widespread failure from the top to the bottom of the third largest bank in the U.S." (Walsh 2018).

Again, one may ask: where were the regulators. They were not watching the practices of banks which grew rapidly, not asking was there anything in their trajectory that warranted a closer look.

In 2018 a new problem was revealed: the unauthorized enrollment of customers in the bank's bill-payment service. Wells signed up more than half a million people for a bill-pay service for which they may not have asked, overcharged them on mortgages, and required that customers pay for life insurance they had not bought. Such unlawful acts were numerous and highly profitable. The revelations kept coming. At the end of 2018, Wells Fargo agreed to pay over $575 million to the fifty states and the federal government in addition to the fines and penalties they had dispatched earlier for a host of such infractions. Wells would disburse another $480 million to settle the class action claims of stockholders harmed by its false statements about the misdeeds. After years of exposure of such substantial wrongdoings, the bank campaigned to win back trust, asserting how comprehensively its culture had changed. Its employees, however, were pressured to persist in practices that the bank no longer defined as quotas but which had to be met. Rather, workers were told they were "not doing enough to help their customers," with management pressuring them to increase such "services" as adding fees even when not in the clients' best interest. One person, after quitting in disgust, found that her clients had been informed by the bank that she would be teaming up with another Wells Fargo employee to handle their account. The former employee asked the bank to retract the letter. They refused. After adverse publicity the bank spokesman claimed that the "letter went out in error" (Flitter and Cowley 2019).

Wells was sanctioned by regulators for improper mortgage fees; a Bloomberg analysis of Home Mortgage Disclosure Act data revealed that the bank had by far the worst record among major lenders when it came to refinancing mortgages for black home owners, based on the latest information available in 2022. The criteria used by banks more generally discriminated against Blacks wishing to finance and refinance mortgages, with as Wells showing itself in this area as well to be imposing the harshest terms (Donnan, Choi, Levitt, and Cannon 2022). The corrective, after the damage was done fines did not begin to compensate for the cost to bank clients who rarely received proper compensation.

It is difficult to know how common the many abusive practices revealed in the case of Wells occur in banking more largely, along with analogous ones in corporate America among firms that manage to avoid scrutiny. As Warren Buffett told an interviewer, "There's never just one cockroach in the kitchen" (Cowley 2017). Using large data systems, other leading financial companies tailor credit cards and home equity loans to individual consumers on a massive scale and then target the marketing of these products. What presumably separated Wells Fargo from competitors may be the length to which they went to push unwanted products at inflated cost onto their customers, as revealed by their internal practices. Perhaps others abused the faith their customers had placed in them more subtly and so avoided adverse publicity, even as manipulations were reported elsewhere among the financial giants involving issues with bank accounts, overdraft fees, prepaid debit cards, credit cards, mortgages and home equity loans, as well as lines of credit.

Economic theory accords little attention to the prevalence of the more common-place criminality in American capitalism that is not policed. Indeed, deregulation to remove constraints on companies often enables them. While there is a specialized literature on the economics of crime (Becker and Landes 1974), it has had little or no relevance to the practitioners of mainstream price theory and the theory of the firm. The dominant approach stresses that contracts between buyers and sellers, and among businesses, employers, and individual workers, can be enforced by the legal system; thus, any dishonesty can be remedied. However, the expense of litigating with a bank or a health care insurance company can be large and the chances of winning not auspicious, although here too the Biden administration took steps to prevent the requirement of forced arbitration and other tactics employed by the dominant side in such contests (see Chapter 5). These practices are coercive; indeed one might view them as interference in the market, as neoclassical theory should suggest.

Other costs come from the support by banks of criminal individuals and organizations. From 2008 to 2014, Bank of America paid $91.2 billion in legal settlements and regulatory fines. It was hardly alone in overstating its regulatory capital and in its sale of toxic mortgage-backed securities. Bank of America was also fined by the Consumer Financial Protection Bureau based on allegations that it forced customers to sign up for extra credit card products – as were other banks besides Well Fargo. The International Consortium of Investigative Journalists uncovered U.S. government documents revealing that JPMorgan Chase, HSBC, and other large banks flouted crackdowns on money laundering by moving staggering sums of illicit cash on behalf of shadowy characters and criminal networks that spread chaos and undermined democracy around the world. These records reveal that five global banks – JPMorgan, HSBC, Standard Chartered Bank, Deutsche Bank, and Bank of New York Mellon – kept profiting by moving "dirty" money even after US authorities had fined them, and other financial institutions, for their failure to stop money laundering. "In some cases the banks kept moving illicit funds even after U.S. officials warned them they'd face criminal prosecutions if they didn't stop doing business with mobsters, fraudsters or corrupt regimes."

The International Consortium of Independent Journalists' FinCEN Files and its sixteen-month investigations offer details and insight into a secret world of international banking, with anonymous informants revealing that big banks continue to play a crucial role in moving money tied to corruption, fraud, organized crime, and terrorism. "By utterly failing to prevent large-scale corrupt transactions, financial institutions have abandoned their roles as front-line defenses against money laundering," Paul Pelletier told ICIJ. A former senior U.S. Justice Department official and financial crimes prosecutor, he reported that banks know "they operate in a system that is largely toothless" (Tatone 2020).

Almost all large banks have misled investors and customers. They have rigged bidding for bonds, colluded in setting rates, engaged in money laundering, and discriminated against minority-group borrowers. High-profile criminality has been found in the way bankers secretly fixed key interest rates, most importantly the London Interbank Offer Rate (LIBOR), the benchmark against which other rates were set. Many smaller banks have been determined to be abusive as well. Their crimes include cheating would-be homeowners by extending mortgages that could not be serviced and selling collateralized loan obligations based on those shaky mortgages to naive investors around the world who believed in the appraisals of the rating agencies (paid by the banks).

Financialization imposes greater costs on the economy than its gains or its ability to compensate for the damage it causes. The financial regime that has been sanctioned for so long amounts to a net negative for the economy, which will be understood when all of the costs it has imposed are demonstrated in the next chapter. As individuals, the leaders of the industry do very well from their self-serving, anti-social decisions. Edward Kane (2015) suggests that the rules "of the financial game must acknowledge that it is wrong for individual managers to adopt risk-management strategies that willfully conceal and abuse taxpayers' equity stake in megabanks." But no senior bankers have been penalized for antisocial or illegal actions. Another major obstacle is the financial capitalists who prioritize their own interests and the incentives that guide their actions.

There have been efforts to nudge capital to better behavior. Larry Fink, the powerful head of BlackRock, the world's largest asset management firm, had used his widely read annual letter to the investor community to suggest that global warming was an issue that required attention, a position that was being embraced by many potential and actual customers of his firm's services. He soon retreated from this stance under the pressure of political initiatives that would cost his firm money.

When Texas passed a law barring the state's retirement and investment funds from doing business with companies that the state comptroller said were boycotting fossil fuels, it targeted BlackRock. Larry Fink, the chief executive of BlackRock, has been outspoken, using his annual letter to corporate leaders to implore them to look beyond the bottom line and make a positive contribution to society and saying that there is a sound business rationale for taking up the fight against climate change and imploring other companies to act. However, with the prospect of losing business from Texas and other states, the mammoth entity told a different story. "We are perhaps the world's largest investor in fossil fuel companies, and, as a long-term investor in these companies, we want to see these companies succeed and prosper," Black-Rock's head of external affairs, Dalia Blass, wrote in a letter to Texas regulators. BlackRock had ninety-one billion dollars invested in Texas fossil fuel companies, Ms. Blass stressed, listing BlackRock's sizable holdings, including Exxon Mobil, ConocoPhillips, and Kinder Morgan. Further, BlackRock said it would support fewer stockholder proposals calling for climate action because "we do not consider them to be consistent with our clients' long-term financial interests."

Fink's revised stance was that

Stakeholder capitalism is not about politics. It is not a social or ideological agenda. It is not "woke." It is capitalism, driven by mutually beneficial relationships between you and the employees, customers, suppliers, and communities your company relies on to prosper. This is the power of capitalism.

(Henney 2022)

One might skeptically reverse his statement. Stakeholder capitalism is about appearing woke as part of a rhetorical and ideological agenda to gain public credibility and discourage any thought of prior antisocial behavior. Fink was cited because his annual letter is a bellwether for financialized capitalism, which continues to dissemble even as the costs of its business model are destroying the planet and the economy.

Olúfẹ́mi Táíwò's description of Fink's guidance to CEOs, as "something of an unofficial State of the Union for the global nation of capital," would seem insightful (2022). Benjamin Braun's (2022) argument is that the new asset manager capitalism "constitutes a distinct corporate governance regime" and illuminates the power over the political economy that BlackRock exerts as a "universal owner" of the American economy. This suggests that Ellen Brown's (2020) injunction too should be born in mind: "No private, unelected entity should have the power over the economy that BlackRock has, without a legally enforceable fiduciary duty to wield it in the public interest." While BlackRock is the largest in the world by the measure of assets under management (at this writing more than six trillion dollars and owning a stake in nearly every listed company in the world), there are also other giants with trillions of dollars of assets under management as well as a great many other smaller, but hardly small, firms in the industry to which people with money entrust their funds.

To sum up, this chapter has argued that the financialized economy illustrates the symbiotic and corruptive relationships that governments form with powerful economic interests. The abuses of banking and finance more led Anat Admati (2021) to charge that "[c]apitalism as practiced has undermined governance across economic and political systems. Institutions and processes are too opaque, the rules too often work poorly, and accountability is lacking." It is difficult to disagree with her conclusion: "Ultimately, governments must address the harms brought about by financialized capitalism so that corporations can help the economy and serve society without creating distortions and undermining key institutions of democracy." Because of the manner in which American election campaigns are funded and the influence of lobbyists on who are chosen for regulatory positions, the American political system may most accurately be termed a finance-dominated democracy or, perhaps from a wider perspective, a capitalist democracy, rather than a liberal democracy. The consideration of financialization offered in this chapter surely supports such a view. But the costs that financialization has imposed go well beyond what has been discussed. In the next chapter, the burdens imposed by the crashes resulting from the power of finance are discussed.

References

Ackerman, Andrew. 2022. "Financial Policy Stymied as Biden Faces Confirmation Struggles." *Wall Street Journal*, April 9.

Admati, Anat R. 2021. "Capitalism, Laws, and the Need for Trustworthy Institutions." *Oxford Review of Economic Policy*, 37(4).

Adrian, Tobias and Hyun Song Shin. 2010. "The Changing Nature of Financial Intermediation and the Financial Crisis of 2007–09." *Federal Reserve Banks of New York Staff Reports No. 439.* https://www.annualreviews.org/doi/abs/10.1146/annurev.economics.102308.124420

Appelbaum, Benyamin. 2011. "Spending Cuts Seen as Step, Not as Cure." *New York Times*, August 2.

Armstrong, Rob and Laura Noonan. 2020. "Largest US Banks Double Profits in Past Decade; Lenders Shrug Off Worries about Regulation, Low Interest Rates, and Technological Disruption." *Financial Times*, January 18.

Assa, Jacob. 2016. *The Financialization of GDP: Implications for Economic Theory and Policy.* Routledge.

Banerjee, Ryan and Boris Hofmann. 2018. "The Rise of Zombie Firms: Causes and Consequences." *BIS Quarterly Review*, September.

Becker, Gary S. and William M. Landes, eds. 1974. *Essays in the Economics of Crime and Punishment.* National Bureau of Economic Research.

Becker, Gary S. and Richard A. Posner. 2009. *Uncommon Sense: Economic Insights, from Marriage to Terrorism.* University of Chicago Press.

Berger, Allen N. and David R. Humphrey. 1997. "Efficiency of Financial Institutions: International Survey and Directions for Future Research." *European Journal of Operational Research*, 98.

Boone, Simon, Joachim Fels, Òscar Jordà, Moritz Schularick and Alan M. Taylor. 2022. *Debt: The Eye of the Storm.* Centre Economic Policy Research Press.

Braun, Benjamin. 2022. "Asset Manager Capitalism as a Corporate Governance Regime." In Jacob S. Hacker, Alexander Hertel-Fernandez, Paul Pierson, and Kathleen Thelen, eds. *The American Political Economy: Politics, Markets, and Power.* Cambridge University Press.

Braun, Benjamin and Daniela Gabor. 2020. "Central Banking, Shadow Banking, and Infrastructural Power." In Philip Mader, Daniel Mertens, and Natascha van der Zwan, eds. *The Routledge International Handbook of Financialization.* Routledge.

Bresser-Pereira, Luiz Carlos. 2010. "The Global Financial Crisis and a New Capitalism?" *Journal of Post Keynesian Economics*, 32(4).

Brown, Ellen. 2020. "Meet BlackRock, the New Great Vampire Squid." *Common Dreams*, June 22.

Buera, Francisco and Juan Pablo Nicolini. 2014. "Liquidity Traps and Monetary Policy: Managing a Credit Crunch." *Working Paper No. 2014–14*, Federal Reserve Bank of Chicago.

Buiter, Willem. 2009. "The Unfortunate Uselessness of Most 'State of the Art' Academic Monetary Economics." *Maverecon*, February 6.

Carney, Mark. 2014. "Inclusive capitalism – Creating a Sense of the Systemic." Conference on Inclusive Capitalism, Bank for International Settlements, London. May 27. https://www.bis.org/review/r140528b.pdf.

Çelik, Serdar, Gul Demirtaş and Mats Isaksson. 2020. "Corporate Bond Market Trends, Emerging Risks and Monetary Policy." *Organization for Economic Cooperation and Development, Capital Markets Series, Paris.* https://www.oecd.org/corporate/Corporate-Bond-Market-Trends-Emerging-Risks-and-Monetary-Policy.htm.

Coppola, Frances. 2021. "The Political Economy of Inflation." *European Journal of Economics and Economic Policies: Intervention*, 18(3).

Cowley, Stacy. 2017. "Tally of Suspect Accounts at Wells Fargo Grows by 1.4 Million." *New York Times*, September 1.

Cynamon, Barry Z. and Steven M. Fazzari. 2015. "Rising Inequality and Stagnation in the US Economy." *European Journal of Economics and Economic Policies: Intervention*, 12(2).

Dávila-Fernández, Marwil J. and Lionello F. Punzo. 2022. "Some New Insights on Financialization and Income Inequality: Evidence for the US Economy, 1947–2013." In Malcolm Sawyer and Jonathan Michie, eds. *Capitalism: An Unsustainable Future?* Routledge.

Donnan, Shawn, Ann Choi, Hannah Levitt and Chris Cannon. 2022. "A Racial Refinancing Gap at Wells Fargo." *Bloomberg Businessweek*, March 14.

Epstein, Gerald A. 2006. "Introduction: Financialization and the World Economy." In Gerald A. Epstein, ed. *Financialization and the World Economy*. Edward Elgar.

Flitter, Emily and Stacy Cowley. 2019. "A Bank Says It's Reformed. Workers Differ." *New York Times*, March 10.

Foroohar, Rana. 2022. "The Fed Needs Diversity of Thought." *Financial Times*, January 23.

Fox, Matthew. 2020. " 'I'm so Bearish, I'm Bullish': BofA Says 'Maximum Liquidity' will Push Stocks to New All-Time Highs, but a COVID-19 Vaccine will Mark the 'Big Top'." *Markets Insider*, August 7.

Gara, Antone. 2017. "Another Disaster for Wells Fargo: Troubled Bank Admits Charging Unnecessary Auto Insurance." *Forbes*, July 28.

Godechot, Olivier. 2020. "Financialization and the Increase in Inequality." In Philip Mader, Daniel Mertens, Natascha van der Zwan, eds. *Routledge International Handbook of Financialization*. Routledge.

Gorton, Gary and Andrew Metrick. 2012. "Securitized Banking and the Run on Repo." *Journal of Finance*, 104(3).

Gray, Alistair. 2018. "Wells Fargo Reveals It Overcharged Wealth Management Clients." *Financial Times*, March 1.

Haldane, Andrew G. 2010. "The $100 Billion Question." *Comments by Mr Andrew G Haldane, Executive Director, Financial Stability, Bank of England at the Institute of Regulation & Risk, Hong Kong*. https://www.bis.org/review/r100406d.pdf.

Haltenhof, Samuel, Seung Jung Lee and Viktors Stebunovs. 2014. "The Credit Crunch and Fall in Employment during the Great Recession." *Board of Governors of the Federal Reserve Finance and Economics Discussion Series*, February. https://www.federalreserve.gov/econres/feds/the-credit-crunch-and-fall-in-employment-during-the-great-recession.htm

Henney, Megan. 2022. "BlackRock CEO Larry Fink Says Stakeholder Capitalism Is Not 'Woke'," *Fox Business*, January 18.

Irwin, Neil. 2021. "Nobody Really Knows How the Economy Works. A Fed Paper Is the Latest Sign." *New York Times*, October 1.

Jayadev, Arjun, Josh W. Mason and Enno Schröder. 2018. "The Political Economy of Financialization in the United States, Europe, and India." *Development and Change*, 49(2).

Jo, Tae-Hee, Lynne Chester and Carlo D'Ippoliti, eds. 2017. *Handbook of Heterodox Economics; Theorizing, Analyzing, and Transforming Capitalism*. Routledge.

Jomo, Kwame Sundaram. 2020. "Finance's New Avatar." *Development*, 63.

Kaldor, Yair. 2022. "Financialization and Fictitious Capital: The Rise of Financial Securities as a Form of Private Property." *Review of Radical Political Economy*, 54(2).

Kane, Edward J. 2015. "A Theory of How and Why Central-Bank Culture Supports Predatory Risk-Taking at Megabanks." *Institute for New Economic Thinking Working Paper Series No. 34*.

Karwowski, Ewa, Mimoza Shabani and Engelbert Stockhammer. 2020. "Dimensions and Determinants of Financialisation: Comparing OECD Countries since 1997. *New Political Economy*, 25(6).

Kay, John. 2015. Other People's Money: The Real Business of Finance. *PublicAffairs*, p. 69.

Keynes, John M. 1936. *The General Theory of Employment, Interest, and Money*. Harcourt, Brace and Company.

Konczal, Mike and Nell Abernathy. 2015. *Defining Financialization*. Roosevelt Institute.

Kotz, David M. 2019. "The Rate of Profit, Aggregate Demand, and the Long Economic Expansion in the United States since 2009." *Review of Radical Political Economics*, 51(4).

Kuhn, Thomas. 1962. *The Structure of Scientific Revolutions*. University of Chicago Press.

Kuttner, Robert. 2018. "Restoring Social Investment Is Key." *Social Europe*, May 23.

Lee, Isabelle. 2022. "Legendary Investor Jeremy Grantham Predicts S&P 500 will Crash 50% after 4th US 'Superbubble' in the Past Century Pops." *Business Insider*, January 20.

Mader, Philip, Daniel Mertens and Natascha van der Zwan, eds. 2020. *Routledge International Handbook of Financialization*. Routledge.

McKinsey & Company. 2021. "Private Markets 2021: A Year of Disruption." *McKinsey's Private Markets Annual Review*, April 21.

Natarajan, Sridhar and Matt Robinson. 2019. "Goldman's Unwelcome Streak: A String of Insider Trading Charges." *Bloomberg*, October 21.

Nygaard, Kaleb B. 2020. "The Federal Reserve's Response to the 1987 Market Crash (U.S. Historical)." *Journal of Financial Crises*, 2(3).

Palladino, Lenore. 2018. "Corporate Financialization and Worker Prosperity: A Broken Link." *Roosevelt Institute*, January 17.

Palley, Thomas I. 2021. "Financialization Revisited: The Economics and Political Economy of the Vampire Squid Economy." *Review of Keynesian Economics*, 9(4).

Parramore, Lynn. 2022. "Our Economic System Is Making Us Mentally Ill." *Institute for New Economic Thinking*, March 18.

Petrou, Karen. 2021. "A Central-Bank Mandate for Our Time: The Fed's De Facto Fiscal Role and Its Anti-Equality Impact. *Prepared for the 39th Annual Monetary Conference: Populism and the Future of the Fed*. November 18, Cato Institute. https://fedfin.com/wp-content/uploads/2021/11/Karen-Petrou-Cato-Institute-A-Central-Bank-Mandate-for-Our-Time_The-Feds-De-Facto-Fiscal-Role-and-Its-Anti-Equality-Impact-11.18.2021.pdf

Philippon, Thomas. 2019. *The Great Reversal: How America Gave Up on Free Markets*. Harvard University Press.

Phillips, Matt. 2020. "Businesses Are Supposed to Cut Debt in a Downturn. Why Not Now?" *New York Times*, July 20.

Popularis, Joe. 2022. "How to Stop Inflation From Hurting America's Working and Middle Class." *The Federalist*, March 3.

Prins, Nomi. 2017. *A Decade of G7 Central Bank Collusion and Counting*, August 29. http://www.nomiprins.com/thoughts/2017/8/29/a-decade-of-g7-central-bank-collusion-and-counting.html.

Robbins, Lionel. 1932. *An Essay on the Nature and Significance of Economic Science*. MacMillan & Co.

Robinson, Austin. 1934. "The Problem of Management and the Size of Firms." *Economic Journal*, 44(174).

Rudd, Jeremy B. 2021. "Why Do We Think That Inflation Expectations Matter for Inflation? (And Should We?)." *Finance and Economics Discussion Series 2021–062*, Board of Governors of the Federal Reserve System.

Saharan, Shubham and Max Reyes. 2022. "Banks Bristle as a Tough Stress Test." *Bloomberg Businessweek*, August 1.

Schultz, Randy. 1998. "Travelers, Citicorp to Unites." *CNN Money*, April 6.

Schumpeter, Joseph A. 1954. *History of Economic Analysis*. Oxford University Press.

Shaw, Christopher W. 2019. *Money, Power and the People*. University of Chicago Press.

Smialek, Jeanna, Peter Eavis and Emily Flitter. 2019. "Banks Want Efficiency. Critics Warn of Backsliding." *New York Times*, August 20.

Smith, Adam. 2002 [1759]. *The Theory of Moral Sentiment (ed. Knud Haakonssen)*. Cambridge University Press.

Stockhammer, Engelbert. 2004. "Financialization and the Slowdown in Accumulation." *Cambridge Journal of Economics*, 28(5).

Storm, Servaas. 2018. 'Financialization and Economic Development: A Debate on the Social Efficiency of Modern Finance." *Development & Change*, 49(2).

Sweezy, Paul M. 1994. "The Triumph of Financial Capital." *Monthly Review*, June 1.

Tabb, William K. 1999. *Reconstructing Political Economy: The Great Divide in Economic Thought*. Routledge.

Táíwò, Olúfẹ́mi. 2022. "How BlackRock, Vanguard, and UBS Are Screwing the World." *New Republic*, March 7.

Tatone, Alicia. 2020. "Global Banks Defy U.S. Crackdowns by Serving Oligarchs, Criminals and Terrorists." *BuzzFeed News*, September 20.

Tercioglu, Remzi Baris. 2021. "Rethinking Growth and Inequality in the US: What Is the Role of the Measurement of GDP?" *International Review of Applied Economics*, 35(3–4).

Tymoigne, Éric. 2009. "Securitization, Deregulation, Economic Stability, and Financial Crisis, Part I: The Evolution of Securitization." *Levy Economics Institute Working Paper No. 573*. https://www.levyinstitute.org/pubs/wp_573_1.pdf.

Walsh, Ben. 2018. "Weighing the Regulatory Risk at Wells Fargo," *Barron's*, February 10.

Woetzel, Jonathan, Jan Mischke, Anu Madgavkar, Eckart Windhagen, Sven Smit, Michael Birshan, Szabolcs Kemeny and Rebecca J. Anderson. 2021. "The Rise and Rise of the Global Balance Sheet: How Productively Are We Using Our Wealth?" *McKinsey Global Institute*, November 15.

3
THE COSTS OF FINANCIAL SYSTEM FAILURE

Estimates of the total amount of funding provided by the Federal Reserve to bail out the financial system in response to the Great Recession include the Fed's claim of only 1.2 trillion dollars, Bloomberg's estimate of 7.7 trillion dollars (just allocated for the largest banks), and the tally by the Government Accountability Office of 16 trillion dollars. Nicola Matthews and James Felkerson's detailed examination of the raw data "pried" from the Fed by lawsuit and congressional order found that the Fed committed more than 29 trillion dollars in the form of loans and asset purchases to prop up the global financial system (Wray 2011). Further cataloging the toll of the Great Recession, William Dudley (2017) stresses the nine million lost jobs and the eight million housing foreclosures. It took eight years after the financial collapse for the unemployment rate to drop to a level consistent with the Fed's employment objective. Those who had lost their jobs were confined to lower earnings well into the future, with many former homeowners of necessity becoming long-term renters.

Gerald Epstein and Juan Antonio Montecino estimate that the U.S. financial system will impose an excess cost of as much as 22.7 trillion dollars between 1990 and 2023, making finance "in its current form a net drag on the American economy." (The calculation was offered before the 2020 financial crisis.) Their research extends beyond the outlays resulting from the 2008 crash to include rents, or excess profits enjoyed by the financial sector, and "misallocation costs," the price of diverting resources away from non-financial activities. The total includes financial rents totaling from 3.6 to 4.2 trillion dollars between 1990 and 2005. This sum does not include "anticompetitive practices, the marketing of excessively complex and risky products, government subsidies such as financial bailouts," and fraudulent activities from which bankers received inordinate pay and profits. Epstein and Antonio Montecino (2016) point out that a relatively small number of owners and operatives in the financial sector benefit from significant salaries, bonuses, and profits as a result of these practices.

DOI: 10.4324/9781003385240-3

While at the Bank of England, Andrew Haldane declared that without a government bailout, losses due to the 2008 collapse would lie "anywhere between a large number and an unthinkably large number." He estimated that in money terms, the output loss of the Global Financial Crisis ranged between 60 and 200 trillion dollars for the world economy. Assuming that such events occur every twenty years, there is no way that the banks can compensate society for their actions with the total market capitalization of the largest global banks being only around 1.2 trillion dollars. For them to pay damages for the output costs of financial crises would "risk putting banks on the same trajectory as the dinosaurs, with the levy playing the role of the meteorite" (Haldane 2010).

The likelihood of governments fundamentally restructuring finance would increase substantially if people both knew of these costs and understood that there is a better alternative to allowing financial institutions to take such high risks with other people's money and for the regulators to make good on such losses. Since banks cannot compensate for output losses, let alone for the emotional trauma suffered by those losing their jobs and homes when the financial system crashes and lives are shattered, it might make sense to substantially limit their ability to take excessive risk and endanger the world economy. The costs of crises and the significant subsidies extended to banks when they run into trouble, Haldane suggested, are "a real and large social problem." It is a "problem" that recurs because, to repurpose the metaphor, the huge beasts that prowl the global economy would require a meteorite to end their reign, perhaps the political revolution that Bernie Sanders advocates.

On learning that the losses suffered from the 2008 financial crash amounted to the equivalent of between 60 trillion and 200 trillion dollars in output, and that the banks paid penalties and fines of only 150 billion dollars over ten years for their various illegal practices (less than a third of what they earned in 2007 alone), one reader of the *Financial Times* wrote, "Jail costs $75,000 a year. $150bn pays for 200,000 bankers for ten years. Let's get busy." Such reactions, Yves Smith comments, "are yet another sign of an intensifying legitimacy crisis. The educated and presumably prosperous readers of the *Financial Times* aren't buying the idea that banks and bankers were treated badly post crisis" (Smith 2017).

As formulated by Walter Bagehot in 1873, in a period of financial panic monetary authorities should lend unsparingly but at a penalty rate to illiquid but solvent banks against sound collateral. This would prevent a decline in the money stock protecting the financial system. Illiquid banks could be helped but only at penalty rates and against high-quality collateral. The central bank would thus be protected against supporting poor business decisions by bankers (Jeffers 2010). Another cost of the response to financial crises in the Fed is the abandonment of this criteria and the Fed's taking over from the market the determination of risks with its new policy of guaranteeing all assets in a downturn. This involves a very different interpretation of the role of lender of last resort than the one originally put forward at the start of the 19th century by Henry Thornton and famously articulated by Bagehot, and which governed until 2007. To safeguard the financial system, the government needs to wrest control from the market, setting interest rates and regulating liquidity. No longer disciplined by market forces, investors and financial institutions have come to expect help from central banks and Treasury departments when problems develop from their assumption of irresponsible risks and their flights of poor judgment. Who is able to access central bank loans, the quality of the collateral that is found acceptable, and the rates at which central banks lend are all issues that are rarely discussed in a serious way by ordinary people. If they did so they would be aware that the Fed's activities "to save the financial system" have both distributional and political consequences. Throughout its history, as Lawrence Jacobs and Desmond King (2021: chapter 16) explain, "Fed Power" has been used to pick winners and losers in the American economy.

If financial institutions had to bear the cost of taking excessive risks or buying private insurance to cover possible losses in their trading activities (should the market actually be able to muster the resources to do this), instead of being bailed out each time by the Fed they would not undertake them, or certainly not on the scale of their current operations. The economy would be safer as a consequence. The 21st-century financial system that has been allowed and encouraged by policy makers increased the interdependence among banks so that risk was spread widely, with the distinction between illiquidity and insolvency having disappeared for all practical purposes; the consequence has been that finance has grown to such proportions that the Fed and other central banks have had no choice but to bail out significant financial institutions whose failure could bring down other substantial players and even major non-financial corporations.

The Fed's balance sheet grew from $700 billion dollars before the Great Recession to 4.3 trillion dollars in mid-March 2020 and then with the next financial crisis to 8.2 trillion dollars by late July 2021. This figure was equivalent to forty percent of nominal U.S. GDP, a level last seen during World War II – and it is ballooning still further as new facilities were created to backstop small and medium-sized banks in danger of collapse following the Silicon Valley Bank debacle. The U.S. was hardly alone in its response; most striking was the crisis of Credit Suisse that not many days after that needed rescuing by the government of the country that had made banking its leading industry. By then the euro system's balance sheet was the equivalent of more than 60 percent of the Eurozone's GDP while the balance sheet of the Bank of Japan reached 130 percent of that country's GDP. The quality of the assets on these balance sheets was a troubling question.

Lessons Learned?

Congress passed the Dodd-Frank Act in response to the 2008 financial crisis. It established the Financial Stability Oversight Council (FSOC), which identifies risks that affected the entire financial industry in 2010. If any firm becomes too big, the FSOC was mandated to remand it to the Federal Reserve for closer supervision. The Fed could require a bank to increase its reserve requirement, making sure it had enough cash on hand to prevent bankruptcy. But reform did not take place; the FSOC proved toothless, with the Fed instead removing all reserve requirements. Other provisions of the law established a wide range of reforms throughout the entire financial system which were designed to prevent a repeat of the 2007–2008 crisis and the need for further government bailouts. But over time these too were compromised; the law was not changed to address new system vulnerabilities as it should have been.

Following the Great Recession, the U.S. experienced its longest (albeit slow and weak) expansion on record despite the continued low interest rates promoted by the Fed to encourage recovery. As a result, at the end of 2019 the Global Research unit of the Bank of America warned that "[w]e enter the next decade with interest rates at 5,000-year lows, the largest asset bubble in history, a planet that is heating up, and a deflationary profile of debt, disruption and demographics." The researchers continued, "The social, political and economic responses to these challenges, all heading to a boiling point this decade, will overhaul traditional paradigms." Among the current developments, they observed: "Monetary policy measures are proving less and less effective at boosting corporate and household animal spirits" (Strauss 2019).

In the fall of 2021 Robert Shiller (2021), without making a timing prediction which he knew would be foolhardy, wrote that the prices of stocks, bonds, and real estate, the three major asset classes in the U.S., "are all extremely high. In fact, the three have never been this overpriced simultaneously in modern history." He also noted a popular tendency to think that "any apparent uptrend in speculative prices, even a short one, is a sign of economic strength or even renewed national greatness and that it can be extrapolated indefinitely." Shiller (2021) warned that with assets already seeming overpriced, investor prudence, not celebration, was required.

The downturn that occurred was blamed on Covid. This was not wrong. The pandemic indeed had triggered the collapse, but the overextension of debt and heightened risk to the system might well have brought a crisis without the precipitating impacts of the disease. It is on the basis of the understandings expressed by Schiller, the Global Research unit of the Bank of America, and observations chronicled here, that it has been suggested that even without the pandemic and the war in Ukraine, the American economy was in serious trouble, likely soon to experience a new financial crisis. It will be up to future investigators after the dust settles on the current period's crisis to parcel out relative responsibility for what may happen before the inflation threat is dealt with and a new normal emerges. It may be that at least some of them will decide to continue to follow their existing understandings as economists' textbook models almost totally ignore real-world finance, a perspective that led most of the profession to view the 2008 financial crisis as a "Black Swan" event (Taleb 2007), unlikely to happen and unpredictable, as the Queen had been told.

In a joint statement, David Colander, Michael Goldberg, Armin Haas, Katrina Juselius, Alan Kirman, Thomas Lux, and Brigitte Sloth (2009) offer what for readers may at this point provide a familiar critique of such a position: "If one browses through the academic macroeconomics and finance literature, "systemic crisis" appears like an otherworldly event that is absent from economic models. Most models, by design," they wrote, "offer no immediate handle on how to think about or deal with this recurring phenomenon. In our hour of greatest need, societies around the world are left to grope in the dark without a theory. That, to us, is a systemic failure of the economics profession."

Phillip Stevens (2015), an opinion writer for the *Financial Times*, offers a not dissimilar evaluation in a blunt commentary. He writes of what was being taught and learned by students that "[a]ll the guff they had learnt about a new financial capitalism, self-equilibrating markets and the end of boom and bust was shown to be, well, guff" (The question is: what should replace such "guff"?)

One key point of an alternative understanding (to be developed in Chapter 6) is that assets are frequently bought with borrowed money, often without the hope that even the interest on the transaction can be paid. The logic of the investment is that due to a rising market it will be worth more and so can be sold at a profit high enough to cover the loan principle plus interest, leaving a profit on the investment, or it can be held anticipating a further rise in its market value. The same logic stands for buying companies with borrowed money and engaging in cost-cutting restructuring, anticipating that they will then be worth more. Yet such Ponzi financing invites a Minsky Moment of recognition – that the game can no longer continue, with the collapse of the asset bubble becoming foreseeable to some and soon evident to all.

The people who contribute to this collapse typically, and correctly, argue that they are not personally to blame. They are prisoners of what is expected of them. As Charles "Chuck" Prince, then head of Citigroup, told the *Financial Times* in July 2007, even when global liquidity is enormous and a significant disruptive event can create a serious downturn for the leveraged buyout market and the investors the bank has lent to, "[a]s long as the music is playing, you've got to get up and dance." As the economy was about to crash, he added, "We're still dancing." It would have been wise to have left the floor. It was not much later that Prince resigned, following the disastrous performance of his bank. Subsequently, he explained his comment to the Financial Inquiry Commission: "The quote itself related to the leveraged lending business, and I specifically asked the regulators if they would take action in regard to that." Prince claimed at the time that "private equity firms were driving very hard bargains with the banks . . . the banks individually had no credibility to stop participating in this lending business." He continued, "[I]t was not credible for one institution to back away from this leveraged lending business." Rather, it was the regulators who "had an interest in tightening up lending standards," and, he told them, "You didn't do it" (Aspan 2010). That the banks lobbied against such regulations then, as now, was somehow not relevant.

At the Citigroup emergency board meeting in which he announced his resignation, Prince told a different story: "Given the size and nature of the recent losses in our mortgage-backed securities business, the only honorable course for me to take as chief executive officer is to step down." Prince acknowledged his responsibility –

and accepted a golden parachute. After having presided over the evaporation of roughly sixty-four billion dollars in market value, he departed with ninety-nine million dollars in vested stock holdings and a pension, in addition to the fifty-three million dollars salary and bonuses he had received during his four-year tenure as head of the bank (Pomorski 2015). The taxpayers bailed out Citigroup, which soon returned to the same high-risk strategies it had practiced before the crisis. The problem was not Mr. Prince but rather the system itself, one in which excess is integral to its normal functioning. The history of capitalism is replete with such booms and financial speculation failures. As the new decade began, central banks continued to accommodate financial institutions, increasing their liquidity, watching their debt grow and their fragility increase. They believed that if they did not preserve the financial institutions the system would collapse, to the mutual ruin of all.

The consequence, however, is that the Fed and other central banks have become trapped in a situation difficult to escape. Each time they save the banks and weaker banks are merged with institutions that are already too large and other entities deemed too big to fail are given greater aid, flooding even more money into the system, the scale of the debt overhang increases. The risk grows yet again. The low-interest environment that followed the 2008 crisis led investors to even more risk-taking in search of yield, accompanied by a pattern of dishonest accounting that was recognized by government statisticians thereafter. These were not novel practices.

By the summer of 2002, following the crash of the dot-com boom, the national income and products accounts of the Bureau of Economic Analysis had revised downward the profits for 1998, 1999, and 2000 by "11.0 percent, 9.3 percent, and 8.9 percent," respectively. Over this period, a threefold increase in stock options had occurred – to about 200 billion dollars in 2000. In mid-2002, a retired J. P. Morgan vice president estimated that about half the declared sum comprised a significant overestimation of earnings, one consequence of the failure to record options as expenses. The other half involved the straight manipulation of earnings. This breakdown was confirmed in a study by researchers at the New York Federal Reserve Bank, who calculated that half of the correction in profits came from stock options and the rest from aggressive accounting (Elliot 2010).

None of this is new, Veblen (1997[1923]) discussed such practices while a less famous figure, William Z. Ripley's (2018[1927]) descriptions of corporate misdeeds at the time were more colorful. He wrote of their "prestidigitation, double shuffling, honey-fugling, hornswaggling, and skullduggery." In his day, as in the current era, corporations diluted their shares, gave sweetheart contracts to their directors, took away shareholders' voting rights, operating without transparency "cloaked and hooded like the despicable Ku Klux Klan" so the individual identities of corporate malefactors remained obscured (Lemann 2020). During the Great Depression, such corruption and fraudulence was widely revealed.

As the economy experienced increased turbulence, it was again reported that manipulation of earnings by Corporate America "is on the rise, an ominous omen for the U.S. economy" (Zumbrun 2023). That is the conclusion of research on accounting fraud, using a technique that had earlier anticipated the dramatic collapse of Enron after its earnings manipulations several years before the energy company's spectacular 2001 failure. It was predicted by the Beneish model that again pointed to a period of misreporting on a wide scale in the second decade of the 21st century predicting recession. (Messod Beneish's M-Score is calculated from eight ratios on a company's balance sheet, all numbers that public companies report quarterly, and comparing the ratios to earnings statements from a year earlier.) The M-score suggested that serious trouble could be ahead for the American economy (Beneish, Farber, Glendening, and Shaw 2022).

The appropriation of surplus from others was most evident in the financial sector where profits were premised on such practices. John Kay (2015: 126) calls attention to a seemingly unthinkable truth: "The possibility that financial institutions do not really make lots of money is difficult to grasp. Look at the salaries, the bonuses, the marbled reception areas, the corporate jets. All the trappings of an exceptionally profitable industry are there. Can it really be the case that the industry is not, in fact, exceptionally profitable?" This question moves the inquiry to the rate of return for financial institutions, and how this measure of profitability is calculated and manipulated.

There are two ways of improving the rate of return on equity. The more difficult is to increase earnings on the same amount of equity. The other is widely practiced. It involves decreasing the size of the denominator, reducing equity through share buybacks, and increasing debt as a source of capital. Since this is so commonplace smart investors do not take rate of return seriously as a reliable measure of firm profitability. This practice unfortunately has wider consequences. The collapse of the financial bubble that occurred in 2007–2008 stemmed from the creation of too much borrowing, too much unpayable debt. Soon enough, global debt had risen to new record highs and not only in the U.S. Non-financial sector debt of twenty key advanced and emerging economies was almost forty percent higher by 2017 than a decade earlier, according to the Bank for International Settlements (BIS). Jaime Caruana, General Manager for the BIS, warned of a looming new debt bubble (Rapoza 2017). The Institute of International Finance reported that global debt of all kinds had reached a record of $217 trillion by 2017, up by 70 trillion dollars from a decade earlier when the financial crisis first broke (if we date that from the collapse of the large lender Northern Rock in the U.K.). Such a development suggested a new crash in the offing. The point, that even without the economic damage brought by Covid a crisis had been feared, suggests that further efforts, by expanding the money supply to limit the impact of a downturn, did not succeed in strengthening the economy for long.

This is confirmed by the data. From 2007 to the end of 2012, central banks flooded the world with more than eleven trillion dollars in liquidity with the object of supporting asset markets and keeping banks solvent after the Global Financial Crisis. Interest rates at historic lows (a fraction of a percent above zero in some countries and held below zero by extensive bond purchases in others) allowed defaults to be minimized. Yet despite these efforts, the global economy experienced only a slow recovery. Lower borrowing costs stimulated not real investment in the production of goods and non-financial services so much as speculation, which pushed up asset valuations. The financial analyst Anthony Crescenzi speaks of "monetary morphine," a global expansion of money creation that with each new injection produces a "high" for stock prices but does little to address the underlying weaknesses of the real economy (Sender 2012). Such a conclusion raises the question of how many of the seemingly successful financial conglomerates were in fact zombie banks, kept from their demise by governments. No matter that they purchased derivatives, which lost value in a financial collapse; their national central bank supported them. Nonetheless, even as economic growth fell for two quarters in 2022, signaling a recession to some, bank profits reached new heights.

Very few countries took the harsh action of allowing the market to work, and when corruption was discovered sending the miscreants to jail. Iceland was an exception. Their banks had grown twentyfold between 2001 and 2008 until they dwarfed the ability of the country to bail them out. When the three main Icelandic banks failed, they made Moody's list of the eleven largest bankruptcies in history. Iceland's government had privatized banks in 2003 (prior to that they had been run like government departments in a low-key, unexciting manner), leaving decision-making to the free market. By 2007 its three largest banks had made loans equal to nine times the size of the country's total economy. (Some of these, it turned out, were described as "strange" loans given to government ministers.) In response, voters decisively repudiated the eighteen-year rule of the conservative Independence Party, putting into office the interim alliance of the Social Democrat and Left-Green parties. The new government arrested the corrupt bankers and others involved.

After years of appeals, in 2015 the Supreme Court of Iceland and the Reykjavík District Court sentenced three top managers of Landsbank and two of Kaupþing Bank, along with a prominent bank investor, to prison for crimes committed. Taken together, twenty-six bankers and financiers had been sentenced to prison for crimes relating to the financial collapse, with a combined prison time of seventy-four years. Icelandic President Olafur Ragnar Grimmson best summed it up when asked how his country had recovered from the Global Financial Crisis: "We were wise enough not to follow the traditional prevailing orthodoxies of the Western financial world in the last 30 years. We introduced currency controls, we let the banks fail, we provided support for the people and didn't introduce austerity measures like you're seeing in Europe" (Syrmopoulos 2015).

It was not audacious to predict that as a result of central banks raising interest rates in 2022 to fight inflation, an economic downturn would once again reveal unwise and illegal practices by banks and other financial institutions and that as inflation recedes, the process would begin again – unless, as Iceland chose to do, lessons presumably learned were actually applied to prevent financialization from continuing to guide the economic system. But it is also hardly a risky forecast to expect that the banks and bankers are likely to come through unscathed, given their political influence, regardless of the impacts on lesser institutions, communities, and individuals. As larger U.S. banks understand, they will be cared for, avoiding the indignities experienced by their Icelandic colleagues.

Political Corruption and the Consequences of Buybacks

In the U.S., and indeed in cases that could be cited in many other countries as well, incidences occurred of what might be considered routine political corruption. One such incident involved the misallocated public resources in the rescue bill that Congress passed in the waning days of the Trump administration. Senate Republicans had inserted an easily overlooked provision (on page 203 of the 880-page bill) that permitted wealthy investors to use paper losses generated by real estate to minimize their taxes on profits. This was "a potential bonanza" for America's richest real estate investors, who stood to benefit from such depreciation losses (which assumed land was worth less over time instead of rising in value). The cost of the provision for the taxpayer was estimated over ten years to be 170 billion dollars. A congressional report found it to be the second-largest tax giveaway in the stimulus package. Other industries, including oil, gas, and commodities trading, were also major beneficiaries.

The Trump administration refused to disclose the names of the companies that had received corporate bailouts. Treasury Secretary Mnuchin told the Senate Committee on Small Business and Entrepreneurship that he would reveal neither the data nor the model. "We believe that that's proprietary information, and in many cases for sole proprietors and small businesses, it is confidential information," he asserted (2020). Republican supporters claimed that "the deep state" investigating the president was politically motivated. Insisting on transparency, his outraged critics demanded to know who was being protected, suggesting that it was Trump's minions and friends.

Public Citizen was sharply critical of Mnuchin's stance, finding his refusal to disclose businesses receiving PPP funds to be "unconscionable, jaw-dropping corruption." Bartlett Naylor, a financial policy advocate for Public Citizen, asserted that "[m]aking sure trillions in aid goes to workers, not profiteers, begins with knowing where the aid goes. . . . Zero transparency is a red carpet for hucksters, schemers, and battlefield scavengers." Small-business advocates, members of Congress from both parties, and the Inspector General of the Small Business Administration (SBA) all raised concerns that the implementation of the Paycheck Protection Program (PPP) may have made it more difficult for certain groups to access its resources, including minorities and business owners in rural areas. As 2020 ended, the SBA released details of who had benefitted from the PPP and by how much. Its report revealed that merely one percent of the over five million borrowers had received a quarter of the more than half a trillion dollars distributed by the program – which had presumably been targeted for small struggling businesses. It had taken an order by Judge James Boasberg of the U.S. District Court in Washington to force the SBA to release the data (Fox News 2020). The paycheck assistance, it turned out, did not go to workers who had lost their jobs; rather it provided a windfall for larger business owners and shareholder. In 2022, two years after lawmakers approved the Covid downturn rescue funds, it was reported that within the previous month examples of rampant fraud had included a guilty plea for using part of a four-million-dollar loan to purchase a Porsche, a Mercedes, and a BMW – not for providing any help to those impacted by the crisis, as required by the program. Another case involved the invention of employees, inflated wages, and tax filings fabricated to collect one million dollars in loans. Still another featured the sentencing of a man who had obtained $800,000 on behalf of nonexistent businesses. Hundreds of similar cases of obvious fraud were found. "There is no question that the immense fraud . . . took place." It was "the largest oversight challenge the Biden administration inherited," reported Gene Sperling, the president's chief coordinator for stimulus spending. He stressed that the administration was taking "significant steps to strengthen anti-fraud controls" (Romm 2022). A great deal of the money could not in fact be traced; Washington acknowledged that it had chosen not to establish a system for checking the merit of government expenditures (except for those of low-income welfare recipients, who were monitored carefully). Other spending, such as by the Pentagon, was similarly plagued by overpayment and underperformance, again without consequence.

Then there is the matter, beyond criminality, of where the profits go in U.S. capitalism that are not targeted to expanding output. The answer is in large measure to the purchase of company shares, which inflates the wealth of the group at the top. This includes senior management, who receive most of their compensation in the form of stock options. Their "sell strategy" is timed to upticks in the value of their holdings, impacted by their own announcements and by policies that inflate short-term growth, sometimes at the expense of the long-term health of the company (Lazonick 2017).

CEO compensation came to be dominated by stock options on the theory that the strategy offers executives incentive to maximize the equity of owners. Their compensation grew to more than half of total compensation (fifty-three percent) in 2009 and greater than three quarters (seventy-seven percent) in 2015. By 2017 the discrepancy between executive compensation and employee pay had grown dramatically, largely driven by the stock market since about eighty percent of CEO compensation was then provided by stock options. The CEOs of the top 350 companies each earned on average almost nineteen million dollars a year or 312 times the median pay for employees in their industries. In 1960, the comparable ratio had been twenty to one (Mishel and Schieder 2018). Stock buybacks hit a new record in 2021. In the first two months of 2022, S&P 500 companies disclosed authorizations to buy back 238 billion dollars in stock – a record pace, according to Goldman Sachs, which expected one trillion dollars of buybacks for the year, an all-time high.

The firm TipRanks uses an algorithm to sort through the Securities and Exchange Commission (SEC) filings required of insider executives, filtering out what it terms "uninformed" transactions – that is, those that seem to have no predictive value – compared to a list of top insiders who do especially well in the market. Reporting on its findings, its CEO Uri Gruenbaum commented that "someone might pick heads five times in a row, but to do it 20 times or 50 times is really hard" (Vaughan 2021). Even the average "insiders" have profited. Purchases they made outperformed the S&P 500 over the ensuing twelve months by an average of five percentage points between 2015 and 2020, according to TipRanks analysis. (An "insider" is defined as a senior executive, board member, or any shareholder who owns ten percent or more of a company. There are about 82,000 of them. Each of their trades, which must be disclosed on a Form 4 within two days of the transaction, is available on the website of the SEC.) "The gap might seem scandalous to those with only a passing acquaintance with U.S. insider trading rules, which make it illegal for insiders to trade using material – financially significant – information," Vaughan writes, "and yet on Wall Street it's long been an open secret that insiders trade on what they know."

Daniel Taylor, head of the Wharton Forensic Analytics Lab, persuaded the SEC to give him a 300-page list of the probes opened between 2000 and 2017, which he and colleagues cross-referenced with Form 4 disclosures. They reported that

> despite the undisclosed and economically material nature of these investigations, we find that insiders are not abstaining from trading. In particular, we find a pronounced spike in insider selling among undisclosed investigations with the most severe negative outcomes; and that abnormal selling activity appears highly opportunistic and earns significant abnormal returns.
>
> *(Blackburne, Kepler, Quinn, and Taylor 2020)*

As Vaughan (2021) writing in *Bloomberg Businessweek* explains, "When an executive learns his company is about to lose its well-regarded CEO and offloads shares to an unwitting pension fund, or a board member hears about a potential takeover on the distant horizon and sets up a plan to start buying, they're profiting at the expense of regular people. He quotes Professor Taylor, commenting on his findings that "there is a lack of appreciation for the amount of opportunistic abuse that exists under the current system, the amount of egregiousness"; he concludes, "Most Americans today believe the stock market is rigged, and they're right."

Under the Securities Exchange Act of 1934, executives who abuse their access to nonpublic information by trading on it themselves or passing it along to someone else can be charged with fraud. But they are rarely charged and even less often penalized. Regulators and lawyers say it is difficult to get a conviction for such crimes – in contrast, for example, to holding up a bank. Insider trading laws and their enforcement "haven't kept up with the crooks," as those with prosecutorial experience recognize (Bharara and Jackson Jr. 2018). Indeed, the laws have changed to enable such inside trading. In 1981, Ronald Reagan, intent on the deregulation of finance and other sectors of the economy, appointed John Shad, the first securities firm executive to head the agency in fifty years, to run the SEC. Under Shad's leadership, the SEC adopted rule 10b-18, which provides a "safe harbor" for companies in stock buybacks. That is, it allows buybacks under specified conditions rather than complying with the intent of the New Deal legislation that declared such activity to be illegal. From then on, buybacks increased substantially.

Firms that engage in greater buybacks prove more vulnerable when a downturn occurs. Buybacks drive up the stock market at the expense of dividends, internal growth, long-term investment, and job creation. As William Lazonick and Ken Jacobson (2018) explain, "[h]aving wasted billions on buybacks, many firms incurred huge losses and required mass layoffs to avoid bankruptcy." They argue that if Congress and regulators "do not take action to rein in buybacks, the rampant economic inequality that already afflicts the United States will only get worse."

Everyday Investor Corruption

Interestingly, there are far louder outcries when public officials seem to benefit from insider trading, as when it was revealed that Dallas Fed President Robert Kaplan had carried out multiple million-dollar trades in individual stocks in 2020. He then owned thirty-two individual stock, fund, or alternative asset holdings, including twenty-seven valued at more than one million dollars, according to disclosures filed by Fed officials. Boston Fed President Eric Rosengren insisted, as did Kaplan, that he had complied with the Federal Reserve ethics rules, but he also announced that in the future he planned to invest the proceeds of individual stock sales in diversified index funds or hold them in cash: "I have decided to address even the appearance of any conflict of interest by taking (these) steps," he promised (Miao 2021). Both men resigned. Richard Clarida did not have to resign since his questionable trades were not discovered until nearly the end of his term as vice president of the Federal Reserve. He had rapidly moved money out of the market before public statements by the Fed that would send the market down – and then re-bought the same assets just before announcements that would encourage investors to purchase them. He stated this to be a matter of rebalancing his portfolio, not a consequence of insider information. He also acknowledged that he had noticed "inadvertent errors" in his initial filings. Others found it to be "peculiar" that he sold stocks just days before Clarida moved back into them. Millions of dollars were moved this way, making him a great deal of money (Smialek 2022).

After these revelations, the Fed adopted a set of ethics rules to prevent such trading activity by top officials, along with 45-day prior announcements of trades (that were not retractable by the official) to increase transparency; moreover, investments were to be held for at least a year. Financial disclosures by the twelve regional bank presidents who partake in policy decisions were also tightened. They were required to post financial disclosure statements on their bank's websites as well as to comply with other rules revealing security transactions. The new rules would apply to an array of personnel with access to sensitive information (Board of Governors of the

Federal Reserve 2022). With the Fed's credibility at stake, the rules laid out were impressively rigorous. Congress, which had the same problem of trading on insider information, lagged behind in imposing such standards on its own members. Similar laws do not exist to restrain corporate executives and board members of banks and other financial institutions.

Those making investments in an array of complex financial products depend on the ratings they are offered by presumably reputable sources. However, the auditors who are meant to reassure investors that financial disclosures can be trusted, and to alert them of misleading disclosures, are paid by the same corporations they audit. The presumption is that low ratings and any identification of questionable practices would lead to their being fired. Consequently, highly risky assets receive high ratings. In this way, the major auditing firms fail the investors and others interested in the safety of their financial products. After the firm Arthur Andersen ended its role as auditor of public companies in 2002 following its conviction of obstruction of justice for shredding and doctoring documents related to Enron audits, only four accounting firm giants remained.

After the remaining Big Four auditors (which together control two-thirds of the entire auditing business) had been fined following the Arthur Andersen collapse for various practices seen as violating the laws on the books, with new leadership in 2022 regulators undertook "a sweeping investigation of conflicts of interest at the nation's largest accounting firms, asking whether consulting and other nonaudit services they sell undermine their ability to conduct independent reviews of public companies' financials" (Michaels 2022). The SEC's scrutinized financial-market gatekeepers (accountants, bankers, and lawyers) calling attention to their duties under federal investor-protection laws. They could not risk another failure of the remaining auditing firms. As a result, flaws may have been dealt with quietly and not been made public. The firms, seeking consulting business may have ignored some improprieties in their auditing roles.

Occasionally because a prominent individual is involved, a smaller firm commands headlines, as when the accounting firm Mazars fired the Trump Organization as a client after suddenly deciding that a decade's worth of statements regarding the financial situation of ex-President Donald Trump "should no longer be relied upon," this as the New York attorney general's office revealed in a court filing that the Trump organization and three of the ex-president's adult children running the business may have committed fraud. Mazars, which for years had prepared Trump's income tax returns, informed the Trump Organization of this as investigators closed in on likely Trump illegalities – with which Mazars evidently preferred not to be associated. The office of Attorney General Letitia James, investigating how the Trump Organization valued certain real estate assets in its applications for loans, insurance policies, and tax-related issues, asked a state judge to order the Trump Organization, Donald Trump Jr., Ivanka Trump, and others to comply with subpoenas seeking documents and testimony.

While campaigning for the presidency, Donald Trump had bragged about how few taxes he paid. He did not mention that he had also declared corporate bankruptcy six times – which had reduced the number of banks willing to do business with him. By the spring of 2022 he was no longer borrowing from a major bank but only from Axos Financial, an obscure, internet-only institution based in San Diego and Las Vegas (Morgenson 2022). Bankers tend to shun the flamboyant posturing of borrowers bragging about how smart they are in avoiding taxation and regulations and choose not to do business with such clients who stick them with bad loans. This does not mean that the same bankers do not service money laundering for more discreet customers. The extent of such practices justifies the existence of the *Journal of Money Laundering Control*, which for over a quarter of a century has chronicled the tax avoidance efforts of governments, corporations, and wealthy individuals.

The power accorded to the leaders not only of banks but of other corporations leads to additional kinds of abuse. Admati (2017) suggests that "the history of corporate governance includes a parade of scandals and crises that have caused significant harm." After each, most key individuals minimize their own culpability. Common claims from executives, boards of directors, auditors, rating agencies, politicians, and regulators include: "we just didn't know, we couldn't have predicted," and "it was just a few bad apples." She goes on to criticize economists who may react to corporate scandals and crises with their own version of "we just didn't know" – but it is their models rule out such possibilities.

Biden administration officials, committed to pursuing white-collar crime, made probes "easier to start, faster to finish, and more punishing." The Department of Justice increased pressure on big banks to look for market abuses and to inform on staff and clients. There was also a growing willingness among prosecutors to employ federal laws against Wall Street transgressors that had been used to target gangsters. The SEC sought larger civil penalties; its senior leaders "have stopped accepting ad nauseam meetings with defense attorneys looking to talk their clients out of trouble" (Schoenberg, Robinson, and Natarajan 2022). This might make many feel that some justice has been done with regard to lawbreaking by those in finance who have evaded responsibility for their crimes. It may even encourage greater caution on their part in taking unconscionable risks with other people's money. There are also numerous ways to appropriate surplus from government and to use privileged, non-public information to engage in insider trading. It seems members of Congress do this with some regularity (Leonhardt 2022; also see Karadas, Schlosky, and Hall 2021). The body has not found it reasonable to end such practices.

The Limits of Financialization

Regarding financialization as an accumulation strategy, Wolfgang Streeck (2017) suggests that it has undergone three stages over the last half century, each of which offset stagnation for a decade or more before the contradictions it produced grew to dangerous proportions. The first is inflation in the 1970s, which gave the illusion to working people of being better off – until they became wise to money illusion (the reality that their higher money wages did not mean a higher standard of living, since price increases were robbing their dollars of purchasing power). The second involved the use of increased public debt to pay for growth that had reached its limits, with governments then having to abandon the expansion of the public sector, instead adopting austerity measures. The third was private debt, borrowing to finance spending and maintain or increase living standards. This strategy reached its limits when the debt burdens became too great. Growth from privatized Keynesianism was thought to be a good thing; such lending by financial institutions was after all a market phenomenon, albeit one allowed and encouraged by government policy. But debt both feeds speculation and produces asset bubbles – internet company stock prices at the turn of the century, mortgages in 2008, and corporate loans and related derivative products in 2020 – that lead to other consequences.

The data support Streeck. The rate of growth over those years resulted from a substitution of debt for labor income. The neoliberal era experienced three long expansions (1982–1990, 1990–2000, and 2001–2007). In each, output per hour rose more rapidly than the real earnings of non-supervisory production workers; profits increased relative to wages; and labor's share of national income fell, with income inequality increasing substantially, reaching levels not seen since before the Great Depression. Between 1973 and 2007 real wages decreased by more than four percent, in contrast to the period 1947 to 1973 of an increase in real wages of seventy-five percent. Household debt rose as a percentage of disposable income from "59 percent in 1982 to 129 percent in 2007" (Kotz 2009).

The exhaustion of such stratagems – inflation, public debt, and private debt with each temporarily reviving the system before producing a serious legitimation crisis – led to increased support for anti-establishment leaders. As Streeck (2017: 173) asserts,

> "[w]hat I feel sure about is that the clock is ticking for democracy as we have come to know it." He raises what "must remain an open question . . . whether the clock is also ticking for capitalism." Neoliberalism, austerity, privatization, and growing inequality undermined the legitimacy that capitalism requires to sustain its credibility. This in turn raises the alternative of a capitalism without democracy – "or at least the capitalism we know."

Consider the extent of support for Donald Trump in a Republican Party in which more than one in three of its partisans contends that violence may be necessary to "save" America. A February 2021 survey by the American Enterprise Institute found that thirty-nine percent of Republicans thought that "if elected leaders will not protect America, the people must do it themselves, even if it requires violent actions" (Cox 2021). Other members of what has been described as the Authoritarian International that has developed in formally democratic countries include the Hungary of Victor Orbán, the Poland of Jarosław Kaczyński, the Turkey of Tayyip Erdoğan, the Philippines of Rodrigo Duterte, and the India of Narendra Damodardas Modi. In Western Europe, in Italy, Spain, and France, candidates of the far right have done very well in recent elections, as they did in the Nordic, nations, Sweden, Finland, and Denmark, where immigration was the most visible target of voters who have grown to feel increasingly insecure. It is left to political scientists and others rather than to economists to consider the relation between macroeconomic policy and these socio-political developments. But it is unthinkable not to recognize the existence of such a connection.

The New Conjuncture: From Les Trente Glorieuses to the Present

There is nothing new about asset bubbles and their collapse. During the tulip mania of the Dutch Golden Age, the price of a fashionable tulip bulb reached extraordinary heights before dramatically tumbling in February 1637, bankrupting many a speculator and impacting the entire economy. London's South Sea Bubble of 1720 ruined thousands of investors. But as capitalism has developed, matters have become more complicated. In terms familiar today, Marx explained that in

> a system of production where the entire interconnection of the reproduction process rests on credit, a crisis must inevitably break out if credit is suddenly withdrawn and only cash payment is accepted, in the form of a violent scramble for the means of payment.
>
> *(Capital, Volume III: Part V, chapter 30, 1894)*

The lack of perfect information can lead to overlending and thence to major bankruptcies, as in the case of the ill-favored mid-19th-century Overend, Gurney & Co., a firm that drew Marx's attention and is immortalized in Volume III of *Capital* in his discussion of the credit system (in chapter 33).

In his time the Bank of England was prevented from making the promiscuous loans now the normal practice of central banks, by the Bank Act of 1844, which "compels it to contract its note circulation at the very moment when the whole world cries out for notes when owners of commodities cannot sell, yet are called upon to pay and are prepared for any sacrifice, if only they can secure bank-notes." The basics were clear in Marx's presentation. As he explains,

> [the] quantity of circulating medium reaches its apex in the period of over-tension and over-speculation – the crisis precipitously breaks out and overnight bank-notes which yesterday were still so plentiful disappear from the market and with them the discounters of bills, lenders of money on securities, and buyers of commodities. The Bank of England is called upon for help – but even its powers are soon exhausted.
>
> *(Capital, Volume III, Part V, chapter 33, 1894)*

We shall return to the implications of Marx's understanding of financial risk in the face of uncertainty, or as he termed it, of a lack of information, in Chapters 6 and 7;

there, the weakness of mainstream macroeconomic policy and monetary policy in the face of the inflation to which central banks were called upon to respond are discussed. As noted earlier, banks rely less on simply lending the money of their depositors than on borrowing themselves by issuing commercial paper to raise funds to lend, leveraging their capital to maximize earnings through increased risk. If they were only to put at risk the capital of their owners, perhaps receiving a one percent return, that would hardly be a performance of which to be proud. But if they borrow an equal amount to put at risk, they increase the return on equity to two percent. If they borrow to increase leverage to four, they quadruple their money when successful; the lower the cost of borrowing, the higher the net profit (when all goes well). With a leverage ratio of twenty, the earnings can be quite impressive. On the other hand, a bad choice can lead to bankruptcy. Just prior to the financial collapse in 2018, leverage ratios were approaching thirty in major financial institutions. However, as the financier expected to be bailed out, the risk surely seemed worth taking.

Under the conditions of too-big-to-fail, finance incentives involving risk-taking continue to favor increasing leverage. As Haldane argues, "If banks know they will be bailed out, those holding their debt will be less likely to price the risk of failure for themselves. Debtor discipline will therefore be weakest among those institutions where society would wish it to be strongest." This, he points out, "encourages them to grow larger still: the leverage cycle isn't merely repeated, but amplified. The doom loop grows larger." He sees the most powerful banks as benefitting from a disguised – and growing – state subsidy. By his estimate, U.K. banks receive a subsidy that amounts to tens of billions of pounds per year that has "often stretched to hundreds of billions" (Haldane 2012). Banks will hardly relinquish such tacit subsidies, which allow them to accrue outsized returns. Without them, their stock price might crash and their CEO compensation significantly diminish.

The Great Recession seemed to signal the end of the redistributive growth model based on financialization – or at least it presented the need to do so. As markets collapsed in 2020, *Financial Times* columnist Gilliam Tett (2020) observed that during "this decade, America's equity market has been like a drug addict. Until 2008, investors were hooked on monetary heroin (i.e., a private sector credit bubble)." When that bubble burst, they turned to "the financial equivalent of morphine" (the trillions of dollars of central bank support). However, to address this "historic equity market crash, they must contemplate a scary question: has this monetary morphine ceased to work?" This is a question that comes up repeatedly as the danger of the recovery itself becomes evident with the incidence of the addiction metaphor multiplied in the financial press.

After the Global Financial Crisis, Peter Boon and Simon Johnson (2010: 274) similarly feared that monetary policy was incapable of solving the deeper impasse of a financialization regime of accumulation, contending that "the most worrisome part is that we are nearing the end of our fiscal and monetary ability to bail out the system. We are steadily becoming vulnerable to disaster on an epic scale." Theirs was a pertinent warning. Another financial crisis will occur at some point, they predict, and "if current patterns hold, not in the distant future. It would be far more provident to reduce debt-to-GDP levels, that is to reduce the extent of fictitious capital that continues to threaten 'disaster on an epic scale'." The cost of this not being done would soon be evident yet again.

Drawing on heterodox models, Barry Cynamon and Stephen Fazzari (2015) argue that the slowdown in the 21st-century growth rate especially since 2007, is a demand-side phenomenon. Their work suggests that if the growth of spending slows significantly, "supply is dragged down as well, reducing potential output" The implication is that demand-side secular stagnation explains slow growth. These models point to the need to turn the neoclassical synthesis "on its head" – and to understand that reduced demand creates less supply. Rising inequality diminishes the propensity to consume for the economy as a whole. The rich have a lower marginal propensity to consume out of income. Not only does this increase speculative investment and feed asset bubbles, but it decreases demand for mass-market goods and non-financial services. And yet, the Federal Reserve allowed banks to take on more risk. This continued to produce overextension and collapse.

The Bailouts Continue Without Reregulation

The bailout of the depositors who had no legal claim to the Federal Deposit Insurance Corporation paying them more than the $250,000 limit per account in 2023 and were made whole by the FDIC raised a debate over whether the collapse of the relatively small institution in question was a threat to the financial system and so requiring such a step. Indeed, the bank had been in the forefront of arguing for greater deregulation on the grounds that banks like theirs weren't actually 'big' and, therefore. didn't need strong oversight.

Three days before Silicon Valley Bank's failure on March 10, 2023, after months of hard work, big bank lobbyists and executives had celebrated convincing important Republican lawmakers to publicly warn Federal Reserve Chair Jerome Powell against tightening regulations on the industry; the political impact of Signature Bank, the second-largest bank failure since 2008 was seen as "the equivalent of a lake of water being dumped on the fire that seemed lit under some Republicans to pressure the Fed," Brookings Institution senior fellow Aaron Klein, a former Treasury Department official and Capitol Hill economist declared.

In the last few months before these failures, Fed Vice Chair for Supervision Michael Barr, appointed by President Biden had initiated a "holistic review" of existing capital rules suggesting lenders should be subject to higher requirements. It was this that mobilized the Bank Policy Institute, the Financial Services Forum and the Securities Industry and Financial Markets Association to mount their seemingly campaign arguing that increasing capital requirements would harm the economy. "SVB's stunningly quick collapse should put an end to the nonstop attempts by banks, lobbyists and their political allies to weaken capital and other financial regulations that protect depositors, consumers, investors and financial stability," said Dennis Kelleher, president and CEO of the nonprofit watchdog Better Markets (Warmbrodt 2023).

Supervisors at the Federal Reserve Bank of San Francisco, which oversaw Silicon Valley Bank, issued six citations before the bank's self-destruction. Those warnings, officially "matters requiring attention" and "matters requiring immediate attention," recognized that the firm was doing a bad job of ensuring that SVB would have enough cash on hand in the event of trouble. But the supervisors did not force the bank to change its high-risk ways. It did not act to prevent the collapse. It has been pointed out that he bank's chief executive, Greg Becker, sat on the Federal Reserve Bank of San Francisco's board of directors until weeks before the collapse.

Amid fears the government was prepared to let SVB and its uninsured depositors go, venture capitalists launched a concerted lobbying effort. They argued that it not making them whole would not only have big economic repercussions, but would have geopolitical ramifications. The tech industry that would experience severe losses if the bank was not bailed out, cried that innovation would be undercut, the economy would suffer from the innovations that would not happen if they were not made whole. Their theme was: "this is not a bank," as one person involved in the lobbying campaign declared. "This is the innovation economy. This is the US versus China. You can't kill these innovative companies." This from an industry that decried regulation when it came to limiting its own dangerous risk taking. The tech companies that had banked with SVB because it lent money to risky startups to which no other bank would lend had taken risks that had come back to haunt them. It, and many other banks held a large part of their assets in fixed interest government bonds the value of which fell as interest rates rose. These had been left unhedged.

Less attention than should have been the case was paid to two other banks that collapsed that week. Signature Bank, shut down by regulators, was one of the top commercial real-estate lenders in the U.S., especially in New York, where it had a 12% market share. The half empty office towers of many downtown business districts devalued the asset portfolios of such banks and made them vulnerable to potential collapse. Silvergate, another bank that made loans to cryptocurrency companies announced it would cease operations and liquidate its assets. That regulators allowed such banks, specialized on a narrow economic and highly risky segment to do business at all was not considered a problem by the F.D.I.C. Such banks were exempted from the regulations applying to the large systemically important banks.

In the aftermath of the 2008 financial crisis, Congress passed to protect consumers and ensure that big banks could never again take down the economy and destroy millions of lives. Wall Street chief executives and their armies of lawyers and lobbyists hated this law. They spent millions trying to defeat it, and, when they lost, spent millions more trying to weaken it. Greg Becker, the chief executive of Silicon Valley Bank, was one of the many high-powered executives who lobbied Congress to weaken the Dodd-Frank Act.

Given the impressive sums the financial sector threw at legislators and the pressure of their warnings that tighter regulation would slow economic growth by limiting the banks' capacity to make loans, a bipartisan group agreed and in 2018 President Donald Trump signed a law passed by a Republican-controlled Congress in 2018, cheered on by a chorus of financial institution executives – and Federal Reserve Chair Jerome H. Powell – to ease critical parts of Dodd-Frank. Elizabeth Warren (2023) describes the change as having "made a bad situation worse, letting financial institutions load up on risk." The repeal of the regulations governing these banks was a bipartisan affair. Seventeen Democrats voted for the bill, and without Democratic support, it would not have prevented a filibuster and would not have reached Trump's desk. The political calculation seemed obvious enough. Democrats in tough re-election races would do these banks a favor, the banks would give them a lot of campaign cash.

After SVB's failure was widely attributed to regulatory failure and the bank's irresponsible risk taking, Republican hopefuls offered a very different understanding of why the bank had failed. It invoked what was an all-purpose theme of their 2024 presidential primary contest – the problem had been wokeness (Breuninger 2023). Ron DeSantis, suggested that diversity, equity and inclusion initiatives were to blame for the bank's failure: "This bank, they're so concerned with DEI and politics and all kinds of stuff, I think that really diverted from them focusing on their core mission," DeSantis said in a Fox interview. Representative **Marjorie Taylor Greene** offered a similar but more drastic assessment of the "woke" policies that supposedly triggered the bank's downfall and Donald Trump, Jr. tweeted along similar lines (Ecarma 2023).

The steps taken to make depositors whole were criticized on more substantial grounds by among others Kenneth Griffin, the founder of hedge fund Citadel. He said that the rescue package for Silicon Valley Bank showed American capitalism "breaking down before our eyes." He told the *Financial Times* that the U.S. government should not have intervened to protect all SVB depositors. "There's been a loss of financial discipline with the government bailing out depositors in full," Griffin said. "Losses to depositors would have been immaterial, and it would have driven home the point that risk management is essential," he said (Agnew, Fletcher, and Jenkins 2023). He and other critics of the rescue package pointed to the risk of moral hazard that comes from making all depositors whole on the money they have with SVB. Banks would continue to take risks. Large depositors would not worry about the solvency of the banks and more such events would transpire requiring other bailouts. On the one hand, Mr. Griffin was right, on the other the perceived alternative, another deep financial crisis was a worse choice the government had concluded. The fear was that depositors in other regional banks and cause bank failures that could set off a financial collapse more broadly.

At the end of 2022, the U.S. banking industry was sitting on a total of about $620 billion in unrealized losses as a result of the rise of interest rates according to FDIC Chairman Martin Gruenberg (2023). Studies by academic economists put the figure much higher. They estimated that the U.S. banking system's market value of assets is two trillion dollars lower than suggested by their book value of assets accounting for loan portfolios held to maturity. Even if only half of uninsured depositors decide to withdraw, almost 190 banks were at a risk of impairment to insured depositors, with potentially $300 billion of insured deposits at risk. If uninsured deposit withdrawals "cause even small fire sales," substantially more banks are at risk. Overall, these calculations suggest that recent declines in bank asset values very significantly increased the fragility of the US banking system to uninsured depositor runs (Jiang, Matvos, Gregor, Piskorski, and Seru 2023).

Steve Keen (2010: 39) insists that in the finance regime exists to create debt, to encourage as many participants in the economy to take it on. If they were funding productive investments with this money "there wouldn't be a crisis in the first place – and debt levels would be much lower, compared to GDP, than they are today." But this hardly serves the interests of those whose business model is one of high leverage (which from a societal standpoint involves dangerous risk-taking). "Instead they have enticed us into debt to speculate on rising asset prices, and the only way they can expand debt again is to re-ignite bubbles in the share and property markets once more," he argued. This was especially the case in a Covid economy in which the pandemic had interrupted supply.

That Covid is implicated in the most recent instance of major economic crisis obscures the relevance of this assessment but makes it no less accurate. Discussion of the impacts of the inflation unleashed by the consequences of the Covid pandemic is postponed until Chapter 7. But the changed macroeconomic context resulting from inflation should not distract attention either from the longer-term developments, the strains produced by neoliberalism, or from the conditions in which neoliberalism and financialization rose to prominence.

Late 20th- and early 21st-century economic crises were not the result of over-production, as in the phase of capitalism in which manufacturing was dominant, but rather of speculative excess and the collapse of asset bubbles. As this chapter has detailed, the cost of financial bailouts is considerable. In the core countries and to a significant extent in the nations on the periphery of the world system, the current stage of financial capital is characterized by disinvestment from the production of goods, replaced by asset speculation. What is also clear is the lack of healthy system reproduction, along with the emergence for the first time since the Great Depression of secular stagnation.

Secular Stagnation

Larry Summers argues that the "core of the problem is that there is not enough private investment to absorb, at normal interest rates, all the private saving." In this context he introduced the concept of "secular stagnation" to a wide audience. Summers explains that the term "refers to the idea that the normal, self-restorative properties of the economy might not be sufficient to allow sustained full employment along with financial stability without extraordinary expansionary policies" (Klein 2014). He regards secular stagnation as a long-term problem that extends beyond short-term business cycles, the result of "extremely low interest rates, weak demand, and low growth and inflation, along with the bidding up of the price of existing capital assets" (Summers 2019).

Summers' version of secular stagnation offers an understanding of the difficulties faced by monetary policy in trying to attain the natural interest rate (the rate at which savings and investment are equal at full employment). His explanation is that it is the zero lower-bound constraint which makes it difficult for central banks to bring the interest rate to a level low enough (i.e., negative) to ensure full employment. The efforts and consequences of using QE (the central bank buying bonds to make liquidity available to financial institutions and investors) suggest the limits to his thinking since, as discussed, it does not lead to greater borrowing for productive investment (Di Bucchianico 2021). The argument here is that it is the overaccumulation of capital and the anarchy of production – concepts foreign to mainstream thinking – that constitute the problem.

While Summers brought secular stagnation back into the purview of economic debate, historians of economic thought have returned not only to Keynes but to the arguments regarding secular stagnation as articulated by Marxists (Kalecki 1968[1935]; Stendl 1952). In the contemporary literature there are demand-side and supply-side versions of secular stagnation (Summers 2015; Gordon 2015; Eichengreen 2015). Others focus on the hypothesis of "financial cycle drag," which suggests the inability to restrain financial booms that, once they turn to bust, cause huge, long-lasting economic damage: deep and protracted recessions, weak and drawn-out recoveries, and persistently slower productivity growth (Borio 2017). Other economists have deployed secular stagnation theory to explain the functional income distribution in the industrial sector of the economy as determined by markup pricing of firms in incompletely competitive markets (Hein and van Treeck 2010). There are many variants of the secular stagnation thesis. Here the emphasis is on the extent to which the social surplus has gone to asset speculation and the financial crises its collapsing booms have produced. The policy implication is that financialization is a poor accumulation regime, especially in combination with neoliberal globalization.

Possible outlets for the surplus that in a longer-term perspective could offset secular stagnation have been explored by Paul Baran and Paul Sweezy. The lesson they draw is quite different from that of Summers. They provide the system critique that "monopoly capitalism is a self-contradictory system" (Magdoff 1967). In the 1980s, Harry Magdoff and Sweezy found the growth of financialization to be the result of economic stagnation – with financial over-leveraging producing unsustainable household, business, and public indebtedness accompanied by instability and crisis (Magdoff and Sweezy 1987).

In this *Monthly Review* usage, "secular stagnation" is defined as the tendency toward long-term sluggishness in the private accumulation process of the capitalist economy, manifested in rising unemployment, excess capacity, and a slowdown of growth. A key part of this definition is that it is a "tendency," one that is a phenomenon not merely of business cycles but potentially present at all times. Secular stagnation theorists understand that factors limiting growth can prevail over countertrends, that the potential of the economy is often not being reached, and that the composition of growth can be wasteful, even harmful, in major respects.

Monopoly capital can appropriate rents which cannot be profitably reinvested in productive activities. This surplus is absorbed in advertising, product obsolescence, war and preparation for war, financial speculation, or more constructively, in the "epoch-making innovations" that offer growth opportunities – major breakthroughs such as the railroad and the automobile. Such developments involve the creation of new industries and different spatial fixes requiring large investments in the built environment that offset the tendency to stagnation. In the *Monthly Review* understanding, the normal state of capitalism is one of overaccumulation (Sweezy and Baran 1966).

Capital generally receives more of the social surplus than it can profitably invest, hence its tendency to wasteful uses if such breakthroughs are not in the offing. Well before most observers, Sweezy found a rising rate of exploitation along with a significant expansion of finance in monopoly capitalism in the mid-1970s in contrast to the earlier, competitive stage of the system (1994). Finance has substantially replaced manufacturing as the leading sector where profits accrue; it thus represents a new accumulation regime (Krippner 2005). Most theorists discussing secular stagnation call for major government interventions to promote stable growth, as will be proposed in the concluding chapter.

The consequences of such developments (beyond their generating more frequent and costly economic crises) include the extraction of surplus linked to financialization (the topic of Chapter 5). Such practices are also the cause of an increased inequality of income, wealth, and political power that will be explored in the next chapter.

References

Admati, Anat R. 2017. "A Skeptical View of Financialized Corporate Governance." *Journal of Economic Perspectives*, 3(13).

Agnew, Harriet, Laurence Fletcher, and Patrick Jenkins. 2023. "US Capitalism is 'Breaking Down Before Our Eyes', Says Ken Griffin." *Financial Times*, March 13.

Aspan, Maria. 2010. "Ex-Citi CEO Defends 'Dancing' Quote to U.S. Panel." Reuters, April 8. Autor, David, David Cho, Leland D. Crane, Mita Goldar, Byron Lutz, Joshua K. Montes, William B. Perman, David D. Ratner, Daniel Villar Vallenas, and Ahu Yildirmaz. 2020. "The $800 Billion Paycheck Protection Program: Where Did the Money Go and Why Did It Get There?" *National Bureau of Economic Research Working Paper 29669*.

Beneish, Messod D., David B. Farber, Matthew Glendening, and Kenneth W. Shaw. 2022. "Aggregate Financial Misreporting and the Predictability of U.S. Recessions and GDP Growth." *The Accounting Review*. https://doi.org/10.2308/TAR-2021-0160.

Bharara, Preet and Robert J. Jackson, Jr. 2018. "Insider Trading Laws Haven't Kept Up with the Crooks." *New York Times*, October 9.

Blackburne, Terrence, John D. Kepler, Phillip J. Quinn, and Daniel J. Taylor. 2020. "Undisclosed SEC Investigations." *Management Science*, 67(6).

Board of Governors of the Federal Reserve. 2022. "FOMC Formally Adopts Comprehensive New Rules for Investment and Trading Activity." *Press Release*, February 18. https://www.federalreserve.gov/newsevents/pressreleases/monetary20220218a.htm.

Boon, Peter and Simon Johnson. 2010. "Will the Politics of Global Moral Hazard Sink Us Again?" In Adair Turner, Andrew Haldane, Paul Woolsey, Sushil Wadhwani, Charles Goodhart, Andrew Smithers, Andrew Large, John Kay, Martin Wolf, Peter Boone, Simon Johnson and Richard Layard, eds. *The Future of Finance; The LSE Report*. London Publishing Partnership.

Borio, Claudio. 2017. "Secular Stagnation or Financial Cycle Drag?" *Keynote Speech to the 33rd Economic Policy Conference*, Washington, DC, March 5–7, Bank for International Settlements.

Breuninger, Kevin. 2023. "GOP Presidential Contenders Cast Blame for Silicon Valley Bank Collapse." *cnbc.com*, March 13.

Colander, David, Michael Goldberg, Armin Haas, Katarina Juselius, Alan Kirman, Thomas Lux, and Brigitte Sloth. 2009. "The Financial Crisis and the Systemic Failure of Academic Economics." *Critical Review*, 21.

Cox, Daniel A. 2021. "After the Ballots are Counted: Conspiracies, Political Violence, and American Exceptionalism." *Survey Center on American Life, American Enterprise Institute*, February 11.

Cynamon, Barry Z. and Steven M. Fazzari. 2015. "Rising Inequality and Stagnation in the US Economy." *European Journal of Economics and Economic Policies: Intervention*, 12(2).

Di Bucchianico, Stefano. 2021. "The Impact of Financialization on the Rate of Profit." *Review of Political Economy*, 33(2).

Dudley, Willliam C. 2017. "Lessons from the Financial Crisis." *Remarks at The Economic Club of New York*, November 6. https://www.newyorkfed.org/newsevents/speeches/2010/dud100208.html.

Ecarma, Caleb. 2023. "Republicans are Blaming Silicon Valley Bank's Collapse on the 'Woke' Left." *Vanity Fair*, March 13.

Eichengreen, Barry. 2015. "Secular Stagnation: The Long View." *American Economic Review*, 105(12).

Elliot, Larry. 2010. "Forced Bank Break-up Makes Sense, Says Financial Stability Chief." *Guardian*, March 30.

Epstein, Gerald A. and Juan Antonio Montecino. 2016. "Overcharged: The High Cost of High Finance." *Roosevelt Institute*. https://rooseveltinstitute.org/publications/overcharged-the-high-cost-of-high-finance/

Fox News. 2020. "Judge James Boasberg of the U.S. District Court in Washington to Force the SBA to Release the Data." December 2.

Gordon, Robert J. 2015. "Secular Stagnation: A Supply-Side View." *American Economic Review*, 105(5).

Gruenberg, Martin. 2023. "Remarks by FDIC Chairman Martin Gruenberg at the Institute of International Bankers." *Federal Deposit Insurance Corporation*, March 6. https://www.fdic.gov/news/speeches/2023/spmar0623.html.

Haldane, Andrew G. 2010. "The $100 Billion Question." *Comments by Mr Andrew G Haldane, Executive Director, Financial Stability, Bank of England at the Institute of Regulation & Risk, Hong Kong*, March 30.

Haldane, Andrew G. 2012. "The Doom Loop." *London Review of Books*, February 23.

Hein, Eckhard and Till van Treeck. 2010. "'Financialisation' in Post-Keynesian Models of Distribution and Growth: A Systematic Review." In Mark Setterfield, ed. *Handbook of Alternative Theories of Economic Growth*. Elgar.

Jacobs, Lawrence and Desmond King. 2021. *Fed Power: How Finance Wins*. Oxford University Press, Second Edition, Chapter 16.

Jeffers, Ester. 2010. "The Lender of Last Resort Concept: From Bagehot to the Crisis of 2007." *Revue de la Régulation*, Autumn.

Jiang, Erica Xuewei, Gregor Matvos, Tomasz Piskorski, and Amit Seru. 2023. "Monetary Tightening and U.S. Bank Fragility in 2023: Mark-to-Market Losses and Uninsured Depositor Runs?" March 13, 2023. https://www.nber.org/papers/w31048.

Kalecki, Michael. 1968[1935]. *Theory of Economic Dynamics*. Monthly Review Press.

Karadas, Serkan, Minh Tam Tammy Schlosky, and Joshua Hall. 2021. Did Politicians Use Non-Public Macroeconomic Information in Their Stock Trades? Evidence from the STOCK Act of 2012." *Journal of Risk and Financial Management*, 14(6).

Kay, John. 2015. Other People's Money: The Real Business of Finance. *PublicAffairs*.

Keen, Steve. 2010. "Deleveraging is America's Future." *Real-world Economics Review*, 54.

Klein, Ezra. 2014. "Larry Summers on Why the Economy is Broken – And How to Fix It." *Washington Post*, January 14.

Kotz, David M. 2009. "The Financial and Economic Crisis of 2008: A Systemic Crisis of Neoliberal Capitalism." *Review of Radical Political Economics*, 41(3).

Krippner, Greta R. 2005. "The Financialization of the American Economy." *Socio-Economic Review*, 3(2).

Lazonick, William. 2017. "The New Normal is 'Maximizing Shareholder Value': Predatory Value Extraction, Slowing Productivity, and the Vanishing Middle Class." *International Journal of Political Economy*, 46(4).

Lazonick, William and Ken Jacobson. 2018. "End Stock Buybacks, Save the Economy." *New York Times*, August 23.

Marx, Karl. 1894. *Capital*. Frederick Engels.

Lemann, Nicholas. 2020. "Institution Man: How Corporations Came to Dominate the US Economy." *ProMarket*, November 22.

Leonhardt, David. 2022. "Personal Profit in Congress; Some Members of Congress have Strangely Good Timing when it Comes to Stock Investments." *New York Times*, January 24.

Magdoff, Harry. 1967. "Reviewed Work: Monopoly Capital by Paul A. Baran, Paul M. Sweezy." *Economic Development and Cultural Change*, 16(1).

Magdoff, Harry and Paul M. Sweezy. 1987. *Stagnation and the Financial Explosion*. Monthly Review Press.

Miao, Hannah. 2021. "Fed Presidents Kaplan, Rosengren to Sell Individual Stock Holdings to Address Ethics Concerns." *CNBC*, September 9.

Michaels, Dave. 2022. "Big Four Accounting Firms Come Under Regulator's Scrutiny." *Wall Street Journal*, March 15.

Mishel, Lawrence and Jessica Schieder. 2018. "CEO Compensation Surged in 2017." *Economic Policy Institute*, August 16. https://www.epi.org/publication/reining-in-ceo-compensation-and-curbing-the-rise-of-inequality/.

Mnuchin, Steven T. 2020. "Statement of Secretary Steven T. Mnuchin, Department of the Treasury Before the Committee on Small Business and Entrepreneurship." *United States Senate*, June 10.

Morgenson, Gretchen. 2022. "The Trump Organization Used to Borrow from Major Banks. Now Look Who's Lending It Money. *Yahoo! News*, April 7.

Pomorski, Chris. 2015. "Former Citigroup CEO: Golden Parachute from Park Avenue Co-op." *Observer*, April 20.

Rapoza, Kenneth. 2017. "Bank for International Settlements Warns of Looming Debt Bubble," *Forbes*, February 10.

Reinhart, Carmen M. and Leora Klapper. 2022. "Private-Debt Risks Are Hiding in Plain Sight." *Project Syndicate*, May 2. https://www.project-syndicate.org/commentary/pandemic-debt-moratorium-and-ukraine-war-boost-debt-distress-by-carmen-m-reinhart-and-leora-klapper-2022-05

Ripley, William Z. 2018[1927]. *Main Street and Wall Street*. Forgotten Books.

Romm, Tony. 2022. "'Immense Fraud' Creates Immense Task for Washington as It Tries to Tighten Scrutiny of $6 Trillion in Emergency Coronavirus Spending." *New York Times*, February 17.

Schoenberg, Tom, Matt Robinson, and Sridhar Natarajan. 2022. "Wall Street isn't Ready for the Crackdown Coming Its Way," *Bloomberg*, May 4.

Sender, Henny. 2012. "Risky Assets Are Hooked on Monetary Morphine." *Financial Times*, March 30.

Shiller, Robert J. 2021. "Stock, Bond and Real Estate Prices are all Uncomfortably High." *New York Times*, October 1.

Smialek, Jeanna. 2022. "Fed Official Didn't Reveal Full Extent of Trading." *New York Times*, January 7.

Smith, Yves. 2017. " Quelle Surprise! Financial Firm Fines are Way Down Under Trump." *Naked Capitalism*, August 7.

Stendl, Josef. 1952. *Maturity and Stagnation in American Capitalism*. Monthly Review Press.

Strauss, Daniel. 2019. "Bank of America: 10 Main Themes Will Define the Next Decade. Here Are the Winners and Losers for Each." *Market Insider*, December 4.

Streeck, Wolfgang. 2017. *Buying Time: The Delayed Crisis of Democratic Capitalism*. Verso, Second Edition.

Summers, Lawrence H. 2015. "Demand Side Secular Stagnation." *American Economic Review*, 105(5).

Summers, Lawrence H. 2019. "The Risk to Our Economy from Secular Stagnation." *Washington Post*, March 7.

Sweezy, Paul M. 1994. "The Triumph of Financial Capital." *Monthly Review*, June 1.

Sweezy, Paul and Paul Baran. 1966. *Monopoly Capital: An Essay on the American Economic and Social Order*. Monthly Review Press.

Syrmopoulos, Jay. 2015. "Iceland Just Jailed Dozens of Corrupt Bankers for 74 Years, the Opposite of What America Does." *The Free Thought Project*, October 21.

Taleb, Nassim Nicholas. 2007. *The Black Swan: The Impact of the Highly Improbable*. Random House.

Tett, Gillian. 2020. "Markets Contemplate a Future in which Stimulus Does Not Work." *Financial Times*. March 13.

Vaughan, Liam. 2021. "Most Americans Today Believe the Stock Market Is Rigged, and They're Right." *Bloomberg Businessweek*, October 4.

Veblen, Thorstein. 1997[1923]). *Absentee Ownership: Business Enterprise in Recent Times – The Case of America*. Routledge.

Warmbrodt, Zachary. 2023. "Banks Fought to Fend Off Tougher Regulation. Then the Meltdown Came," *Politico*, March 12.

Warren, Elizabeth. 2023. "Silicon Valley Bank is Gone. We Know Who is Responsible." *New York Times*, March 13.

Wray, L. Randall. 2011. "$29,000,000,000,000: A Detailed Look at the Fed's Bailout of the Financial System." *Levy Institute of Bard College*. https://www.levyinstitute.org/publications/9000000000000-a-detailed-look-at-the-feds-bailout-of-the-financial- system.

Zumbrun, Josh. 2023. "Accounting-Fraud Indicator Signals Coming Economic Trouble; A Tool to Identify Corporate Earnings Manipulation Finds the Most Risk in Over 40 Years." *Wall Street Journal*, March 24.

4

INEQUALITY AND FINANCIALIZATION

Historically, inequality has not preoccupied academic economists, or at least not those in the dominant neoclassical tradition. The focus has instead been on efficiency to increase the size of the pie maximizing the use of available resources rather than delving into how it is divided (Berman 2022). Robert Lucas (2004) famously offered the rationale behind this position: "The potential for improving the lives of poor people by finding different ways of distributing current production is *nothing* [italics in the original] compared to the apparently limitless potential of increasing production." (Such a view, once standard in the profession, still prevails, especially among economists who lean to the right). This conservative position on fairness and inequality has been expressed by Michael Tanner (2018), a senior fellow at the Cato Institute. As he argues, "We have become obsessed with economic equality at the expense of economic growth. Inequality is said to be the transcendent issue of our time. Yet a society that is rich and unequal still beats one that is poor and equal any day of the week." The unstated assumption is that inequality promotes productive capital formation rather than harmful asset speculation and that a more equal distribution of income slows growth. In the economy that exists in the extended present, this is not true.

To many economists, macroeconomic theorists especially, inequality is beyond their remit. But as James Galbraith maintains,

> We do not study inequality because it is shocking. We study inequality mainly because it is informative. We study it because it enables us to understand the economic world in which we live, in ways that were not accessible to us before. One of the most important of those ways is precisely the neglected linkage between inequality and instability, between finance and society, and between economic and social differences and the risk of financial crisis.
>
> *(2012)*

DOI: 10.4324/9781003385240-4

It is these aspects of inequality that are central to any serious consideration of the impacts of financialization and the misleading claims that have gone along with it as finance has become a profit center based on the distribution rather than the production of surplus.

> The investor class has encouraged the view that inequality is necessary for the accumulation of capital, both to create jobs and to promote growth. But this argument is contradicted by considerable contemporary evidence. The models still taught to economists in training assume that the savings of the wealthy are used to fund investment, which is essential and responsible for economic growth. Such an assumption was valid during earlier stages of capitalism but not today, however, when the surplus is directed largely to the purchase of financial assets. Indeed, the current accumulation model fails to lift all boats; rather it distributes wealth upward, slows growth, and generates pessimism
>
> *(Kohler, Guschanski, and Stockhammer 2019)*

Long-standing thinking that privileges growth as an uncontested goal has been doubly discredited. First, on economic grounds: the conclusion that greater inequality promotes faster growth has been shown to be simply incorrect. Second, a great majority of citizens believe that as a matter of justice, the rich should be taxed more and the wages of working people should increase. This conviction is consistent with the conclusion that slow growth is caused by a rise in inequality due to the stagnation/decline of purchasing power by working-class Americans and so can be replaced by investment in different jobs that are ecologically sustainable and are components of a care economy.

It was long the conventional wisdom that there is a trade-off between efficiency and equality. The consensus of liberals as well as conservatives was prominently propounded by Arthur Okun, a senior advisor to President John Kennedy (1975). The evidence now demonstrates that such a trade-off is incorrect. The harm done by rising inequality refutes this "common sense," although it is still argued by conservative economists. The thesis of much contemporary empirical analysis, in contrast, asserts that inequality today is slowing growth and increasing the likelihood and duration of socioeconomic crises. The available surplus could contribute substantially to the improvement of the living conditions of those who suffer from a lack of decent work and basic necessities – except that the structures that create and perpetuate extreme inequality not only prevent such distributional measures but impede growth. However, increasingly within the economics profession it has been accepted that inequality has harmful impacts on economic prospects (van Treeck 2020).

"Net wealth became overvalued, and high asset prices gave the false impression that high levels of debt were sustainable. The crisis revealed itself when the bubbles exploded," Jean-Paul Fitoussi and Francesco Saraceno (2011) explain. They emphasize that although the crisis may have emerged in the financial sector, its roots are much deeper, lying in a structural change in income distribution that have continued for a quarter century. Thomas Piketty suggests that one consequence of increasing inequality has been

> [the] virtual stagnation of the purchasing power of the lower and middle classes in the United States, which inevitably made it more likely that modest households would take on debt, especially since unscrupulous banks and financial institutions, freed from regulation and eager to earn good yields on the enormous savings injected into the system by the well-to-do, offered credit on increasingly generous terms.
>
> *(2014: 273)*

While others were blaming the Great Recession on greedy bankers, Branko Milanovic (2009) pointed out that the origin of the crisis may rather be found in the marked increase of inequality over the prior thirty years in practically all countries in the world, and in the U.S. in particular. Noting that in America the top one percent of the population doubled its share in national income from around eight percent in the mid-1970s to almost sixteen percent in the early 2000s, he suggests that the phenomenon "eerily replicated the situation that existed just prior to the crash of 1929, when the top 1 percent share reached its previous high watermark of American income inequality over the last hundred years." While the people of that period whose relative income had fallen could buy less, the rich with their limited demand funneled their wealth into financial speculation that brought about the collapse of 1929. There is reason to fear a repeat.

The neoliberal era experienced three long expansions (1982–1990, 1991–2000, and 2001–2007). In each, output per hour rose significantly more rapidly than the real earnings of nonsupervisory production workers; profits rose rapidly relative to wages; and labor's share of national income fell as income inequality substantially increased, reaching levels not seen since before the Great Depression. The politics of wage austerity, a shrinking government, deregulation, and regressive tax cuts that have characterized the policy mix of the period since 1980 created conditions such that the economic collapse of 2008 triggered the most unequal recession in modern U.S. history.

To place the blame on Donald Trump, as many liberals have done, is hardly sufficient or, from a longer-term perspective, accurate. During Bill Clinton's administration in the 1990s, the wealthiest one percent garnered forty-five percent of the increase in disposable national income. The pattern accelerated in the 2000s under George W. Bush when the one percent received seventy-three percent of the increase. The top one percent captured ninety-five percent of the income gains in the first three years of the Obama recovery. As Obama left office, the top one percent owned more private net wealth than the bottom ninety percent of Americans (Saez 2013). Because data on inequality soon become dated, readers may wish to consult the University of California, Berkeley website that updates information on income, wealth, and labor inequality (www.realtimeinequality.org/).

The Obama administration bestowed the task of helping those with underwater mortgages to the very banks and companies primarily responsible for originating the mortgages; they packaged them into derivatives and sold them to investors who then took on what turned out to be substantial risk, well beyond what was projected by the rating agencies paid by the banks – which thus profited both from the housing bubble and from its collapse (Dayen 2015). Rather than offering the help promised to suffering families, the banks profited yet again. It would not be unexpected to hear a "Thank you, Obama" from those cynically regarding his liberalism.

As Yves Smith (2010) has written, Obama in effect repudiated his campaign promise of change, turning his back on any meaningful reform of the financial services industry. Instead, he worked

> fist in glove with the banksters, supporting and amplifying their own, well established, propaganda efforts. Thus Obama's incentives are to come up with "solutions" that paper over problems, avoid meaningful conflict with the industry, minimize complaints, and restore the old practice of using leverage and investment gains to cover up stagnation in worker incomes.
>
> *(2010)*

She saw "Potemkin reforms dovetail with the financial service industry's goal of forestalling any measures that would interfere with its looting."

Obama and the Democrats were responsible for millions losing their homes, then denying they had done any damage, claiming rather that they had helped people – when it was obvious that the only ones helped were beneficiaries in the financial sector. Barack Obama, Matt Stoller (2022) tells us, "clothed with authority granted by the public in the election of 2008, used that authority to destroy the lives of tens of millions of people with policy decisions around housing and financial power." Enamored then and now with Obama, Democrats have never grasped his responsibility and that of the Democratic Congress for causing so many to lose their homes to the banks. Major investors bought up the devalued inventory to rent to former owners unable to purchase homes again.

As to the banks themselves, their pay structure encouraged excessive risk-taking. The top executives at Lehman Brothers and Bear Stearns, the two investment banks that failed spectacularly (as noted earlier), were rewarded for behavior that led to the demise of their firms; using SEC data, Lucian Bebchuk and Holger Spamann (2009) found that the senior executives of the failed banks profited handsomely. Over the 2000–2007 period, the top five executives at Bear received cash bonuses in excess of $300 million and at Lehman of over $150 million. These numbers do not include what they received from the sale of company shares, which they sold before the downfall of the banks. Unloading their banks' stock netted the ten executives an additional two billion dollars. By 2008, when the collapses occurred, they had sold more shares than they retained.

When the profit picture darkens, executives moving quickly to dispose of company stock holdings that might be considered a leading indicator of their company's financial difficulties. U.S. corporate insiders sold a record sixty-nine billion dollars in shares before 2021 was over – and almost fifty of these "bigwigs," as the *Financial Times* termed them, "pocketed more than $200m each." This was a thirty percent increase over the year before and seventy-nine percent more than the prior ten-year average. Brooke Masters (2021) argues that insider selling "is also a red flag at a time when soaring indices mask the fact that more than 1,380 companies are trading at or near 12-month lows." Unscrupulous executives can introduce plans to buy and then secretly cancel when they have reason to expect disappointing earnings. Corporate insiders who reap the rewards of a bull market "should no longer be allowed to slip out the backdoor before bad news hits. While the selling top executives claimed this was a result of automatic plans, this looked very much like insider trading."

A study of 10b5–1 trading plans (presumably passive so that the executives are not actively managing them and so are not trading on inside information – in theory at least) by 10,123 executives at more than 2,000 companies revealed that rather than involving long-term strategies, half the "plans" relied on just one trade. Even more dubious, almost forty percent of those executives started selling within sixty days, including fourteen percent who cashed out in the first month. Such short-term trades were not only much larger than those of plans that waited longer but also, on average, they avoided losses of two and a half percent because the executives sold shares before or as the share price of the company declined. "The plans that tend to be most opportunistic and abusive are those that go into effect on Friday and sell on Monday," reported the study's co-author Daniel Taylor, head of the Wharton Forensic Analytics Lab, which carried out the research (Blackburne, Kepler, Quinn, and Taylor 2020).

Apparently believing that if it weren't for buybacks companies would invest in job creation (regardless of market conditions), liberal Democrats spearheaded passage of a one percent tax on buybacks. It is unlikely that such a tax will change corporate behavior, as optimistic liberals have argued, by "nudging" greater investment, something opponents of the tax professed to fear. Analysis of data from S&P Capital IQ revealed that during the prior decade, companies in the S&P 500 stock index had repurchased over five trillion dollars of their own shares. Before the end of 2021, those companies announced more than one trillion dollars in share buybacks, according to Goldman Sachs. The investment bank argued that the impact of a one percent tax on buybacks would be "marginal."

While there are those who disagree, little evidence exists that buybacks crimp investment. Research by Charles Wang demonstrates that corporate investment has remained roughly constant as a percentage of company sales in recent years. For this reason the failure of companies to make greater investments is not an issue. They had the capacity to do so even with all the buybacks. "After all, in 2019, public firms held about $5.2 trillion in cash," he notes (Eavis 2021). This suggests an important conclusion: that the problem for U.S. capitalism is the upward distribution of wealth to corporate America and to the one percent who have gained most from this development. Substantial new real investment (as opposed to financial investment) is limited by the extent of demand in the market.

Between 2014 and 2018, the twenty-five wealthiest Americans collectively earned $401 billion but paid just $13.6 billion in taxes, according to a ProPublica investigation. The researchers calculate that each of the top eleven averaged over one billion dollars in income annually from 2013 to 2018. (They point out that the typical American would have to work for 25,000 years to make 1 billion dollars.) About a fifth of the top 400 earners were managers of hedge funds, making them the largest group identified. Executives and founders of private equity firms were also conspicuous in the findings, commonly reporting a high percentage of income from long-term capital gains, which lowered their tax rate. They also benefitted from the carried-interest loophole that allowed them to treat fees from managing their clients' money as investment income. Critics argue that these fees should be taxed as ordinary income. While running for office politicians have also spoken out against this loophole. When running for the presidency, Donald Trump said he would end it; in office he did not take steps to do so, nor have other politicians who received large contributions from the industry's leading beneficiaries. Researchers commented that generally in the American system a marked difference exists between how wages and investments are taxed. Income from financial assets is generally taxed at a lower rate, indeed, at almost half the rate (twenty percent to an average of thirty-seven percent for ordinary high income). The advantage of receiving capital gains is thus evident since the extra income goes primarily to buying financial assets rather than investing in increased production that creates jobs (Kiel, Ngu, Eisenger, and Ernsthausen 2022).

The discrepancy between the billionaires and the group Occupy Wall Street termed the ninety-nine percent suggests the need for a wealth tax – a complicated proposition to effectively codify, as economists have explained (Scheuer and Slemrod 2021). Yet the justification seems clear. During the first year and a half of Covid, from the start of 2020 to the middle of 2021, while the bottom half of Americans gained $700 billion in wealth, the wealth of the richest one percent grew by ten trillion dollars (Petrou 2021b). The total wealth of American households is about one hundred trillion dollars or more than three quarters of a million dollars for every American household if divided equally. In actuality, half of all American households have zero or negative wealth. This disproportion has provided the rationale for Biden's effort to raise taxes on corporations and wealthy individuals and to eliminate as much tax avoidance as possible.

Having obtained a vast trove of Internal Revenue Service data covering more than fifteen years on the tax returns of thousands of the nation's wealthiest citizens, ProPublica was able to compare the taxes that the twenty-five richest Americans paid each year with how much *Forbes* estimated their wealth grew during that same time period. ProPublica researchers then designated their true tax rate. According to *Forbes*, those twenty-five Americans saw their joint worth rise by $401 billion from 2014 to 2018.

Over those five years they paid a total of 13.6 billion dollars in federal income taxes, according to the IRS data. "That's a staggering sum, but it amounts to a true tax rate of only 3.4%." The researchers were able to gain an inside look at the financial lives of the likes of Tesla founder Elon Musk, at this writing the wealthiest person in the world, who paid no federal income taxes in 2018. When Jeff Bezos was the richest, he matched this zero-payment rate (Eisinger, Ernsthausen, and Kiel 2021).

With the recession that began in 2020, the Bloomberg Billionaires Index recorded its largest annual gain in the history of the list to date, a thirty-one percent increase in the wealth of the richest people for the year. Nine of the top ten richest people live in the U.S.; taken together, their assets are valued at more than 1.5 trillion dollars. This list of the world's richest people changes with events in the global economy. For example, the "giant leap" in global food prices caused by Russia's invasion of Ukraine enhanced the wealth of three Cargill family siblings, great-grandchildren of William Wallace Cargill, who founded the Cargill Company in 1865. They joined the Bloomberg Billionaires list of the world's 500 richest people. A contrast to their colossal wealth is offered by Eric Muñoz, Oxfam America's senior policy adviser for agriculture, who asserts, "Right now we're seeing food prices skyrocket, which is taking a devastating toll on the most vulnerable communities. Exorbitant food prices, alongside the Covid-19 pandemic, are pushing families in countries like Ethiopia, Somalia, Kenya and South Sudan to the breaking point." Stressing this impact, he continues, "Meanwhile, the richest have seen their profits soar. We must see urgent action to save lives now and to address the inequality, broken food system and other root causes that are driving this crisis" (Neate 2022).

There is also the need for a reminder with regard to the Federal Reserve. In addition to the market forces that government has allowed to play out, the Fed is responsible for increasing inequality and "the destructive social-welfare, macroeconomic, and systemic implications of persistent downward mobility," as Karen Petrou argues. She demonstrates that "even extra-stimulative fiscal policy will do little to reduce near-term economic inequality given the force of countervailing Fed de facto fiscal intervention" (Petrou 2021a). Any thought that a separation exists between the government and the presumed independent central bank on the one hand and market causes of inequality on the other requires close inspection. The middle class has been shrinking while the proportion of Americans classified as low-wage workers has increased; to observers, the role of the Fed in producing this disparity is clear (Petrou 2021b).

The point is frequently reiterated that the Fed makes "mistakes" and needs to learn from them. For example, Neil Barofsky, watchdog for the flawed 2008 Troubled Asset Relief Program, offered an explanation of how things went wrong in 2020: "Clearly, the government has failed to learn from its mistakes during the 2008–09 financial crisis. Back then, it also funneled money through the banks, encouraging them to use bailout funds to increase lending to smaller companies that had been frozen out of the banking system, and to provide relief to homeowners struggling under the weight of the foreclosure crisis."

These were the recommendations made after the fact, with the Great Recession fresh in people's minds. Such lessons were ignored and soon forgotten. As Barofsky writes:

> Rather than follow the recommendations from oversight bodies to attach some strings to require or incentivize the banks to carry out its intended goals, the Treasury simply trusted that the banks, on their own initiative, would do so. Without any incentives or formal rules, the banks instead used the funds to further their own goals, not those of the Treasury.
>
> *(2020)*

He maintained that although lessons were discussed repeatedly in the aftermath of the financial crisis, including in his own agency's oversight reports. The Treasury and the Small Business Administration took no heed of them when setting the rules for the 2020 relief program and in 2023 basically ended risk for depositors of whatever amount they held in banks. He pointed out that "the incentives they did include only drove the banks to prioritize their most profitable and established customers over the little guys. The bigger the Paycheck Protection Plan loan, the bigger the fee." In the "rescue of homeowners in the earlier rescue their had been such perverse incentives. The regulators increased the incentive for bankers to continue to take high risks knowing their depositors were unlikely to panic since the Fed would protect them.

One suspects that Barofsky was not surprised either by what happened in 2020 or in the next rescue and inadequate efforts at regulation. Indeed, he has shown a sophisticated understanding of the self-interested culture of the financial community and of the many who move from the private sector to become regulators and then return to Wall Street (Sirota 2021). He understands regulatory capture, even as he has fought against it. Not acting on lessons supposedly learned is not a mistake; it is how the system functions. To say that "for the good of the system we must be fairer to the majority" ignores the capacity of the system to deceive ordinary people while retaining, if not their enthusiastic loyalty, their acquiescence. It is difficult for most people to think beyond the order that exists. It is even more difficult for non-specialists to comprehend how financialization has distorted the economy. Nor, although they have felt the impacts, do ordinary people grasp how extreme American inequality has become. There is a shared belief that the system is unfair – that the few at the top take advantage of them. However, Americans are deeply divided over what solutions should follow.

(De)Regulation: The State's Enabling Role and Revolving Doors

In 2005 Raghuram Rajan, Director of the IMF's Research Department, spoke in Jackson Hole, Wyoming, to the annual symposium of the Federal Reserve Bank of Kansas City, a gathering of notables in the world of finance theory and policy making. He explained that while bank managers were often rewarded when they took on large risks and won their gambles, in fact their herd behavior threatened the financial system. In response, Larry Summers pronounced Rajan a "luddite." It was the sort of dismissal for which Summers was famous when his own views were challenged. Rajan pointed out that financial institutions "have too little ability to penalize a manager who follows the herd into disaster. After all, it is easy for the manager to get a job in another fund, blaming the collective crash for his poor performance" (Hirsh 2013). Rajan's explanation proved prescient regarding the way the new financial order would further increase economic hazards.

Even earlier, at an April 21, 1998 meeting of the President's Working Group on Financial Markets, Brooksley Born, "the little-known chairwoman of a little-known agency" (the Commodities Futures Trading Commission) expressed concern about the growth of credit default swaps; she urged the regulation of these financial products. Alan Greenspan, the libertarian head of the Federal Reserve System at the time and an Ayn Rand acolyte in his youth; Robert Rubin, Secretary of the Treasury and former Goldman Sachs co-chairman; and his deputy Larry Summers, whose personal wealth came primarily from serving hedge funds, all warned that financial markets would not welcome, and indeed would respond badly, to such a proposal. Born suggested that her agency conduct a study of the way this marketplace had evolved.

Even to do this was sacrilege. Rubin and Greenspan "were passionate about the key lesson they had learned from the Street and brought to Washington: finance must be allowed to flow, markets to operate unencumbered, and regulation kept at bay. Finance was the engine of innovation, America's greatest strength." Earlier, after an angry dressing down from Summers, Born told a colleague: "That was Larry Summers. He was shouting at me" (Hirsh 2010). Summers channeled the views of Wall Street's finest. They had been alarmed that even a hint of regulation would send derivative trading overseas, costing America business.

Summers told Born that he had trade association reps in his office complaining that it was doing enormous damage to their business for her even to ask these questions; he wanted to let her know she should just stop doing it. Born responded: "I was astonished a position would be taken that you shouldn't even ask questions about a market that was many, many trillions of dollars in notional value – and that none of us knew anything about" (Hirsh 2010). It was the unspoken assumption in those years that what was good for Wall Street was good for the U.S. economy and vice versa.

The day she made the recommendation for a study of the issues involved, her male colleagues disseminated a statement expressing "grave concerns" about the Commodity Futures Trading Commission intervention. Congress quickly passed a law that banned regulation of swap contracts that President Clinton signed. Born resigned (Bair 2012). In 2014, when the Clinton Library released handwritten notes of the 1998 meeting, the headline in *Bloomberg Businessweek* read: "Top Clinton Aides Blew a Chance to Avert the Financial Crisis" (Coy and Brush 2014).

"The committee to save the world" had laid the groundwork for further serious crises as they released Wall Street from supervision and made its priorities those
of the U.S. government. Brooksley Born had been correct regarding the need to
regulate the dangerous products Wall Street was creating that could intensify future
financial crises. The faux saviors personified regulatory capture, the half century-old
theory introduced by George Stigler (1971). Stigler had proposed that the form that
regulation takes is instituted by government in response to the demands of well-
organized interest groups acting to maximize their own well-being at the expense of
diffuse public interests. When in the current period there are calls for the regulation
of Big Tech, it is sensible to predict that such action would only add to cost and not
decrease consumer dissatisfaction. Regulatory capture, including the details of the
restrictions Congress is likely to mandate, would turn out to favor the companies
to be regulated (Dudley 2021). In Europe matters are different, in significant part
perhaps because the firms in question are American.

Writing after the meltdown, John Kay offers the observation that

> a remarkable feature of the global financial crisis is that most people in finance
> seemed to regard it as self-evident that government and taxpayers had an obli-
> gation to ensure that the sector – its institutions, its activities and even the ex-
> ceptional renumeration of the people who work in it – continued to operate in
> broadly its existing form. What is more remarkable still is that this proposition
> won broad acceptance among politicians and the public.
>
> *(2015: 4)*

The same might again be said after the 2020 financial crisis and again in the 2023
difficulties.

The climate emergency aside, there is the reality that financialization is producing profit without prosperity for the majority. Lacking the regulation that Born and
others saw (and see) as necessary, companies continue to borrow large amounts to
purchase their own stock; remember that from 2007 to 2016, ninety-three percent
of all the profits of the Fortune 500 went to buybacks and dividends. Yet the dominant economic growth policy until the Biden administration involved tax cuts to
stimulate job creation without imposing sufficient government guidance on which
investments should be subsidized and what conditions should be imposed in exchange. Nonetheless, the Biden embrace of industrial policy was a major turning
point that can be advanced if and when a progressive Congress is seated.

The actual impacts of government tax initiatives and subsidies must be scrutinized. For example, the 2017 tax cut, which brought hundreds of billions of dollars
held by American corporations back to the U.S., was supposed to provide significant
job creation. Little of it did. Instead, the largesse went overwhelmingly to companies
buying their own stock (Coy 2019). Such transactions benefitted the CEOs and the
ten percent of Americans who own eighty-four percent of all household-held stock
(Wartzman and Lazonick 2018). Among proposals for essential change, Edward

Kane (2016) focuses on the financial incentives that, difficult to alter, need to be subjected to serious regulation. Others point to the possibility and even the necessity of replacing the incentives of those companies. Among such economists, Lazonick and Jang-Sup Shin (2020) recommend rechanneling capital to innovative enterprise, offering suggestions for the strategic controls required to combat predatory value extraction and promote sustainable prosperity. Instead, when the Biden administration acted to support R&D, it did so through increased tax incentives, requiring compromises that were undesirable but politically necessary. Public pressure and electoral outcomes will influence whether industrial policy will be equitable for taxpayers, who fund investments and must have major inputs into how these are made.

Three levels of analysis may be suggested regarding the enabling function of the state with regard to financialization. The first concerns the role of the appointed policy makers who oversee financial regulation. They almost invariably have come from, and return to, leading positions in major financial corporations. Or they are politically ambitious officials heavily dependent on special interests, most singularly Wall Street, for campaign funding. As discussed, the Biden administration broke with this long-standing pattern by choosing critics of financial system abuse. A second level of analysis suggests that in the contemporary conjuncture, finance has become misleadingly understood to be the leading growth sector and thus the force most committed to economic expansion. Here too the Biden team was able to pass legislation that increased spending on social needs as well as environmental protection and needed infrastructure, suggesting what more could be done with a large liberal Congressional majority. On the third level, allocation of society's economic surplus need not be carried out primarily by financiers and private investors; rather, in an economic democracy, it can be subject to the preferences of citizens. This, as will be suggested, is the social democratic next step that the left-center and the left in American politics ought to pursue. Unfortunately, the campaign priorities of the Democrats avoided this and other pro-working-class policies (Sanders 2022).

The past choices of the Democratic establishment have proven costly. At the level of the revolving door, it is not simply that Robert Rubin came from Goldman Sachs and that after leaving government service he moved on to Citigroup, where he became chairman of its executive committee and of the board of directors. It must also be noted that while he was Bill Clinton's Secretary of the Treasury, the federal government injected forty-five billion dollars of taxpayer money into Citigroup and guaranteed 300 billion dollars of its illiquid assets. Taxpayers temporarily received a twenty-seven percent stake in the bank, although it can be argued that given its financial shape at the time, they paid enough to have owned the company outright. After the bank became healthy as a consequence of government actions, it was quietly privatized again. Policy making by such revolving-door public servants takes place in the circumstance of decision-making that is notably friendly to banks.

Before Rubin became Clinton's secretary of the Treasury, Henry Paulson, who had been Chairman and CEO of Goldman Sachs, was secretary of the Treasury under George W. Bush. Jack Lew, Mr. Obama's selection for that position, was the chief operating officer of Citigroup's Alternative Investments unit, a proprietary trading group that under his leadership had invested in a hedge fund which bet on the housing market to collapse (Mahanta 2012). The impact of the revolving door is also lucrative for the lawyers who leave a firm where they work for tax-minimizing clients for brief stints in government at relatively low pay and where they can exert a major influence on tax policy often helping their former and future clients. These lawyers and accountants typically return to their firms with promotions and significantly higher pay (Drucker 2021). Many of the lawyers that Biden's administration has called upon to serve are law school professors rather than members of practices representing the industries to be regulated, as has been the traditional pattern. They are intent on serving the public interest and not the tax evaders and avoiders that the more common appointees have favored.

The general practice of such appointees is confirmed in a study that found at least thirty-five examples from the four administrations preceding Biden's of lawyers from the largest accounting firms who went to work at the Treasury department's tax policy office and then returned to their firm. Many of those lawyers "granted tax breaks to their former firm's clients, softened efforts to clamp down on tax shelters and approved loopholes used by their former firm. In nearly half the examples, the officials were promoted to partner upon rejoining their old firm." This pattern was found in both Republican and Democratic administrations – in the Treasury department during the Obama administration as well as those of the Trump, George W. Bush, and Clinton administrations. After carrying out their own inquiry, Senator Elizabeth Warren and Representative Pramila Jayapal called for the inspector general to investigate the revolving door, offering some pointed questions to be asked (Drucker 2022). Capitalist democracy continues to prevail, although it must be said that the Biden administration made impressive efforts to address the heavy thumbs on the scale of economic justice that characterize what is called America's liberal democracy.

The Fed and Inequality

The financial sector showed higher returns in the wake of the economic collapse accompanying the 2020 coronavirus pandemic, just as it had after the financial crash in 2008. The Fed bailed out overextended firms with below-investment grade bonds, buying them to prevent the ruin of their lenders. The holders of these securities would otherwise have spiraled downward, along with the assets that were thrown on the market by those desperate for liquidity to meet their own obligations. One suspects that the market power of the large financial institutions supported by the Fed's protective shield produced the high profits that were revealed as the pandemic raged. Because the cost of punishing those who had taken dangerous risks and lost their bets would have brought down the entire edifice of finance, it was thought that there was really no choice but to extend whatever support was required to save the financial institutions. Their leadership was similarly left in place. The Icelandic alternative was simply unthinkable.

Wall Street's largest banks reported record profits for 2021. They benefited from "blockbuster" investment banking fees, a consequence of global mergers and acquisitions that had reached their highest levels since records had been kept (Franklin 2022). The expectation of increases in interest rates by the Federal Reserve in 2022 fed optimism that banks were positioned for another favorable year. However, there remained a significant downside risk. What was worrying about the financial sector was that it had lent promiscuously on questionable security. Financiers looking for high returns in a low-interest (and negative real interest) environment had bought and held the debt of high-risk borrowers. Many of these came to be seen as so-called zombie firms, companies unable to cover the costs of debt servicing from current earnings and unlikely to return principal. Their numbers rose as interest rates dropped. Investors seeking better returns bought the higher interest-paying debt of those risky companies. When interest rates increased to fight inflation, a debt trap became apparent (Chapter 7).

Banks that had acquired such assets were loath to write off losses, rolling over the debt of the zombies that could not be collected. Two years before coronavirus struck, former chair of the Fed Janet Yellen had expressed her concern about the systemic risk associated with these essentially bad loans. Such a situation also prevailed in Europe; there, however, most companies had held investment-grade credit at the turn of the century, but two decades later most did not. The fear was that if central banks were to stop buying risky bonds and attempted to sell others they already held as part of the campaign to raise interest rates to reduce inflation, the zombies would be in major trouble. IMF economists worried that the damage that could be expected in poor and middle-income countries would be substantial if steps were not taken to confront the coming economic debacle of unpayable debts and banks refusing new loans (Reinhart and Klapper 2022).

Using data on listed firms in fourteen advanced economies, researchers at the BIS found what they termed "a ratcheting-up" in the prevalence of zombies. In the early 1990s, the zombie rate had been just two percent. By 2018, twelve percent of all companies globally had become zombie firms, according to the BIS. Sixteen percent of U.S. companies were then zombies (Edwards 2018). Should creditors press for repayment, the firms whose profits were lower than the interest payments on their debt would clearly go out of business (Banerjee and Hofmann 2018). This was the situation before the pandemic, with creditors continuing to hold their paper even as it became less safe in the downturn, not wanting to acknowledge losses on their balance sheets and expecting to be protected against such losses by action of the Fed. Under the rules of the market, borrowers and many creditors should have failed. Instead, the coronavirus provided cover for the Federal Reserve to do what it would have done in any case had there been a threatened downturn: buy large quantities of bonds, holding their value well above what a market free of such a sizable intervention would have assessed. Should such firms have been allowed to fail, not only would the owners and creditors have suffered but also the workers and their communities.

The problems afflicting the zombies were not that they did not have ready cash to meet their obligations, although they did not, but that they were not solvent. They were the living dead – surviving only on borrowing that could not continue if interest rates rose and they were unable to rollover debt. The largest firms were not immune to reduced internal reserves. Companies in the S&P 500 index of major U.S. corporations spent more than two trillion dollars buying back their own stock in the three years preceding the outbreak of the coronavirus, thus undermining their prospects should the economy turn down. Many did not have the reserves to weather a crisis and turned to the taxpayer for a handout when their business ran into trouble, trouble that was much greater due to the buybacks undertaken to increase the payouts to stockholders and top company officials.

Airlines, for example, had spent ninety-six percent of their free cash during the prior decade to buy back their own stock in order to drive up its price – with no regard for possible future obligations and, as it turned out, a decline in passengers due to Covid. They demanded and received far greater help than they might have needed had they kept the money in reserve, which they had instead spent on stock buybacks. As their business picked up again when people increased travel for business and pleasure, there was no thought of paying taxpayers back.

Members of the public were unaware of such largess, nor, when confronted with the extent of the cost of these buybacks, were they knowledgeable on the issue; as a result, they were not politically activated to confront what the opportunity cost had been for the financialized economy, money that could have been repurposed to the provisioning of public goods. What historians term "finance politics" was a powerful movement in the U.S. from the middle of the 20th century, when Americans struggled to make banking more democratic, as Christopher Shaw (2019) has shown; however, a formerly prominent politics had faltered and almost disappeared. The triumph of finance has left many Americans working in low-waged jobs in which productivity was not increased in a slow-growth economy. But with the Republican Party becoming an authoritarian vehicle, "semi-fascist" as President Biden called the MAGA Republicans, a populism seized the foreground of American politics. One consequence was that the deregulation agenda was substantially supported as part of a broad anti-government agenda.

The deepening of the 2020 crisis, the realities of the deteriorating economic situation led regulators in other advanced economies, including the European Central Bank and the Bank of England, to tell their banks to suspend dividends, buybacks, and discretionary bonuses. Sheila Bair (2020), former head of the Federal Deposit Insurance Corporation, found this sensible: "Every dollar of capital a big bank distributes to shareholders and top executives is a dollar that does not support credit which struggling businesses and households need. Why hasn't the Fed put banks under similar restrictions?" She urged that "To compensate their shareholders, banks could consider paying dividends in shares, which would not compromise their lending capacity. But they should suspend cash dividends and bonuses until this crisis is over. That," she maintained, "would be a good way to prove to a cynical public that

Wall Street is capable of putting the public's interest above its own. Why the Fed does not require them to do so remains a mystery."

The significance of Bair's suggestion was made clear by Neel Kashkari, President of the Federal Reserve Bank of Minneapolis and overseer of the Troubled Asset Relief Program. Well before the Great Recession, he wrote that "the most patriotic thing" large banks could do "would be to stop paying dividends and raise equity capital" to ensure that they could withstand a deep economic downturn without needing additional Fed support. Unlike ordinary Americans, banks have the ability to protect themselves against such a crisis: "They should do so now" (Kashkari 2020). But they had not complied, as he and other government officials had urged them to do, when financial strains emerged in 2007, nor when he continued to urge such action. They did not comply in 2020 either.

Banks prefer not to follow such advice. It reduces their profits, their stock price, and their compensation to top executives. Regulators who come from and return to the industry can weaken standards by lowering capital requirements and easing stress tests, allowing for greater dividend payments and more stock buybacks. They will bear responsibility for the consequences when the next financial crisis comes. For decades such pro-financial institution rule changes were presented as regulatory "corrections," with "tailoring," "tweaking," and other circumlocutions used to suggest that they involved only the most marginal changes that would, however, improve the efficiency of finance. Steps desired by banks already earning historically large profits worried a number of experts, including past Fed governors, who spoke publicly against such practices (Smialek, Eavis, and Flitter 2019).

Fed chair Jerome Powell saw no reason to impose conditions on the banks that would reduce their profitability and ability to increase the compensation of their top executives. The Fed loosened post-crisis regulations established to ensure that banks had sufficiently large financial cushions to continue lending. Offering cheap funding programs, it relaxed borrowing caps and encouraged banks to dip into their capital. It stood ready to do whatever it could in the hope that this strategy would prompt banks to lend more. Banks would of course do what they judged to be in their own interest. As part of a policy of deregulation stretching over decades, the Treasury and the Fed made it easier for them to employ such self-interested tactics.

Long-time observers noted that the Fed went even further in subsidizing the financial sector in 2020 than it had during the 2008–2009 financial crisis, using tools "more creative, in fact, than any Fed leaders since the birth of the central bank in 1913" (Coy 2020). Their "creativity" included establishing at least eleven special lending facilities with a combined capacity to spend more than 2.3 trillion dollars. This is more than ten percent of the 2019 U.S. GDP. It made free money available to virtually any business, large or small, responsible or irresponsible – including the zombies. Interest rates were already in the range of zero to one quarter of one percent, lending the trillions of dollars available on any quality of collateral, making loans directly to companies, and continuing bond buying under QE. These steps exposed the Fed to potentially large losses as it attempted to return growth to the financial markets.

The policy, authorized by Section 13(3) of the Federal Reserve Act, grants the board of governors of the Federal Reserve the power in "unusual and exigent circumstances" to make loans to "any individual, partnership or corporation" through a program or facility with broad-based eligibility. Total funding, backed by the Treasury and so the taxpayer, was quantitatively far greater than any other rescue, and like previous programs under similar conditions, it favored Wall Street over basic protections for Main Street (Jarsulic and Gelzinis 2020).

Jim Cramer (2020), host of CNBC's "Mad Money," which provides stock picks and interviews with finance industry insiders, offered the remarkable statement (given the source) that the coronavirus pandemic had produced "one of the greatest wealth transfers in history." He surmised that "The bigger the business, the more it moves the major averages, and that matters because this is the first recession where big business . . . is coming through virtually unscathed." He continued, "I think we're looking at a V-shaped recovery in the stock market, and that has almost nothing to do with a V-shaped recovery in the economy." There might be plentiful jobs; however, despite rising wages, inflation robbed workers of purchasing power.

Wages, Financialization, and Market Concentration

Between 1973 and 2007 real wages fell by less than four and a half percent, in contrast to the 1947–1973 years of National Keynesian during which real wages rose by seventy-five percent. Both the number of better-paying jobs and the level of benefits declined during the reign of global neoliberalism, along with decreased union density and greater monopsonistic power in regional labor markets. Concession bargaining and pay freezes had become more frequent even before the Great Recession, which further intensified pressure on workers for concessions. More jobs were converted to short-term contract work and part-time employment. Large numbers of workers were excluded from unemployment benefits. Income and job precariousness increased as a consequence. Using the *Distributive Financial Accounts* along with the *Flow of Funds* financial accounts of the Federal Reserve and the Survey of Consumer Finances, Matt Bruenig finds that between 1989 and 2018, the top one percent increased their total net worth by twenty-one trillion dollars while the bottom fifty percent saw their net worth decline by $900 billion (2019).

Corporate profits, which comprised seven percent of U.S. GDP in 2001 (at the start of the previous cyclical upturn after the dot-com crash), had risen at their peak to a little over twelve percent by the beginning of 2006, when the median income was three percent lower in real terms. Between 2001 and 2005, American families added to their debt at a rate that was sixty percent greater than the growth of the overall economy. Before 2010, the middle class owned more wealth than the top one percent. Since 1995, the share of wealth held by the middle class has steadily declined, while the share at the top has steadily increased. Actually, over the period between 1989 and 2018, the top one percent increased its total net worth by twenty-one trillion dollars, more than the entire U.S. GDP in 2018. As noted, the decline in income going to working people led to indebtedness and borrowing – which could not be sustained. The combination of the inability of many to meet payments on subprime mortgages, which had triggered the Great Recession, and the lack of spending were felt as a crash not only of the financial system but of the possibility of the American Dream. The share of U.S. national income going to wages and salaries reached its lowest recorded level (until then) in 2005–2006 (Bruenig 2019).

In the aftermath of the Covid crisis, labor shortages produced a rise in wages. But in terms of real income the gains were limited to some segments of the labor force and remained slight compared to labor's long-standing losses and the impact of the rising prices of consumer goods. Federal assistance made a large difference, allowing consumer demand to endure and thus promoting growth and a quick recovery, although contributing to inflation. After the gains resulting from government assistance in the worst part of the Covid pandemic, most Americans were once again beaten down by the cost increases in "the three H's" – housing, health care, and higher education, sectors in which costs rose well beyond the rate of the Consumer Price Index.

Even as workers were being squeezed by inflation, unemployment was low and working people had more power in the labor market. In October 2021, when the jobs report from the U.S. Department of Labor elicited stories in the media regarding the trouble employers were having in finding workers, and there was a rising concern about the inflation resulting from increased wages – despite wages lagging the rate at which prices were increasing. Robert Reich (2021) wrote that "[a]cross the country, people are refusing to return to backbreaking or mind-numbing low-wage jobs. . . . You might say workers have declared a national general strike until they get better pay and improved working conditions." The quit rate had risen to a record high since such data had first been collected, with workers leaving poorly remunerated tasks and bad working conditions to look for better opportunities in the new labor market. Reich's analysis of what has been termed "the Great Resignation" is that "[c]orporate America wants to frame this as a 'labor shortage'." This, he argued, was incorrect. What was really going on "is more accurately described as a living-wage shortage, a hazard pay shortage, a childcare shortage, a paid sick leave shortage, and a healthcare shortage. Unless *these* shortages are rectified, many Americans won't return to work anytime soon."

Indeed, after decades of the rising share of national income going to capital along with its dominance over labor as unionization declined, *Bloomberg Businessweek* reported on a pattern of burned-out millennials and Gen Zers quitting their jobs by the millions (Hancock, Dmitrieva, Look, and Takeo 2021). David Dayen (2021) preferred "the Great Escape" as the term for the phenomenon, which he regarded as people simply wanting the dignity and respect they had been denied for so long. He pointed to the daily toll for those enmeshed in dead-end, low-wage jobs and the constant surveillance they endured. This analysis was supported by a Pew survey, which found that while the major reason workers left jobs in 2021 was that "pay was too low," only slightly behind this was that they "felt disrespected at work"

(Parker and Horowitz 2022). Dayen noted that "overfinancialization has added to the pain. More than 11.7 million U.S. workers, most of them low-wage, [are] now working for companies owned by private equity firms." He offered a parallel to the Black Plague of the 14th century with its severe death toll, which had produced a labor shortage and consequently, rising wages, despite the attempts of employers and governments at the time to force people to work under past terms. He pointed to Republican state legislatures "allowing 14-year-olds to work as late as 11 p.m., along with other rollbacks of long-standing protections in the interest of increasing the labor force while holding down labor costs."

With the weakness of trade unions, most quits and group walkouts were instigated by individuals who had just had enough; they were not part of an organized resistance. Many videotaped their actions, which encouraged others. The most famous "quit" video is Shana Blackwell's. Ms. Blackwell earned a little over eleven dollars an hour as a night stocker at a Walmart in Lubbock, Texas. She filmed herself resigning over the store's public address system: "Attention, all Walmart shoppers"; she proceeded to call out managers and colleagues for inappropriate behavior, declaring, "This company fires Black associates for no reason. This company treats their employees like shit . . . . Fuck the managers, fuck the company, fuck this position . . . I fucking quit." Her video received more than 50,000 likes and over 11,000 retweets, along with other "I'm not a robot" Amazon quit videos. Many other individual proclamations have produced similar online camaraderie. In an environment of labor shortage, they have resulted in better wages and working conditions. It remains to be seen what will transpire in this regard when jobs are filled and the shortage ends; in any event, inflation stole the increases the average worker had achieved. Still, many had moved on to better jobs, often with training provided for candidates rather than employers demanding experience. Qualifications formerly required such as a college degree which were actually unnecessary to perform a job were dropped in the need to hire in a labor-shortage economy.

What was shown during this period of labor shortages, a marked exception from the preceding decades of labor surpluses that had added to the power of capital, was that class struggle does exist and workers do understand that they are exploited. They had not spoken publicly about this until the conditions of supply and demand had changed to favor their class. Despite this situation, the employer class held monopsonistic power in many markets, and especially for workers who did not have skills prized in the market, the inflation that had resulted (Chapter 7) reduced their real income. Even after the temporary gains workers had made, looking at the previous decades it was clear that working people had not fared well.

While many workers could for a time improve their exceedingly poor earnings and unpleasant job conditions, nonsupervisory workers received an average wage that when adjusting for inflation in 2022 that was little different from to what workers had earned in 1968, over half a century earlier. The share of the national income that goes to wages had fallen more than seven percent from the fourth quarter of 1968 to March 2022. Over that time worker productivity had increased significantly, gains that were not shared by labor but went overwhelmingly to occupy Wall Street's 1% – or more pointedly to the one percent of the 1%.

By the later date labor shortage illustrated what happens in a period approaching full employment. It is also the reason that when such a state is reached Fed officials worry about inflation and by increasing interest rates slow of the economy to increase unemployment, reducing the bargaining power of labor and inflicting the pain of addressing inflation onto the working class. Given its pro-labor stance, the Biden administration favored tax increases on the wealthy to cool the economy with those revenues deployed to public goals needing financing rather than a reliance on the monetary policy of higher interest rates.

President Biden proposed a new tax on households making more than 100 million dollars a year, a plan termed the "billionaire minimum income tax." It would impose a twenty percent minimum tax on such realized and unrealized income, including financial investment income. "In 2021 alone, America's more than 700 billionaires saw their wealth increase by $1tn, yet in a typical year, billionaires like these would pay just 8% of their total realized and unrealized income in taxes. A firefighter or teacher can pay double that tax rate, the White House declared in a statement that provided details of the plan" (Aratani 2022). The tax increase included in the 2022 Inflation Reduction Act went some way toward the goal of tax fairness to pay for the changes in spending.

Americans were experiencing a strong level of job security in 2020–2022, given the low unemployment rate and shortage of workers. But because this was a function of the tightness of labor markets and not a structural advantage, it was unlikely to last with the Fed's action of slowing the economy to fight inflation. Although the Fed raising interest rates would restrain growth and the workers' advantage would fade, the period demonstrated how labor could benefit in an economy of full employment. In the 1960s, when workers were more likely to be unionized, wage security had been a greater reality for the twenty-eight percent of workers who were members of labor unions, as well as of others whose wages rose with those of unionized employees. Currently, only ten percent of workers are unionized, as well as only six percent in the private sector, so if the Fed's dramatic hikes in interest rates restrain the economy, wage increases will slow and quit rates will fall. While the Biden administration expressed its support for unionization and its appointees to the National Labor Relations Board made a significant difference in that regard, rebuilding the trade union movement has remained an uphill struggle, led by remarkable grassroots, self-initiated organizing. The quit videos offer a contemporary expression of such changes; if full employment were to continue should a center-left Democratic Party win control of Congress, this would have further ramifications for labor strength and the revival of trade unionism that young workers from Starbucks to Amazon warehouses had initiated.

The important point is that the novelty of "the great resignation," the "great escape," or however this period of worker power is termed, illustrates why full employment is troubling to employers. It gives workers a sense that they do not have to remain in jobs that are demeaning and pay too little to live in dignity – that they have a choice. The classic analysis is offered by Michal Kalecki, who wrote of the opposition by the employer class to full employment and to the use of government resources (public investment and subsidizing consumption), which strengthen labor's bargaining power. Capital dislikes the social and political changes that result from sustained full employment (Kalecki 1943: 2–3).

The Accounting and the Legal Systems

The interactions of corporations, governments, and powerful individuals across political and legal systems broadly influence markets and impact economic outcomes. However, most mainstream economists pay little attention to the institutions that shape markets. But Admati (2017) sees the financial sector as "a stark example of the governance issues at the heart of the crisis in capitalism and democracy." She believes that the imperviousness of economists to "frictions" connected to governance, law, and politics may be related to the supposition articulated by Ronald Coase (1937) that private contracting is all that is needed for efficient outcomes. However, this bland assurance ignores the cost of such private contracting – that it is between parties of equal bargaining power and influence in the legal system. Coase's "solution" requires an unrealistic understanding of costly litigation practices and the impediments facing everyday individuals and smaller firms confronting larger, more powerful entities. For these reasons what is called the Coase Theorem provides a weak crutch for economists who do not choose to address asymmetric power in contracting and the extent to which it ignores the wider social interest.

Contracting is complicated. It presumes transparency and an honest sharing of relevant data. Consider that close relations and mutual dependencies between companies and their accountants offer another problematic aspect of the growth of financialization. The opportunity for fraudulent presentation of data is an area of concern. In times of economic crisis, the illusion of accounting exactitude comes to be seen as fraud when such strategies are revealed to be misrepresentations expressly calculated to mislead investors.

The most famous corporate collapse in recent U.S. history involves the bankruptcy of Enron in 2001. It brought down its accounting firm, Arthur Andersen, which had approved the company's fraudulent balance sheet numbers. (Its demise left four remaining accounting firms of any consequence.) This was not Andersen's only such fiasco. There had also been Waste Management, Sunbeam, and even the interesting case of the Baptist Foundation of Arizona. As this is written, it is not clear that investors are any safer putting confidence in the remaining presumed watchdog accounting firms. "You have four international behemoths. They act and operate as though they're too big to fail, and regulators are fearful of going out and doing anything about it," stated Lynn Turner, Chief Accountant of the SEC from 1998 to 2001. In the next downturn, it was feared that the consequence of government timidity would be made all too clear (Farrell 2021). Against strong industry resistance, the Biden administration appointees acted to avoid such outcomes. In doing so the administration was faced with confronting a host of questionable, if not outright corrupt, familiar accounting practices.

Accepting official numbers can be misleading due to commonly employed techniques, which render it difficult to comprehend the true state of affairs that can become more apparent in a downturn after an overly optimistic (and abusive) application of Generally Accepted Accounting Principle – GAAP accounting rules. Most investors pay no attention to the use of mergers and acquisitions as a tool to manipulate earnings and deductions as, for example, taking in-process R&D charges off against taxes (the estimated value of research and development at a purchased firm); pooling good will; the use of pro-forma statements to report large profits (while later reporting huge losses to the SEC); restructuring reserves; channel stuffing (booking profits when goods are sent to a warehouse even if they will not be sold for some time or perhaps forever); vendor financing (lending companies the money to buy a company's products, loans that may not be repaid as happened widely in the telecom meltdown); and using earnings before interest, taxes, depreciation, and amortization (EBITDA) rather than net income as a measure of cash flow (which fails to include cash costs).

By the turn of the 21st century, the backdating of options and the post-dating of sales and related practices, which had come under increasing scrutiny, led to dozens of executives being forced to resign, followed by a widespread restatement of their companies' earnings. By 2006 more than two thousand companies were found likely to have backdated stock options to maximize the incomes of their top executives. Using information from the Thompson Financial Insider Filing database of stock transactions by corporation executives (as reported to the Federal SEC), academic researchers examined nearly forty thousand stock grants over a decade. Based on market probabilities, they estimated that almost thirty percent of the companies had used backdated options to increase executive compensation. Examining returns from fifteen hundred of the largest American corporations between 1992 and 2001, other researchers found that companies dispensing options that were larger than average to their top five executives produced decidedly lower returns to shareholders than did those dispensing smaller option grants. The practice, found to be commonplace, was characterized as "secret compensation" (Anabtawi 2004).

A study by the Boston Consulting Group of companies found guilty of fraud estimated that the value of stock options granted to the CEOs of those firms in the years before the fraud became public was 800 percent greater than the value of those granted to CEOs in comparable firms in which no fraud was found. Nothing, it turns out, correlates as strongly with fraud as stock options. After the downturn in 2007–2008, researchers found that dividends from 2004 through 2006, a seeming indicator of corporate profitability, were covered in a large number of cases with borrowed money, which inflated stock values and artificially increased stock option payouts. From the fourth quarter of 2004 through the third quarter of 2008, the companies of the S&P 500 reported net earnings of 2.4 trillion dollars but paid dividends of $900 billion and repurchased 1.7 trillion dollars in shares – to the benefit of those exercising stock options (Norris 2009). The bonuses were real, the profits a mirage. Again, a restating of profits was required. The incentives were substantial, involving as they did gaming the system in order to increase returns to those receiving stock options.

Both political decisions and the regulatory rules and their enforcement are crucial to how much one should trust Coasian private contracting. Katharina Pistor describes the more arcane processes by which capital is created behind closed doors in the offices of private attorneys and how what is done there is responsible for much of the increased inequality. Demonstrating that the law selectively "codes" certain assets endowing them with the capacity to protect private wealth, she argues that the ability to influence the legal system is one of the most significant causes of the widening wealth gap between the holders of capital and everybody else. As Pistor (2019) elucidates, "if legal coding, rather than the thing itself, is key for capital, then with the right legal coding anything can be coded as capital: not only tangible objects but expectations, ideas, even nature's own genetic code." When people sign noncompete agreements and compulsory arbitration clauses, as well as with the appropriation of their personal data, they are creating capital in the hands of others. She recounts 400 years of property, collateral, and corporate law, the common law trust, bankruptcy and contract law to illustrate how such appropriation has historically been achieved. Important for the purposes of the current discussion is her contention that in this legal creation of debt, complex financial products and other assets are coded to give economic advantage to their holders. There is, of course, a long history of governments creating laws and regulations that protect the financial extraction of wealth from the society by capital (Pistor and Deakin 2017).

In this era of financialization, extraction of surplus takes many forms that depend on whether the political process is quick enough, or even willing, to limit how technologies may be used. Consider that the first financial product patent was issued in 1990 for electronic futures trading. The U.S. Supreme Court validated the patenting of mathematical and business algorithms in the 1998 decision *State Street Bank v. Signature Financial*. For example, State Street, the country's third largest asset manager, patented a system for building an Exchange Traded Fund derivative by bundling other ETFs. By 2014, Bank of America had filed roughly the same number of successful U.S. patents as Novartis and MIT. From 1969 through 2019, Bank of America obtained a total of 2,319 patents; JPMorgan Chase, 814; Goldman Sachs, 244; and Wells Fargo, 226. As in the case of better-known tech and copyright firms, patent litigation is a way for banks to reduce or eliminate competition (Schwartz 2022). The legal system can be utilized by large financial institutions with deep pockets, much as is the case with major corporations in other sectors.

International Financial Weakness

In concluding the discussion in this chapter of how financialization has contributed to increased inequality, attention needs to turn once more to the global picture and the impact of allowing finance to dominate. Policy choices have been made throughout the era of global neoliberalism on the supposition that unrestricted capital mobility increases financial market efficiency. What was not grasped is that reality involves a dense and dangerous network of interpenetrating and overlapping obligations based on the issuance of debt.

By early 2018, global debt had risen to nearly 250 trillion dollars, three times the global income and a substantial increase from the $142 trillion of a decade earlier. It formed part of cross-border transactions in which firms and governments borrowed in stronger foreign currencies. Such debt had to be paid back in the same currencies, over which the borrower had no control. When the U.S. raised interest rates, money that had been lent to poorer economies had to be repaid in dollars, often unexpectedly, and so not easily or without assistance from the World Bank and the International Monetary Fund.

Financial globalization has been presumed to spur development. Instead, it transfers money to the Global North, exacerbating existing inequalities. Perhaps because of such benefits, although most of the intellectual consensus underlying neoliberalism "has collapsed," the idea that emerging markets "should throw their borders open to foreign financial flows is still taken for granted in policymaking circles," as Arvind Subramanian and Dani Rodrik (2019) contend. They offer an analysis of the damage that follows, concluding that until change occurs, the developing world "will suffer from unnecessary volatility, periodic crises, and lost dynamism." They title their essay, "The Puzzling Lure of Financial Globalization." This recurrent trope, "puzzling," is used by economists who recognize the sharp disjuncture between the evidence and continued policy norms endorsed by mainstream economists. Of course, if the puzzle were to be solved by acknowledging that policy makers are guided by the powers of the world and not by the evidence, they would be accused of ideologically motivated work. Indeed, even raising such "puzzles" carries the risk of colleagues intimating that they are giving aid to the radicals (Rodrik 2008).

Cheap, readily available liquidity enables investors to engage in various forms of the carry trade. That is, funds flow into countries where a higher return in local currencies is expected, with profits presumably brought back into the currency from which the funds originated. When fear arises that the return might fall, a sudden exit quickly follows in the movement of such short-term funds. The carry trade gambit can make money for speculators, but the rapid arrival and exit of large sums play havoc with macroeconomic policy in the impacted countries. Such highly liquid funds can, and often do, destabilize economies with painful consequences for local banks and businesses that find themselves with unpayable debt taken out in foreign currency – and also of course for the displaced workers.

The expressed concern of the global state economic governance institutions, the World Bank, the International Monetary Fund, and others with the suffering of the debtors of the Global South has been accompanied by only modest assistance and little recognition that the endorsement of open borders for foreign, short-term speculation has produced a structural problem for these economies in every economic downturn that has afflicted the countries at the center of the world system (Tabb

2004). International capital movements under the regime of global neoliberalism increase inequality within the countries of the Global South, just as financialization has done in the U.S. and other nations of the Global North.

References

Admati, Anat R. 2017. "A Skeptical View of Financialized Corporate Governance." *Journal of Economic Perspectives*, 3(13).

Anabtawi, Iman. 2004. "Secret Compensation." *North Carolina Law Review*, 82(3).

Aratani, Lauren. 2022. "Americans Pay Just 3.4% of Income in Taxes, Investigation Reveals." *Guardian*, April 13.

Bair, Sheila. 2012. *Bull by the Horns: Fighting to Save Main Street from Wall Street and Wall Street from Itself*. Free Press.

Bair, Sheila. 2020. "The Mystery Behind the Fed's Refusal to Suspend Bank Dividends." *Yahoo Finance*, April 14. https://finance.yahoo.com/news/the-mystery-behind-the-feds-refusal-to-suspend-bank-dividends-131547657.html?fr=yhssrp_catchall.

Banerjee, Ryan and Boris Hofmann. 2018. "The Rise of Zombie Firms: Causes and Consequences." *BIS Quarterly Review*, September.

Barofsky, Neil. 2020. "Why the Small-Business Bailout Went to the Big Guys." *Bloomberg*, April 30.

Bebchuk, Lucian and Holger Spamann. 2009. "Regulating Bankers' Pay." *John M. Olin Center for Law, Harvard University Discussion Paper 5-1-2009*. http://www.law.harvard.edu/programs/olin_center/papers/pdf/Bebchuk_641.pdf.

Berman, Elizabeth Popp. 2022. *Thinking Like an Economist: How Efficiency Replaced Equality in U.S. Public Policy*. Princeton University Press.

Blackburne, Terrence, John D. Kepler, Phillip J. Quinn, and Daniel J. Taylor. 2020. "Undisclosed SEC Investigations." *Management Science*, 67(6).

Bruenig, Matt. 2019. "Top 1% Up $21 Trillion. Bottom 50% Down $900 Billion." *People's Policy Project*, June 14. https://www.peoplespolicyproject.org/2019/06/14/top-1-up-21-trillion-bottom-50-down-900-billion/.

Coase, Ronald H. 1937. "The Nature of the Firm." *Economica*, 4(16).

Coy, Peter. 2019. "CEOs Get a Buyback Bonus." *Bloomberg Businessweek*, December 9.

Coy, Peter. 2020. "The Fed Loves Main Street As Much As Wall Street This Time." *Bloomberg Businessweek*, April 20.

Coy, Peter. and Silla Brush. 2014. "Top Clinton Aides Blew a Chance to Avert the Financial Crisis." *Bloomberg BusinessWeek*, May 1.

Cramer, Jim. 2020. "The Pandemic Led to a Great Wealth Transfer." *The CNBC Video*, June 4.

Dayen, David. 2015. "Obama's Foreclosure Relief Program Was Designed to Help Bankers, Not Homeowners." *The American Prospect*, February 14.

Dayen, David. 2021. "The Great Escape." *The American Prospect*, November/December.

Drucker, Jesse. 2021. "A Revolving Door Keeps Tax Policy on Clients' Side." *New York Times*, September 20.

Drucker, Jesse. 2022. "Leaders Want Treasury to Examine Hiring Issues." *New York Times*, February 23.

Dudley, Susan E. 2021. "Let's Not Forget George Stigler's Lessons about Regulatory Capture." *ProMarket*, May 20. https://www.promarket.org/2021/05/20/george-stiglers-lesson-regulatory-capture-rent-seeking/. Coy, Peter. 2019. "CEOs Get a Buyback Bonus." Bloomberg Businessweek, December 9.

Edwards, Jim. 2018. "The 'Zombie' Problem: Low interest rates and 'leveraged loans' sustain a vast number of lousy companies which should have gone to the wall years ago." *Business Insider*, October 29. https://www.businessinsider.in/The-zombie-problem-Low-interest-rates-and-leveraged-loans-sustain-a-vast-market-that-keeps-thousands-of-lousy-companies-afloat-that-should-have-gone-to-the-wall-years-ago/articleshow/66400669.cms.

Eisinger, Jesse, Jeff Ernsthausen and Paul Kiel. 2021. "The Secret IRS Files: Trove of Never-Before-Seen Records Reveal How the Wealthiest Avoid Income Tax." *ProPublica*, June 8.

Farrell, Greg. 2021. "The Next Accounting Fiasco." *Bloomberg Businessweek*, December 6.

Fitoussi, Jean-Paul and Francesco Saraceno. 2011. " Inequality, the Crisis and After." *Rivista di Politica Economica*, 1.

Franklin, Joshua. 2022. "Wall Street Banks Set to Report Record Profits for 2021." *Financial Times*, January 8.

Galbraith, James K. 2012. *Inequality and Instability: A Study of the World Economy Just Before the Great Crisis*. Oxford University Press.

Hancock, Tom, Katia Dmitrieva, Carolynn Look, and Yuko Takeo. 2021. "A Global Urge to Lie Flat." *Bloomberg Businessweek*, December 13.

Hirsh, Michael. 2010. "Capital Offense: How Washington's Wise Men Turned America's Future Over to Wall Street." *New York Times*, December 13.

Hirsh, Michael. 2013. "The Comprehensive Case Against Larry Summers." *The Atlantic*, September 13.

Jarsulic, Marc and Gregg Gelzinis. 2020. "Making the Fed Rescue Serve Everyone in the Aftermath of the Coronavirus Pandemic." *The American Prospect*, May 14.

Kalecki, Michael. 1943. "Political Aspects of Full Employment." *Political Quarterly*, 14(4).

Kane, Edward J. 2016. "A Theory of How and Why Central-Bank Culture Supports Predatory Risk-Taking at Megabanks." *Atlantic Economic Journal*, 44.

Kashkari, Neel. 2020. "Big US banks Should Raise $200bn In Capital Now Biggest Lenders Must Prepare for the Worst to Survive Deep Economic Downturn." *Financial Times*, April 16.

Kay, John. 2015. Other People's Money: The Real Business of Finance. *PublicAffairs*.

Kiel, Paul, Ash Ngu, Jesse Eisinger, and Jeff Ernsthausen. 2022. "America's Highest Earners and Their Taxes Are Revealed." *ProPublica*, April 13.

Kohler, Karsten, Alexander Guschanski and Engelbert Stockhammer. 2019. "The Impact of Financialization on the Wage Share: A Theoretical Clarification and Empirical Test." *Cambridge Journal of Economics*, 43.

Lazonick, William and Jang-Sup Shin. 2020. *Predatory Value Extraction: How the Looting of the Business Corporation Became the US Norm and How Sustainable Prosperity Can Be Restored*. Oxford University Press.

Lucas, Robert E. 2004. "The Industrial Revolution: Past and Future." *The Region, Federal Reserve Bank of Minneapolis*, May.

Mahanta, Siddhartha. 2012. "Flashback: Lew's Time at Citi and Other Disappointments." *Mother Jones*, January 9.

Masters, Brooke. 2021. "Lax Rules Are Allowing Corporate Fat Cats to Dump Stock; US Financial Regulator should Crack Down to Prevent Selling Just Before Share Prices Fall." *Financial Times*, December 22.

Milanovic, Branko. 2009. "Two Views on the Cause of the Global Crisis – Part I." *YaleGlobal Online*, May 4.

Neate, Rupert. 2022. "Soaring Food Prices Push More Cargill Family Members on to World's Richest 500 List." *Guardian*, April 17.

Norris, Floyd. 2009. "Easy Loans Finance Dividends." *New York Times*, January 8.

Parker, Kim and Juliana Menasce Horowitz. 2022. "The Great Job Resignation." *Pew Research*, March 9.

Petrou, Karen. 2021a "Economic Stimulus Is a Gift to the Rich." *New York Times*, July 13.

Petrou, Karen. 2021b. "A Central-Bank Mandate for Our Time: The Fed's de Dacto Fiscal Role and Its Anti-Equality Impact. *Prepared for the 39th Annual Monetary Conference: Populism and the Future of the Fed.* Cato Institute, November 18. https://fedfin.com/wp-content/uploads/2021/11/Karen-Petrou-Cato-Institute-A-Central-Bank-Mandate-for-Our-Time_The-Feds-De-Facto-Fiscal-Role-and-Its-Anti-Equality-Impact-11.18.2021.pdf

Piketty, Thomas. 2014. *Capital in the Twenty-First Century*. Belknap Press.

Pistor, Katharina. 2019. *The Code of Capital. How the Law Creates Wealth and Inequality.* Princeton University Press.

Pistor, Katharina and Simon Deakin. 2017. "Legal Institutionalism: Capitalism and the Constitutive Role of Law." *Journal of Comparative Economics*, 45(1).

Reich, Robert. 2021. "Is America Experiencing an Unofficial General Strike?" *Guardian*, October 13.

Reinhart, Carmen M. and Leora Klapper. 2022. "Private-Debt Risks Are Hiding in Plain Sight." *Project Syndicate*, May 2.

Rodrik, Dani. 2008. "Schleifer the (Counter)Revolutionary," *Dani Rodrik weblog*, February 23. https://rodrik.typepad.com/dani_rodriks_weblog/2008/02/shleifer-the-co.html.

Saez, Emmanuel. 2013. "Striking it Richer: The Evolution of Top Incomes in the United States (updated)." http://elsa.berkeley.edu/~saez/saez-UStopincomes-2012.pdf; The World Top Incomes Database. http://topincomes.gmond.parisschoolofeconomics.eu.

Sanders, Bernie. 2022. "Sanders Warns Democrats Not to Focus Solely on Abortion Ahead of Midterms." *Guardian*, October 10.

Scheuer, Florian and Joel Slemrod. 2021. "Taxing Our Wealth." *Journal of Economic Perspectives*, 35(1).

Schwartz, Herman Mark. 2022. "Global Secular Stagnation and the Rise of Intellectual Property Monopoly." *Review of International Political Economy*, 29(5).

Shaw, Christopher W. 2019. *Money, Power, and the People: The American Struggle to Make Banking Democratic.* University of Chicago Press.

Sirota, David. 2021. "Meltdown." *Audible Podcast.* https://www.audible.com/pd/Meltdown-Podcast/B09J733SQR.

Smialek, Jeanna, Peter Eavis, and Emily Flitter. 2019. "Banks Want Efficiency. Critics Warn of Backsliding." *New York Times*, August 20.

Smith, Yves. 2010. "The Empire Continues to Strike Back: Team Obama Propaganda Reaches Fever Pitch." *Naked Capitalism*, March 10. https://www.nakedcapitalism.com/2010/03/the-empire-continues-to-strike-back-team-obama-propaganda-campaign-reaches-fever-pitch.html.

Stigler, George J. 1971. "The Theory of Economic Regulation." *Bell Journal of Economics and Management Science*, 2(1).

Stoller, Matt. 2022. "Throw the Bums Out Politics." *Big*, July 22.

Subramanian, Arvind and Dani Rodrik. 2019. "The Puzzling Lure of Financial Globalization." *Project Syndicate*, September 25. https://www.project-syndicate.org/commentary/financial-globalization-neoliberalism-discredited-by-arvind-subramanian-and-dani-rodrik-2019-09

Tabb, William K. 2004. *Economic Governance in the Age of Globalization.* Columbia University Press.

Tanner, Michael D. 2018. "The Dangers of America's Obsession with Inequality." *National Review Online*, February 14. https://www.cato.org/commentary/dangers-americas-obsession-inequality#.

van Treeck, Till. 2020. "Inequality, the Crisis, and Stagnation." *European Journal of Economics and Economic Policies: Intervention*, 12(2).

Wartzman, Rick and William Lazonick. 2018. "Don't Let Pay Increases Coming Out of Tax Reform Fool You." *Washington Post*, February 6.

5
VALUE EXTRACTION AND FINANCING MONOPOLY POWER

The ongoing concentration and centralization of capital reflect a development in the increased appropriation of surplus by firms able to gain and abuse market power. Financialization is responsible for the acceleration of this process, with hedge funds and private equity able to access financial markets to accumulate large pools of capital, deploying mostly borrowed money. Relying on the assets of the takeover target as collateral, they have gained control of companies in a continuing process of mergers and acquisitions – with anticompetitive consequences. This process has been sanctioned by antitrust authorities on the grounds that so long as consumers benefit from lower prices, concentration reflects greater efficiency in meeting demand. Such mergers were acceptable to the antitrust authorities before the Biden administration ended this strategy, once again making the prevention of increased market power the governing criteria.

Popular dissatisfaction with the power of large corporations and their abuse of consumers, workers, and suppliers has contributed to a new wave of progressive populism, one that takes many forms. In a Brandeisian spirit, the Biden administration is opposing the continued monopolization of the American economy by challenging anticompetitive mergers, thus attempting a return to the original intent of the antitrust laws. This chapter details how extensively the economy has departed from the competitive model that many presume still applies. It examines how the legal system favors capital at the expense of labor as well as the manner in which financialization provides the vehicle for the accumulation of monopoly power in an era when finance capitalism dominates – a domination that is now under challenge.

While such a focus governs this chapter, it needs to be pointed out that a bifurcation of American businesses has occurred between the most successful and a growing number of marginal companies. New economy firms endowed with innovative products dominate markets, growing with sizable returns to scale in the markets

DOI: 10.4324/9781003385240-5

or market segments in which they have monopoly power. The big five divide the commanding heights of tech. Google dominates search, Facebook social media, Apple phones, Amazon ecommerce, and Microsoft business software. When the firms realized regulators were going to act against their dominance, they edged into each other's territory and are to a significant extent competing in new domains. Some of these forays have not been successful (Facebook into an expensive losing investment in the metaverse, for example).

The search for yield in a period of low interest rates during the slow recovery from the 2008 Great Recession increased the ability of weak firms to borrow by promising high returns to investors. The capacity of those firms to meet the loan obligations they had undertaken was in many cases questionable – as was their capability even to pay interest on their debt. They were kept from defaulting by creditors rolling over their obligations with new lending.

From Invisible Hand to Heavy Hand

The understanding that market competition fosters efficiency is frequently attributed to Adam Smith, who captured the function of the market in one of the two most famous passages in *The Wealth of Nations*:

> Every individual necessarily labours to render the annual revenue of the society as great as he can. He generally neither intends to promote the public interest, nor knows how much he is promoting it. . . . He intends only his own gain, and he is in this, as in many other cases, led by an invisible hand to promote an end which was no part of his intention.

In the book's other widely cited passage, Smith declared, "It is not from the benevolence of the butcher, the brewer, or the baker that we expect our dinner, but from their regard for their own interest." The consumer is sovereign, choosing among the many producers who compete to meet customer preferences; however, Smith imposed moral conditions on the context in which such competition was to function (Tabb 1999: chapter 3).

Smith's description of an 18th-century competitive marketplace of small producers became outmoded long ago. Large enterprises grew to dominate markets and market segments. The early 21st century was one of the most significant periods of mergers and acquisitions in the history of American capitalism. Companies absorbed competitors and potential competitors; they extended their product range, secured vertical linkages to suppliers, forwarded linkages of distributors, and by copying and underselling drove smaller, often more innovative firms out of business if they could not be acquired. The giants with deeper pockets are able to cross-subsidize divisions, accepting temporary losses to destroy smaller competitors. The U.S. was far and away the leader in such practices, its giant corporations benefitting from sheer market power and increasing returns to scale and scope – factors that are absent from the usual model of competitive markets, which presume diminishing returns with size.

Many companies that sell manufactured goods outsource production while retaining patents and valuable brand names; they do not hold inventory themselves but rather manage the supply chains and distributions to stores and online sellers of their products. They maintain strong market positions, often holding monopoly power in one or more areas. Their high valuations mean that they can borrow easily and at low cost when they wish. These valuations also generate a great deal of surplus that they can return to stockholders and top managers, use to buy back their own stock, and invest in financial assets.

The deregulation of finance has allowed such landmark events as the Kohlberg Kravis & Roberts (KKR) purchase of RJR Nabisco in 1988 for twenty-five billion dollars, putting up only 0.06 percent of its own money and borrowing the rest, using the assets of its target as collateral. The political contributions made by KKR and other private equity firms to state officials (the guardian of state worker pension funds) may have been a factor in such deals. In the present moment, there are more private equity-owned companies than there are companies listed on public stock exchanges. This important development has for the most part been under the radar of economists, who have dismissed Senator Sanders' Stop Wall Street Looting Act, which would have forced these giants to assume liability for the debt they imposed on companies and to protect worker pensions of the companies forced into bankruptcy.

Economists have been slow to understand that corporations themselves are commodities, bought and sold like the products they market. Whole industries experience waves of takeovers that result in a few dominant players remaining. Unlike Smith's marketplace, in which consumers choose among the wares of many different sellers, alternatives offered today are often owned by the same large company. Moreover, whereas in Smith's time the small, family-run businesses passed from father to son, today's corporate versions commonly have short-term owners.

Adam Smith's "baker" is thus a very different entity two centuries later. Nabisco, a conglomerate selling Mallomars and Oreos among many other branded products, can trace its origin to Pearson & Sons Bakery, which opened in Massachusetts in 1792. Nabisco is now a subsidiary of Mondelēz International. Product names remain, but they become components of different entities as they are bought and sold. Phillip Morris, the tobacco firm, acquired Nabisco and became RJR Nabisco, obscuring in its new name any association with a certain cancer-producing product. And our baker became part of a new parent – Kraft – until Kraft split and Mondelēz International merged, marketing the snack food and candy segment of what had formerly been Kraft. In the 21st century, as a spin-off Mondelēz sold Ritz crackers and Chips Ahoy! Cookies as well as Philadelphia cream cheese and Halls cough drops among other products, parts of a corporate portfolio that expands and contracts as divisions and brands are bought and sold.

In 2013, Mondelēz was forced to give Trian Fund Management a seat on its board to avoid a proxy fight with that firm's principal, Nelson Peltz, who had suggested that the company merge with the Frito-Lay snack business owned by Pepsi Cola. In 2015 Mondelēz once again became a target when William Ackman's Pershing Square Capital Management announced that it owned a 7.5 percent share of the company and demanded dramatic cost cutting – in fact that Mondelēz sell itself (Langley 2015). Ackman proposed reuniting Mondelēz and Kraft Heinz. Other analysts regarded Nestle as a better fit. In 2016 Mondelēz made a bid to take over Hershey. Peltz and Ackerman had pushed the firm to separate from Kraft (which then merged with Heinz). Kraft's new owners were the Brazil-based 3G Capital and Warren Buffett's Berkshire Hathaway. Needless to say, none of this was about baking a better cookie to meet consumer demand.

With each change the company fired workers, squeezed suppliers, and selected cheaper, often less healthy ingredients. Mondelēz is among the diminishing number of food giants which make money when fresh or semi-processed offerings are replaced by highly processed convenience foods. It follows a business model closely linked to obesity, diabetes, and other diseases. The market power of Big Food extends beyond the consumers to the treatment meted out to farmers, workers, and the planet (Chemnitz 2017).

In 2016, the management of Nabisco's Chicago plant, which had employed generations of Windy City workers, made an announcement to its 1,200-person labor force, by then largely African-American and Hispanic employees with decades of service and membership in the Bakery, Confectionery, Tobacco Workers and Grain Millers International Union (note the forced mergers of once-strong, independent industrial unions); they would have to accept forty-six million dollars in concessions, amounting to cuts of $23,000 per worker – or the company would move its production lines to Salinas, Mexico. Similarly, a highly profitable Mondelēz (run by the hedge fund 3G) was trying to eliminate the union pension plan. It recruited strikebreakers in preparation for a long confrontation (Garver 2016). Although that year's national election campaigns were underway and criticism of disloyal and iniquitous corporations was commonplace, an appraisal concludes that even "considering the vitriol directed toward Big Business on the campaign trail," Mondelēz and its Oreo brand "scored one victory after another in Washington . . . [and] the voters' fury seems harmless" (Coy 2016).

In the summer of 2021 when labor markets were tighter, Nabisco workers in Portland, Oregon, went on strike protesting against demands for concessions, although the company was in fact quite profitable due to greater sales during the pandemic. Workers in similar facilities throughout the U.S. followed them out, affecting every company bakery and distribution center in the country. Members of other unions joined their protests, and a boycott was established. The members of Railroad Workers United refused to deliver baking supplies to the Portland facility when they saw the workers on strike. Support also came from prominent Hollywood actors and elected officials. Using tactics that would have made a Wobbly (a member of the early 20th-century International Workers of the World) proud, protesters blockaded parking lots where suspected replacement workers were boarding and set off car alarms at hotels where the scabs were reportedly staying. After more than a month, a settlement was reached without the concessions that had been demanded; instead, there were pay raises, increased contributions to the employees' 401(k) accounts, and a $5,000 bonus for each worker. Labor shortages had changed the bargaining power of increasingly angry workers, with a large number of strikes reversing decades of concessions to employers. The reversal in the relative power of employer and worker was attributable to the state of the labor market, which reduced the power of capital that financialization normally increases.

When asked whether consumers would accept higher prices for the company's Oreos and Cadbury chocolates, Mondelēz International Chief Financial Officer, Luca Zamamella, responded (in a period of general inflation) that the company had changed package sizing, saying "if you look at the market, you'll see price going up and volume going up. The old concept of elasticity – higher price/lower volume – is not necessarily there anymore" (Riggs 2022). Many other companies with well-established brand loyalty and market power might have responded in a similar fashion. Given the widespread inflation afflicting the consumer, such companies found little difficulty in ramping up their own prices above the cost of labor and their purchased inputs. Their profits increased accordingly.

Mondelēz is only one firm among many that no longer resemble their Adam Smith-world ancestors, having been bought and sold, merged and split, taken public, then private, then public again – events not recognized by consumers, who focus on the brand names of the commodities they purchase while giving little thought to the ownership of the company producing them. Another firm is the descendant of Smith's brewer, the giant Anheuser-Busch InBev with headquarters in Leuven, Belgium, home of Stella Artois. It is the largest brewer in the world, owning an extensive portfolio of brands including once upstart, small, quirky craft beers, as well as major brands – over fifty in total – and holding over forty percent of the U.S. market. It is the world's fifth largest consumer product company. Adam Smith's brewer has metamorphosed into a transnational serial acquirer. (It is also at this writing owned by the gentlemen at 3G Capital.) A merger with SABMiller makes the location of its "home" unclear. While it is registered in Brussels and holds annual shareholder meetings in Leuven and Liege, the company's top management is based in New York City. The company designates St. Louis, where the Budweiser Clydesdales are stabled, as its official U.S. headquarters giving consideration to public relations in its biggest market.

Tradition plays a role in the location of corporate headquarters but far more important is, of course, taxation. AB InBev reported an effective tax rate of eighteen percent in 2014, less than half the forty percent rate that an independent, U.S.-based Anheuser-Busch had reported in 2007. Because London-based SABMiller was subjected to a twenty-six percent tax rate, Belgium with its lower taxes is now its official home (Chaudhuri and Mickle 2015). Subsidiaries are found in several other tax havens, further reducing its taxable income. The mammoth brewer is among the multinational corporations being investigated by European Union officials for tax evasion. EU antitrust regulators are exploring whether the beer behemoth abused its dominant position through unfair and illegal competitive practices. In 2019, it was fined a mere $225 million for such activities (Chee 2019).

The number of U.S. companies owned by private equity firms doubled in the 21st century, currently totaling in the tens of thousands. How should an economy be understood when companies like 3G make such decisions, buying and selling corporations as if they were so many trading cards? These entities, whether owned by private equity, hedge funds, money managers, or other institutional owners and intermediaries, impose financial criteria that are not directly concerned either with sales or with investment in plant and equipment. They make strategic decisions regarding which merger will be more profitable and when spinning off a division is advantageous. Financial capitalists make money from money – with no thought to production but only to short-term market signals.

One, two, three, or four companies dominate most industries and sectors of the American economy. They follow what economists politely term "co-respective behavior," maximizing their collective profits by limiting competition. Over recent decades, cartels have been found fixing the price of a long list of product categories ranging from ball-bearings and seat belts to candle wax, thereby appropriating the earnings of working families, often in violation of federal laws. The push to deregulate, the ideological denunciation of "Big Government interference in the free market," and the vast sums spent by special interests have eviscerated antitrust regulation.

Another aspect of the drive to extract profit from acquisitions involves squeezing the target firms, cutting wages, and selling off assets, leaving a shell of a company with debts they cannot pay, sending them into bankruptcy after much of their value has been extracted. This process has been prominent in retail, where firms that are under pressure from Amazon but own valuable real estate can be purchased at low cost – then, loaded with debt, with their new owners paying themselves lavish fees from borrowed money. Some of the firms that have been bought and destroyed in leveraged buyouts by private equity firms include Toys 'R' Us, Payless ShoeSource, and Gymboree. Many healthy firms have suffered this treatment, even as some failing companies have also been turned around by private equity managers (Appelbaum and Batt 2014).

Private equity firms utilize the money of institutional investors, including pension funds and university endowments, to acquire and restructure companies and even whole industries in a wide array of sectors. In the era of global neoliberalism, the private equity industry "embodies the neoliberal movement's values, while exposing its inherent logic." After they have extracted maximal returns, they declare bankruptcy, destroying jobs, and limiting consumer choice. This has happened to companies with the household names noted earlier.

The rewards for these actions are remarkably large, and they go undertaxed. The Internal Revenue Service rarely conducts detailed audits of private equity firms. Indeed, such audits are "almost nonexistent," asserted Michael Desmond, who stepped down in 2022 as chief counsel of the IRS. The agency "just doesn't have the resources and expertise." As Jesse Drucker and Danny Hakim (2021) explain, "One reason they rarely face audits is that private equity firms have deployed vast webs of partnerships to collect their profits. Partnerships do not owe income taxes. Instead, they pass those obligations on to their partners, who can number in the thousands at a large private equity firm. That makes the structures notoriously complicated for auditors to untangle." Perhaps as a consequence, the United States Treasury Department is estimated to lose seventy-five billion dollars a year from investors in partnerships failing to report their income accurately. Analysts, however, warn that legal and financial intermediaries are sometimes based in countries allowing a great deal of secrecy, with such complexity meaning that it is difficult to gather complete and accurate data (Guyton, Langetieg, Reck, Risch, and Zucman 2021). In 2022 President Biden and the Democrats passed a bill allotting the IRS eighty billion dollars to catch up on audits with a stress on the millionaire class, upgrade its outdated technological capacities, and replace some of the thousands of workers who were expected to retire in the next few years. The agency's enforcement staff had fallen by thirty percent since 2010, with audits on millionaires declining by over seventy percent. It was a more potent investigation and audit of the highest-income Americans that was to be the project of expanded IRS capacity, along with providing better service to ordinary filers needing assistance.

On Trump's social media outlet, Truth Social, the IRS hires were called "thugs" and "terrorists" and likened to "the gestapo." One percent of the new agents would be authorized to carry guns because of the work they would be doing, leading to the charge that the Democrats were weaponizing the agency with agents "trained to kill Americans." Iowa Republican Senator Chuck Grassley, a member of the Senate Finance Committee, warned Fox News viewers that the new IRS agents might be coming with loaded "AK-15s ready to shoot some small business person in Iowa" (Rappeport and Hsu 2022). This was a tactic designed to defend the financial elite and misdirect fear to arouse anger among the party base.

The *Financial Times* inquired editorially about the negative impacts of serial acquisitions. It termed the model "3G's chainsaw capitalism," asking rhetorically, "do the gains really increase welfare, given how much of the profit will go to a handful of rich people while thousands of workers bear the pain?" (Editorial 2017). The "chainsaw capitalism" meme originated in the closing years of the 20th century. Sunbeam CEO Al Dunlap's preferred nickname was "Chainsaw Al" for his willingness to dismember the businesses he acquired, selling off their parts for more cash than he had spent on the purchase. "Dunlap emerged as the mascot of a new kind of capitalism," David Plotz wrote at the time.

> Dunlapism begins and ends at Wall Street. Its sole credo is: "How can we make our stock worth more?" Nothing that is valued by less steely businessmen – loyalty to workers, responsibility to the community, relationships with suppliers, generosity in corporate philanthropy – matters to Dunlap.
>
> *(1997)*

The inspiration for his nom de guerre was the popular 1974 horror film, *The Texas Chain Saw Massacre*, which culture critics were quick to see as a metaphor for the excesses of capitalism (Merritt 2010).

The Growth of Monopoly

The private equity industry attracted trillions of dollars in a world with very low (and in price-adjusted terms) even negative interest rates. Private equity has claimed a thirteen percent annual return over a recent quarter of a century, far more than the S&P 500. Investors find the sector appealing, although there is some concern that the industry exaggerates its returns (Parmar and Kelly 2019). An examination of the approximately 500 businesses taken private from 1980 to 2006, which compared the leveraged buyout cases and a similar number of companies that remained public for a period of ten years, found that about twenty percent of the private equity-owned companies filed for bankruptcy – ten times the rate of those that remained public. Not only do the employees lose in such transactions, but so does the community in which the companies are located. The government also loses because it has to support the former employees. Who wins? "The funds do" (Ayash and Rastad 2021) – and, of course, those who invest in them, attracting still more money to the sector. Private equity firms currently manage at least $3.4 trillion of investor commitments globally, up from less than $500 billion in 2000. These structural developments may explain why the average price markup over the cost of production had risen from twenty-one to sixty-one percent over the past four decades (De Loecker, Eeckhout, and Unger 2020).

Before the end of 2021, private equity firms announced a record $944 billion of buyouts in the U.S., two and a half times the volume for the same period the prior year and more than double that of the previous peak in 2007, according to Dealogic. There had been five ten billion dollar-plus deals, a sum that equals the total in all of 2007. By the end of November of that year, buyout firms had raised $315 billion in capital to invest in North America out of the available cash earmarked for the region, a record $756 billion, according to the data from the Preqin Global Alternatives Reports. The fundraising showed no signs of abating, indicating a continuation of the private equity shopping spree, especially in areas of tech, medical goods, and service companies.

By 2020 the major stock index, the Wilshire 5000, contained fewer than 3,500 companies as a consequence of mergers and bankruptcies. Because they borrow and extract so much from the purchased company, firms owned by private equity are ten times more likely to go bankrupt than their peers. Tracking a sample of 484 public-to-private leveraged buyouts for ten years after the companies went private, researchers found a bankruptcy rate of approximately twenty percent, an order of magnitude greater than the two percent bankruptcy rate for a control sample. The analysis is robust to macro and industry shocks, among other potential explanations for the higher bankruptcy rate (Ayash and Rastad 2021). The business model, not chance, produces such an outcome.

It is assumed on Wall Street that a combination of maximal debt and minimal reserves for the future is an efficient strategy. However, debt limits managerial discretion, imposing inescapable debt-servicing requirements. While corporate leaders may not wish to endanger their company in this way, but they often have little choice in the matter. Pushed by activist shareholders and a desire to raise the price of their stock, many firms take out loans to fund buybacks and dividend payments, assuming increased debt. In the U.S., corporate debt rose from $3.3 trillion before the Great Recession to $6.5 trillion in 2019. Investors eager for yield in a low-interest environment bought bonds from companies with weak prospects, incentivized by their higher rate of return. Moody's Investors Service's Loan Covenant Quality Indicator measures the level of protection that lenders require of borrowers. Such covenants had become more liberal as those with surplus funds sought out borrowers who would pay attractive rates of interest. This index was at its lowest level ever in the U.S. at the end of 2019, weeks before the coronavirus struck the economy. If the Federal Reserve had not bought such company bonds and held them, firms would have had difficulties paying interest on their debt and many would likely have had to declare bankruptcy. Investment grade borrowers could quickly have been reclassified by rating agencies in the downturn. Zombies that would have otherwise died continued to exist. (The last section of the next chapter discusses the significance of zombies in some detail.)

Weakened firms offer easy targets for acquisition. At the start of the second decade of this century, Goldman Sachs President John Waldron spoke of a new merger wave about to unfold: "Politicians are going to be faced with the uncomfortable reality that you're going to have more big business doing better and that there's going to be more losses of jobs along the way." He added, "You are going to see a fairly sizable amount of large-cap M&A coming with stronger, healthier companies being the acquirer and taking advantage of weaknesses in their industry or elsewhere." His important customers would prosper, as would Goldman Sachs. "Our clients are more desirous of playing offense and doing deals. That's a good thing," he told a gathering. He mentioned in passing that large companies will be looking to consolidate smaller companies, which will be "complicated societally" (Stoller 2020).

Acquisitions were defended with the argument of the "failing firm": that struggling businesses could be saved at lower cost, justifying the reduction of employment at the purchased firms and their combination with former rivals, even with the consequent increase in market concentration. Evaluating what was occurring, Austan Goolsbee (2020), who chaired the Obama Council of Economic Advisers, addressed this rationalization, stating that the "largest downturn in 90 years threatens to fundamentally change the competitive balance for decades to come." While liberal policy makers once spoke of a crisis being something they should not waste, believing it offered an opportunity to make changes they favored, large corporations, asset managers, and others that the financialized economy had brought to prominence were the ones who took advantage of the situation in pursuit of their own ends.

In an academic paper that focuses on the junk bond market of the 1980s, George A. Akerlof and Paul M. Romer (1993) refer to bankruptcy for profit as "looting." The conclusion of their essay is worth recalling: "the regulators in the field who understood what was happening from the beginning found lukewarm support at best, for their cause. Now we know better. If we learn from experience, history need not repeat itself." In reality, people do not learn when money can be made by purposeful forgetting. While their paper was occasioned by the Savings & Loan scandals in which this pattern of the misuse of borrowed money had dominated, private equity firms took looting in the Ackerlof and Romer usage to new heights. The coronavirus panic prompted the Federal Reserve to follow past patterns, protecting such firms from losing money and obscuring from the public the extent to which they had been responsible for the widespread bankruptcies of once-healthy companies and the takeovers of many others.

Of course, not all acquisitions were made to sell off company assets. Most assets were retained, offering sources of continued income for the acquirer. At the same time, a downturn or increase in interest rates would render dangerous the debt obligations that the purchases had required. In the fall of 2021, Moody's warned that the private credit industry that provided high-return loans to midsized companies often owned by buyout groups was making loans, which were attractive due to their strong returns (again, assuming they were repaid). "The mounting tide of leverage sweeping into a less-regulated 'grey zone' has systemic risks," the rating agency declared. "Risks that are rising beyond the spotlight of public investors and regulators may be difficult to quantify, even as they come to have broader economic consequences." This was because the industry depended on significant amounts of borrowing. "Private equity's business model relies on leverage," stated Christina Padgett, head of leveraged finance research at Moody's. "We have become more accustomed to leverage in the institutional loan market and bond market. Now we are seeing a higher degree of leverage among smaller companies. . . . At the moment that is fine because rates are low but it introduces a higher degree of risk going forward" (Wigglesworth, Rennison, and Gara 2021). There were many cautions of this type, which emphasized the danger for the stability of the economy that the financialization model of accumulation imposes along with warnings of the defaults that higher interest rates might bring.

The wages of over-exuberance have been discussed, as have the consequences for individuals, financial institutions, and the economy. While the timing of a new downturn cannot be predicted, it may be noted that such margin borrowings in October 2021 were up to forty-two percent from a year earlier, having reached $936 billion according to data from the Financial Industry Regulatory Authority, Wall Street's self-regulator. At the same time, the measure of cash holdings among individual investors fell to forty-six percent of margin balances, the lowest such reading in data going back to 1997. Options trading, which has "exploded" in popularity, is not fully reflected in the data, nor is the debt employed by hedge funds and other institutional investors. As readers might expect, "many investors brush off worries about investor borrowing and other longstanding market risks, such as high valuations and 'crowded' trades that are prone to sudden reversals." Perhaps, ironically, it was among the banks that this happened first in a system endangering manner. The Fed came to see reason for concern but did not act. It had accepted the model, even if it was reluctant to live with the possible consequences of the borrowing on margin premised on the value of the asset only going higher (Wursthorn 2021).

Even as many banks needed Fed bailouts, as interest rates rose, there was remarkable little interest on the part of policy makers for the leverage and risk of asset valuations falling in the real economy. The growth of private equity firms with their abundance of capital has rightly been described as "one of the most profound shifts in the capital markets since the 19th century" when public equity markets first became widely available (Idzelis 2019). Currently, while Walmart employs more people than any other company, the next eight largest employers are private equity groups that own portfolios of companies. Carlyle controls Hertz and AMC movie theaters, for example. It had 900,000 employees in the companies it owned in early 2019. KKR employs 700,000 people and Blackstone 600,000. Private equity firms manage three trillion dollars in assets. They are highly leveraged and should the economy slow marketly they too may face collapse and taxpayer help will be needed. Their investment deals have proliferated dramatically. These firms sextupled in net asset valuations to $1.4 trillion in 2021, surpassing their pre-Great Recession peak. That year a report by McKinsey & Company on private markets found that "the most in-depth research continues to affirm that, by nearly any measure, private equity outperforms public market equivalents (with net global returns of over 14 percent)." This verdict, rather than the skeptical one suggesting that the industry overstates its profits, has garnered greater purchase on the thinking of investors, which accounts for the result that private equity has penetrated almost every area of the economy. Its employees were found collecting rental carts at airports and working at car washes and in dentist offices, auto-repair shops, and dry cleaners. Stoller (2020) has collected examples of the "rollups" of niche industry firms by private equity in a host of industries ranging from portable toilets to martial arts. The "rollup" of small niche companies has moved into all manner of businesses that now include Burger King and Dunkin' franchises, the Boston Red Socks, and the Pittsburgh Penguins. In 2020, one out of every thirteen U.S. workers was an employee of a private equity firm.

Some of the principles directing private equity have flaunted their wealth in a manner not seen since the era of the robber barons, which Mark Twain termed the "Gilded Age of post-Civil War America" when wealth became concentrated and celebrated. Amidst the conservative drive to "own the libs," the doings of the 21st-century robber barons go unappreciated. For example, Stephen Schwarzman, the co-founder of Blackstone, at this writing with a net worth of well over thirty billion dollars, is famous for his multimillion-dollar birthday parties that symbolize the excesses of these masters of the universe. His 60th birthday party at the Park Avenue armory in New York (shortly before the financial crash of 2008) featured performances by Rod Stewart and Patti LaBelle with guests including Barbara

Walters and Donald Trump. The latter was to receive generous contributions from Mr. Schwartzman, who was angry that President Obama had tried to raise taxes on private equity, an event he likened to the worst excesses of Adolph Hitler. Describing Schwartzman's 70th birthday as "brilliantly stimulating," David Koch, a fellow billionaire who attended, was impressed by the acrobats, Mongolian soldiers, and camels. Gwen Stefani sang "Happy Birthday" (Levin 2017).

The over-the-top splendor was paid for by Blackstone's buying up the mortgages on homes that had been defaulted upon and other homes as they came on the market to rent them to people who had once been, if temporarily, homeowners or who no longer could aspire to such a status. Also, prominently, private equity purchased businesses, cutting spending on wages and on other inputs, extracting fees, and in many cases abandoning the remaining shells to bankruptcy proceedings after they had been wrung dry. People became aware of the excess deaths during Covid at nursing homes owned by private equity; this pattern was also a cause for voter anger.

Blackstone is one of the world's largest property owners. Its rental housing and other real estates produce nearly half of its profits. But as Maureen Farrell (2022) writes, Blackstone has grown "into a behemoth with a hand in just about everything: mortgage lending, infrastructure, television and film studios, stakes in entertainment companies, pharmaceuticals, and even the dating app Bumble." Since the 2008 financial crisis, it and its rivals, Apollo, KKR, and Carlyle, have become financial conglomerates; they "have refashioned themselves into the supermarkets of the financial industry," engaging in activities that are traditionally the territory of banks, hedge funds, and venture capital. While banks are more tightly regulated, the shadow banking industry has moved more aggressively into lending. As a result, the Biden SEC considered what new laws may be needed to regulate the shadow banks, which are now lightly supervised. Public comments were sought in what would be a difficult process of extending regulatory oversight.

Health Care, Private Equity, and Market Extractions

One of the areas penetrated by private equity has been experienced by patients who visit an emergency room or are admitted to an in-network hospital by an in-network doctor, only to find that some of the professionals who treat them are not covered by their insurance. This occurs because hospitals outsource emergency room tasks, anesthesiology, radiology, and other specialized services to outside physician practices or staffing firms. They save money, but patients as a result often receive unexpected medical bills that can run into tens of thousands of dollars. These out-of-network services are largely owned by leveraged buyout firms. Such specialist practices have been a logical target for such firms, since patients who need care cannot negotiate over price.

Eileen Appelbaum and Rosemary Batt reported that among other strategies, private equity-owned companies evade state laws that prohibit nonmedical ownership of doctors' practices by setting up "physician management" or "management services" organizations. The doctors do the medicine. The private equity firm that owns the management company handles the billing for the practice. KKR and the Blackstone Group own the two largest physician-staffing firms, employing almost 80,000 health care professionals employed in hospitals and other facilities across the U.S. Appelbaum and Batt (2019) cite a survey which found forty-one percent of Americans reporting that they or a family member had received an unexpected medical bill, with half of them attributing that bill to out-of-network charges. The researchers gathered data on the exorbitant fees imposed by air transport companies and ambulance firms owned by private equity; in an emergency a person whose life may be in danger, or their family, rarely attempts to negotiate price. Surprise ambulance bills occurred eighty-six percent of the time an ambulance took a patient to an emergency room.

The hospitals themselves engage in not dissimilar practices. Essentially it is impossible to know in advance what the full cost of a hospital procedure will be. Those proposing Health Care for All, or any meaningful improvement in cost reduction, will need to confront the private equity giants, the hospital chains, and the drug companies that, operating along similar lines, raise the price of medical care, leading to the charge that hedge funds are "ethically challenged" (Olson 2022). It turns out that such abuses were committed by supposedly nonprofit giant hospital chains as well (Silver-Greenberg and Thomas 2022).

The Covid pandemic has revealed, according to Akexander Sammon (2022), "the profound inadequacy of the uniquely privatized and financialized American system, where for-profit (and 'nonprofit') hospitals and for-profit insurance companies teamed up to help the United States secure its worst-in-the-world national death toll while notching one best-ever earnings call after another." He is especially critical of the billions of dollars vaccine manufacturers accrued using research that was funded by taxpayers and he called for the government to manufacture as well as conduct the research for new drugs, which would end Americans paying by far the highest drug prices in the world.

In 2018 the private equity group KKR agreed to buy Envision Healthcare, one of the largest providers of medical staff to U.S. hospitals, for $9.9 billion, including debt. The transaction was one of the most significant buyouts since the financial crisis. The *Financial Times* reported that the deal "underscores how financial investors are playing a defining role in the U.S. healthcare system that is being transformed by technological change and a years-long legislative tussle over the future of Obamacare." The piece noted that Envision "had faced controversy over billing practices for emergency room patients" (Vandevelde and Platt 2018). The company-owned emergency medicine group, with some 70,000 professionals staffing 540 health care facilities in forty-five states, was found to be in serious financial trouble, even as Congress moved to prevent it from making so much money from surprise bills. Creditors have lost confidence in its ability to repay its huge debt. Envision's $5.3 billion first-lien term loan, due in 2025, was soon trading in distressed-debt territory. Blackstone-backed TeamHealth, which provides emergency-room doctors to hospitals, saw the value of its $2.7 billion loan, due in 2024, also tumble (Rennison and Kuchler 2019).

Weeks before a ban on surprise medical billing was finally set to begin on January 1, 2022, the American Medical Association, the American Hospital Association, and other similarly self-interested groups filed a suit to block elements in it to which they objected. (Consumer groups, employers, insurance companies, and the members of Congress who wrote the law supported it as written.) A mysterious group calling itself Doctor Patient Unity (which listed as its "agent," a person who was also the contact for 150 other political action groups) spent twenty-eight million dollars on television ads and direct mail to voters, encouraging them to tell their legislators not to vote for the bill. The principal support for the campaign against new restrictions was found to be two large firms backed by private equity. The ads generally omitted references to surprise bills. Instead, they warned of "government rate setting" that harms patient care. In one ad, an ambulance crew arrives with a patient only to find the hospital dark and empty (Sanger-Katz, Creswell, and Abelson 2021). Yves Smith (2022) wrote, "[H]ats off to Eileen and Rosemary for not giving ground in this long-running fight." She noted, "With private equity 'research' being heavily influenced and funded by private equity (business school professors can easily make five or ten times their business school pay on private equity 'consulting' gigs), there was only a tiny cohort of private equity skeptics in academia." As a result, "[i]n private equity, flattering studies are the norm." There is widespread agreement with David Dayen's (2022) judgment that "[i]t is genuinely hard to find a more destructive economic force in America today than the private equity industry." The tenacity of Appelbaum and Batt, who have investigated private equity for over a decade, has paid off.

Fortunately for the consumer, most surprise medical bills are now illegal due to bipartisan legislation that was passed over the efforts of special-interest lobbying groups. However, even while the law eliminates the risk of out-of-network doctors or hospitals sending the surprise bills they had been able to do before the public pressured Congress to act, emergency medical care can still be expensive for patients with high deductibility plans. Such patients do not know what their medical care will cost in advance, nor what their insurance plans will cover. Like private equity, the medical establishment continues to fight efforts to restrain its profits.

While surprise bills, Big Pharma, and more recently the suppliers of materials required by hospitals have received considerable attention, it is the mergers among hospitals themselves that are also significant; a single large hospital dominates in much of the country. Such hospital giants and often the national chain that owns them, along with the associated networks that in many places are a major, if not the major employer, may also be the primary contributor to the local congressperson, who is more likely to vote to help the hospital than to force it to keep prices down. A similar dynamic has been at work when it comes to overbilling by insurance companies administering Medicare Advantage programs.

The American health system absorbs twice the percentage of the country's GDP compared to peer countries that provide better outcomes. The American economy is less competitive globally, because excessive health care raises costs of employing labor. Even the reforms that manage to be enacted into law prop up the existing system. They offer subsidies to private insurers, which have the incentive to deny payment for treatment and compete by offering involved plans that are difficult to compare, making wise choices among confusing alternatives challenging even for experts. Franklin Roosevelt, Harry Truman, and subsequent presidents who wanted to create a universal health care system all failed to do so. Improving health care provisioning by government and lowering its cost were resisted by Republicans, who spent years attempting to repeal the Affordable Care Act (ACA), a plan based on Republican Mitt Romney's program when he was governor of Massachusetts. The opposition only faded when Americans had the opportunity to appreciate the benefits of the ACA and the Trump administration with the control of both houses of Congress declined to repeal Obamacare (Cohn 2021).

Eventually, before the healthcare system bankrupts the country, some form of Healthcare for All involving direct negotiation by the government over the cost of pharmaceuticals, medical equipment, and hospital charges will be required. However, the resistance to such a significant change remains strong. Needless to say, the individuals and companies most important to the financialization of the economy are key to this resistance.

Confronting Market Power

Affirming much of what has been discussed here, a study by the American Economic Liberties Project (2021) reveals that virtually every sector of the American economy has grown more concentrated during the era of neoliberalism. Monopoly power, its researchers argued, "is a causal factor in our most serious economic challenges, such as inequality, health care costs, farm bankruptcies, reduced entrepreneurship and productivity, the decline of the free press, and systems of racial discrimination." This occurred because the U.S. basically abandoned antitrust enforcement.

In his State of the Union address of March 1, 2022, President Biden declared that "Capitalism without competition isn't capitalism. Capitalism without competition is exploitation." This was perhaps the most radical statement of its kind from a U.S. president since Franklin Roosevelt. But he assured people that he was indeed a capitalist and he intended that his appointments and policy measures would work to promote and restore competition. The administration was responding to half a century of presidents accepting and endorsing policies that have led to the greater monopolization of the economy.

The president explicitly criticized the Chicago School of free market economics, which contends that only lower prices for consumers matter and that cost-reducing mergers (not eventual market power) comprise the proper antitrust criteria. From the 1970s, Milton Friedman, Gary Becker, and most influentially Robert Bork in his 1978 book, *The Antitrust Paradox*, convinced economists and courts that regardless of a company's size or market share, as long as acquiring competitors leads to lower prices, such acts are pro-competitive and therefore should be permitted.

A memo found by a researcher in the Reagan library titled "Throttling Back on Antitrust: A Practical Proposal for Deregulation," written by leaders of the Chicago School George Stigler and Richard Posner, made the case that Reagan could dispense with the antitrust law if his antitrust chief "just stopped bringing cases. But to do that, they would need a policy change in an obscure document known as 'merger guidelines' that organize antitrust enforcement," as Stoller (2020) reports. The memo said in part that

> President Reagan can throttle back on antitrust enforcement without asking for new legislation or higher appropriations without antagonizing politically influential constituencies. He has only to appoint an Assistant Attorney General in charge of the Antitrust Division . . . committed to enforcing the antitrust laws in accordance with the economic consensus position, i.e., confining enforcement to price fixing and large horizontal mergers. The head of the Antitrust Division could promptly . . . issue modified Merger Guidelines.

In other words, as Stoller summarized,

> they simply needed to rewrite how antitrust was enforced, instead of getting the statute repealed. This would include abolishing prohibitions against most mergers, and then making challenges against all but the extremely obviously bad ones impossible. The DOJ would also cut its own funding over time, and try to intervene in courts to stop private antitrust suits.
>
> *(2022a)*

William Baxter, who directed antitrust enforcement under Reagan called Supreme Court decisions mandating strong antitrust rules "rubbish" and "wacko" and circulated a memo in the department calling one such precedent "idiocy" Baxter's economists and lawyers did not initiate the kinds of cases the law was intended to prosecute in order to prevent market-restricting mergers. Instead, he produced the new guidelines that came to be accepted by the legal system. For forty years such a pro-concentration antitrust policy has governed. It was challenged by the assertive policies of the Biden administration against those with excessive market power.

William French Smith, the corporate lawyer whom President Ronald Reagan had appointed attorney general, famously declared, "We must recognize that bigness in business does not necessarily mean badness." President Reagan also appointed pro-corporate federal judges, including Bork, Richard Posner, and Antonin Scalia. "The letter of the nation's antitrust laws hasn't changed, but those judges rewrote the meaning of the laws," Benjamin Appelbaum states, arguing that it is a mistake "to assume that judges with progressive outlooks on social issues will necessarily favor constraints on corporate power. Some of the most celebrated liberal justices of recent decades, including Thurgood Marshall, Ruth Bader Ginsburg and Stephen Breyer, played key roles in gutting the nation's antitrust laws" (Appelbaum 2022). The Biden administration inherits an economy that prior Democratic presidents had allowed to become overwhelmingly concentrated. One of the results was that the beef, poultry, and pork industries, which have been shown to be responsible for roughly half of the inflation in food prices. Government statistics reveal that just four firms control approximately 55–85 percent of the market for these three products. The firms squeezed suppliers, speeded up workers, and increased prices.

The Biden administration recruited leading antitrust experts who saw the need to actively confront 21st-century monopolists and robber barons. His policies may offer substantive changes in how government treats firms with excessive market power, which has been a significant factor in the increased inequality. Lina Khan was appointed by President Biden as chair of the Federal Trade Commission (FTC) to stop such accommodation. It would prove difficult. On November 9, 2021, she tweeted, "We're on track to receive 3500 merger filings this year – a 70% increase over the average number of filings in recent years. Our funding has not kept up: between 2010–16 it effectively declined, and the agency's total headcount today remains about 2/3 of what it was in 1980." Even so, that the FTC was breaking with its long-standing practice of accommodation with business occasioned the U.S. Chamber of Commerce to issue an "open declaration of war against the FTC" as well as the Chamber's CEO, singling Khan out for condemnation. Its attack "certainly raised eyebrows, even among the Chamber's own members," Stoller (2020) writes, explaining that a small group of firms that run the Chamber's antitrust division, including Google, Apple, Facebook, and Amazon, is under public pressure to alter their policies. It is in the interest of such companies to fund and use the Chamber and other "front groups." Khan proved useful for the Chamber, itself a business, to raise funds by demonizing her. Stoller (2022b) explained of this "Defund the (antitrust) Police" strategy that as much as he hoped it would not work, it presented a real constraint on the agencies. Still, against the odds, the Biden administration was serious about reviving a rigorous approach to antitrust laws in keeping with the original intent of the populists who had led Congress to adopt them.

"Forty years ago we chose the wrong path," Biden insisted. "Following the misguided philosophy of people like Robert Bork, we pulled back on enforcing laws to promote competition. We are now forty years into the experiment of letting giant corporations accumulate more and more power." Biden issued an executive order declaring that the policy of the federal government under his leadership would be to promote fair competition both through antitrust laws and also through a reliance on every agency with authority to structure markets. He explicitly called attention to the lax controls on corporate power as the causal factor behind American stagnation. "What have we gotten from it?" Biden asked rhetorically. "Less growth, weakened investment, fewer small businesses. Too many Americans who felt left behind, too many people who are poorer than our parents. I believe the experiment failed." He listed seventy-two executive actions to address monopoly in many parts of the economy (Stoller 2021).

In terms of antitrust action, the Biden Justice Department offered its view on pending bipartisan legislation aimed at America's largest and most powerful companies. It regarded "the rise of dominant platforms as presenting a threat to open markets and competition, with risks for consumers, businesses, innovation, resiliency, global competitiveness, and our democracy," in the words of a letter written to the bipartisan leaders of the Senate Judiciary signed by the Justice Department's acting Assistant Attorney General Peter Hyun. "Discriminatory conduct by dominant platforms can sap the rewards from other innovators and entrepreneurs, reducing the incentives for entrepreneurship and innovation," as the letter from the department's Office of Legislative Affairs argued. It continued, "Even more importantly, the legislation may support the growth of new tech businesses adjacent to the platforms, which may ultimately pose a critically needed competitive check to the covered platforms themselves" (Tracy 2022). As the tech giants tried to buy major firms in adjacent sectors, the Biden administration took a dim view of their ambitions standing on the side of preserving competition over increased market power.

Its Brandeisian agenda was clear. Market power and the value extraction it allows were seen as harmful to the economy. The administration supported competitive markets; it was opposed by powerful corporate leaders who had no intention of being "led by an invisible hand to promote an end which was no part of his intention," but who chose rather to make decisions only with "regard for their own interest," which may not "intend to promote the public interest." The archetypal profit maximizer "necessarily labours to render the annual revenue of the society as great as he can" – to reprise Adam Smith as cited previously. It is the concentration of contemporary markets that permits the anticompetitive behavior which the Biden regulators sought to combat. But whether anything approaching a market in the spirit of Adam Smith can be recreated is another question.

Khan and Antitrust Division chief Jonathan Kanter launched a project to revamp how the government enforces antitrust law. They were taking a playbook from Ronald Reagan and rewriting the merger guidelines – but in reverse. Khan and Kanter returned competition policy, in contrast to President Reagan's Mr. French, to its original purpose, suggesting that when it comes to corporate power, big is usually bad. The administration took action in a number of concentrated sectors in which collusive practices were to be found. In one instance, the Biden Justice Department targeted the oligopolistic poultry producers who for decades had shared information with which they collectively controlled the prices they paid, forcing them to provide compensation of eighty-five million dollars to workers harmed by their schemes. The firms signed a consent decree promising to discontinue specific practices (Qiu 2022).

In terms of asking for public comments, the process would usually be confined to the province of economists and insiders, ignoring the public's views on big business. But the Biden appointees instead wanted to hear from the public, and they did. Earnest, informed responses came from doctors objecting to the predations of pharmaceutical companies, hospital chains, and insurance companies, and from small-business owners and independent contractors complaining of how large corporations were taking advantage of them; they asked the government to address the asymmetrical power that was exploiting and extorting them. There were reasoned complaints against banks as well, indeed directed at the financial system as it has come to be structured.

One submission read: "I am a screenwriter and the creator of the Netflix show Outer Banks. Mergers in the film industry have been horrendous for artists. It has massively suppressed wages. It has greatly limited creativity." The writer, Josh Pate, explained to the Federal Trade Commission that "There are now essentially 4–5 places to sell shows, a few years ago, there were over 20. The Disney Fox merger should NEVER have been allowed to happen. The media is FAR too consolidated." Another submission contended, "Concentrated corporate power is destroying the profession of pharmacy. After spending many years trying to understand why my chosen profession felt like it was dying, I now know that it is due to oligopolies and subsequent anticompetitive business practices." Both the suppliers and the purchasers (called pharmacy benefit managers or PBMs) for pharmacies and hospitals, it was explained that ninety-five percent of the drug wholesaler market is controlled by just three companies and three chains dispensed over eighty percent of the sale of prescription medications. Moreover, each is vertically integrated with an insurance company and each of these oligopolized markets was created through mergers that it can be argued should not have been allowed. Indeed, that was the put upon pharmacist was telling the FTC to do something about.

Compared to the type of comments sent to the FTC from lobbyists and other industry representatives, the FTC was to receive thousands of such personal entries from ordinary citizens from many walks of life explaining how monopolization was harming them personally. These public comments reflected a public awareness as Stoller (2020) observed that "[a]ntitrust law is essentially the law we use to structure all the money and power in corporate America, because it's the legal framework by which firms can exploit their market power. But for forty years, it's been essentially dormant, which is . . . why our society is so screwed up." He concluded enthusiastically, "that era of lethargy is over." Because the FTC has broad jurisdiction over privacy, consumer protection, and antitrust laws, "it can reorient how virtually every corporation in the country functions. It can write rules against "unfair methods of competition," which can include prohibiting anything from discriminatory pricing in industrial gas markets to addictive or deceptive user interfaces to certain kinds of targeted ads. It is time for progressive government to change each of these areas of abuse.

In carrying out such programs," personnel is policy," as a famous Washington saying has it, and Biden's appointees markedly differed from their typical predecessors. Gary Gensler, Biden's head of the Securities and Exchange Commission, acted quickly to cancel what his Trump-appointed predecessor had engineered to protect corporations from scrutiny. But he went further, requiring companies to disclose additional information about factors concerning climate change, workforce diversity, and political contributions. Under his guidance, the SEC proposed additional disclosures by Special Purpose Acquisition Companies (shell companies created to acquire a target company without the traditional initial public offering) that would ensure investors' understanding of the risks involved. The SEC voted to add yet another requirement, that private funds report details of material events to the agency within one business day. This would prevent the sort of practice mentioned earlier, that firms wait to reveal such information only after considerable time has passed. Such a policy involves what has been described by SEC Commissioner Hester Peirce as a "sea change" in federal regulation; until the Biden presidency, the SEC had not mandated disclosures by hedge funds, private equity funds, and others. Under a new proposal, they would also be required to provide investors with quarterly statements regarding fees and returns. Peirce, who had been appointed by President Trump, voted against these changes. SEC Chairman Gensler and the majority of commissioners argued that such rules would promote greater transparency and competition among the firms. "Private fund advisers, through the funds they manage, touch so much of our economy," Gensler stated. If adopted, "it would help investors in private funds on the one hand, and companies raising capital from these funds on the other" (U.S. Securities and Exchange Commission 2022).

The industry objected to having to disclose this data. As Drew Maloney, president of the American Investment Council maintained, "We are concerned that these new regulations are unnecessary and will not strengthen pension returns or help companies innovate and compete in a global marketplace." A contrary view was offered by reformers: "It's basic transparency," stated Carter Dougherty, a spokesperson for Americans for Financial Reform, an advocacy group. "These Wall Street titans are constantly telling us how great they are. If they object, one can reasonably wonder: What are they hiding?" (Whoriskey 2022). Republican politicians were quick to respond. Mike Lee, the Utah Republican who would head the panel overseeing antitrust enforcement if his party were to take control of the Senate, characterized Khan's "antibusiness agenda" as a "progressive putsch" (Nylen 2022: 19).

Toward the end of 2022, following two years of reconstituting the direction of competitiveness policy and placing a very different group of leaders in charge of the key agencies, the Biden administration began to win major cases. A U.S. district court judge ruled against a merger between Penguin Random House and Simon & Schuster, which if allowed would have reduced the major book publishers from five to four. The Justice Department's Antitrust Division based its argument on the finding that the consolidation would have restricted advances for authors. They would have had fewer companies competing for their services. "That's an argument about the impact of a merger on workers, not consumers, which Robert Bork famously argued was the only thing antitrust enforcement should concern itself with," as David Dayen points out, adding that the Justice Department "also claimed that cultural output would be reduced as a result of the merger, another novel (and correct) application of antitrust law." Jonathan Cantor, head of the division, also announced a guilty plea in a criminal monopolization case under Section 2 of the Sherman Act. It was the first case of its kind in forty-five years. The Justice Department further took steps against the anticompetitive practice of interlocking directorates, which, while clearly illegal, had been ignored for decades under Bork-thinking; as Dayen (2022) writes, "it's just that the section of the law barring the practice was simply forgotten during the decades of corporate domination of government." State attorneys general and Democratic committee chairs in Congress also moved to investigate antitrust violations.

Other developments in the economy requiring attention impacted not only the U.S. but, as in so much else, the rest of the world as well. These included a significant shift in financial intermediation from banks to direct finance, thence to asset managers, accompanied by the introduction of financial market logic into domains where it had previously been absent; this alteration has "not just led to negative developmental impacts, but also changed the 'rules of the game' and facilitated rent-seeking practices of a self-serving global elite," Servaas Storm (2018) asserts. Foremost among these is the trend that has been stressed here. In the 21st century up to 2017, the result was that "for every extra dollar of output, the world economy cranks out almost 10 extra dollars of debt." The trend would continue. Such statistics suggest a structural change in the political economy of our time to "a debt-peonage society" in Paul Krugman's (2005) judgment, one that Gabriel Palma (2009) describes as a "rentiers' delight," and Geoff Mann (2010: 18) finds "difficult to reconcile with any acceptable definition of democracy."

The half-forgotten designation "rentiers" is a term used by Adam Smith, who defined rentiers as capitalists who were able "to reap where they never sowed." In a more recent evaluation, Martin Wolf (2019) informs his *Financial Times* readers that rentier capitalism "means an economy in which market and political power allows privileged individuals and businesses to extract a great deal of such rent from everybody else." Such a critical evaluation deters neither the financiers designing and selling their products nor the investors buying them (Christophers 2020).

The rise of cryptocurrencies, robo-advisers, and the growing prevalence of a host of financial apps and meme trading, all were developments that led Gensler, recognizing that perhaps new multibillion-dollar industries might be emerging, to reexamine decades-old legal tests. How would these new areas be appropriately handled with existing definitions of what constitutes a security, investment advice, and stock recommendation? Would consumers in the new environment need to be protected against being taken advantage of in new ways that break existing laws? (Bain 2022). The criteria here, and in all the areas in which Gensler found material for investors, involved an assessment of the long-existing standard: "What is the substantial likelihood that a reasonable investor would find it significant to a total mix of information?" (Livni 2022). Investors and service buyers needed better protection and the new sector firms needed oversight.

Industry spokespeople and conservative politicians found overreach where Gensler saw the legitimate purpose of disclosing relevant information so that investors could make informed decisions. While it is not our purpose here to examine each of these issues, it is important to point out that the meltdown of cryptocurrencies bought by investors gambling on a rise in their future price (and for tax avoidance) did not seem to be a currency replacement in which private money would, as libertarian enthusiasts claimed, become a means of removing government from intermediation functions and making business and personal transactions less costly – and anonymous, away from the eyes of law enforcement and tax authorities. However, as Nouriel Roubini commented after the collapse of a major cryptocurrency firm in the winter of 2022, "crypto has turned out to be the Mother of All Scams." From a three trillion dollar market capitalization a year earlier it had lost two-thirds of that presumed valuation justifying Gensler's concern (Global Charts 2022).

Whatever the success of the antitrust actions were to be, there remained the structure of the economy that has accelerated the trend to a greater financialization of non-financial corporations, along with the rapid growth of firms focused on "managing" assets. The criteria used by the asset speculating firms have involved short-term returns, which force the actual managers of the units to calculate immediate returns rather than long-term company growth. This is a form of value extraction, which contributes to the slowdown of growth and the loss of U.S. competitiveness that the Biden White House and its appointees in the executive branch agencies were trying to reverse.

Examining these developments permits an interrelated set of arguments that should not be controversial. They are not involved, but they are significant. The first is that the economy has grown more concentrated with fewer, larger firms dominating. A second is that due to their dominance, these firms have the power to appropriate rents, earning well above what economists term "normal profits." A third is that the corruption is structural, integral to actually existing capitalism. Fourth, the usual analyses of financialization miss the degree to which these high-profit financial firms have also built intellectual property-based tollbooths similar to those constructed by the high-profit intellectual property firms, the tech firms dominating the commanding heights of the economy. Innovative startups reaching the scale at which they can challenge the industry incumbents in tech face "unprecedented obstacles." While venture capital is readily available, groundbreaking startups are growing "much more slowly than comparable companies did in the past." "Surprisingly," James Bessen (2022a) writes, "a major culprit is technology" Proprietary information technology suppresses industrial turnover, which has declined sharply over recent decades.

In addition to their financial resources, the big companies have the advantage of large customer bases, a cluster of products, and vast pools of data that have allowed them to increase their market dominance and avoid being overtaken by rivals. This has led to a loss of dynamism with broadly "negative implications for the U.S. economy." Research ties slower growth to substantially slackened productivity growth. This "affects the entire economy, all the way down to personal incomes," as Bessen (2022a) argues in MIT's *Technology Review* (also see Bessen 2022b). In addition, the Biden administration undertook action against tech companies for anticompetitive practices that have contributed to this development.

In the past, new technologies have spread widely either through licensing or as firms independently developed alternatives; these practices enabled greater competition and innovation. Government sometimes helped this process. Bell Labs developed the transistor but was forced by antitrust authorities to license the technology broadly, creating the semiconductor industry. Similarly, IBM created the modern software industry when, in response to antitrust pressure, it began to sell software separately from computer hardware. However, the most important new technologies "are proprietary, accessible only to a small number of huge corporations." Bessen (2022a) suggests that antitrust policy could be employed to "encourage or compel" more large firms to open their proprietary platforms. Loosening the restrictions that noncompete agreements and intellectual-property rights place on employee mobility would also foster a greater diffusion of technology. Their market power arises from a dominance that is a relatively new phenomenon in American capitalism, even as it demonstrates characteristics that echo the power of finance capital in the era of JPMorgan a century ago. It will take a political revolution approaching that of the Progressive Era and the New Deal for Americans to wrest control of their economic future from back the financiers and speculators whose profit seeking irresponsibility threaten further upward redistribution of the social surplus and potentially more devastating economic crises.

The question emerges as to whether the dominant private equity firms and Exchange Traded Funds (EFTs) can be put under social control even while the contradictions of a debt economy and the policy problematic of addressing inflation without provoking a significant economic crash remain. By the end of 2022, inflation had imposed a hiatus on the trends described in this chapter. Higher interest rates have meant many weak corporations deeply in debt had trouble meeting their obligations. If high interest rates persisted, many zombies would actually be dead. U.S. companies that accumulated a debt mountain exceeding ten trillion dollars, much of it as the Fed kept interest rates near zero, would have to produce at least 200 billion dollars in 2022 and 2023 to cover rising interest expenses, according to a *Wall Street Journal* analysis of data from Fitch Ratings of the companies it covers.

In addition to the fallout from the Fed's high interest rate to control inflation there is the concentration of ownership by asset management companies. Institutional investors own eighty-five percent or more of the S&P 500, with EFTs offering a low-cost way to diversify investments. The massive holdings of money managers, most prominently Vanguard, State Street, and BlackRock, make these three collectively the largest owners in more than four fifths of the S&P 500 companies; needless to say, the willingness of these asset managers to make their preferences known to corporate boards and managers has increased with their growth. Their holdings allow them to exert informal pressure, to meet with the management of hundreds of companies, making their views heard beyond stockholder meetings. They are capable of coordinating actions that amount to co-respective behavior among those who collectively exercise great market power. The new trusts are not the same as those the populists confronted in the 19th century, but they are hardly less powerful.

Such dominance has led Benjamin Braun (2022: 271) to argue that "this new 'asset manager capitalism' constitutes a distinct corporate governance regime."

The ability of asset managers to pool financial capital on such a scale allows them a position of control of particular companies while also maintaining a high degree of portfolio diversification. This provides significant structural power. It also explains the longevity, indeed the growing strength, of rentier capitalism. Now the question is the degree of influence they will impose on mergers of weak companies with stronger ones in which they also have large stock holdings.

The next chapter will explain such patterns of asset devaluation and collapse. Chapter 7 returns to a focus on the impacts of inflation and discusses policy responses and their class character.

References

Akerlof, George A. and Paul M. Romer. 1993. "Looting: The Economic Underworld of Bankruptcy for Profit." *Brookings Papers on Economic Activity*, 1993(2).

American Economic Liberties Project. 2021. The Courage to Learn: A Retrospective on Antitrust and Competition Policy During the Obama Administration and Framework for a New Structuralist Approach. *American Economic Liberties Project*, January 12.

Appelbaum, Binyamin. 2022. "When Choosing Judges, Democrats Must Stop Ignoring Economics." *New York Times*, June 1.

Appelbaum, Eileen and Rosemary Batt. 2014. *Private Equity at Work: When Wall Street Manages Main Street*. Russell Sage Foundation.

Appelbaum, Eileen and Rosemary Batt. 2019. "Private Equity Tries to Protect Another Profit Center." *The American Prospect*, September 9.

Ayash, Brian and Mahdi Rastad 2021. "Leveraged Buyouts and Financial Distress." *Finance Research Letters*, 38.

Bain, Ben. 2022. "Gary Gensler Eyes Rules for Robots." *Bloomberg Businessweek*, January 17.

Bessen, James. 2022a. "How Big Technology Systems Are Slowing Innovation: The Great IT Revolution is No Longer Promoting Economic Dynamism. It's Preventing It." *Technology Review*, February 17.

Bessen, James. 2022b. *The New Goliaths: How Corporations Use Software to Dominate Industries, Kill Innovation, and Undermine Regulation*. Yale University Press.

Braun, Benjamin. 2022. "Asset Manager Capitalism as a Corporate Governance Regime." In Jacob S. Hacker, Alexander Hertel-Fernandez, Paul Pierson and Kathleen Thelen, eds. *The American Political Economy: Politics, Markets, and Power*. Cambridge University Press.

Chaudhuri, Saabira and Tripp Mickle. 2015. "Where Should a New Beer Giant Call Home? For the Planned Merger of AB InBev and SABMiller, Deciding on Corporate Addresses is a Challenge." *Wall Street Journal*, December 15.

Chemnitz, Christine. 2017. "The Rise of the Food Barons." *Project Syndicate*, June 15.

Christophers, Brett. 2020. *Rentier Capitalism: Who Owns the Economy, and Who Pays for It?* Verso.

Cohn, Jonathan. 2021. *The Ten Year War: Obamacare and the Unfinished Crusade for Universal Coverage*. St. Martin's Press.

Coy, Peter. 2016. "Open Season on Business." *Bloomberg Businessweek*. February 25.

Dayen, David. 2022. "The Week Corporate Power Started to Dissipate." *The American Prospect*, November 4.

De Loecker, Jan, Jan Eeckhout and Gabriel Unger. 2020. "The Rise of Market Power and the Macroeconomic Implications." *The Quarterly Journal of Economics*, 135(2).

Drucker, Jesse and Danny Hakim. 2021. "A Revolving Door Keeps Tax Policy on Clients' Side." *New York Times*, September 20.

Editorial. 2017. "Buffett, the Brazilians and Chainsaw Capitalism." *Financial Times*, May 8.

Farrell, Maureen. 2022. "The New Financial Supermarkets." *New York Times*, March 10.

Garver, Paul. 2016. "Mondelēz Girds for War Against U.S. Bakery Workers." *Talking Union*, February 25.

Gensler, Gary. 2022. Statement on Private Fund Advisers Proposal." *U.S. Securities and Exchange Commission*, February 9. https://www.sec.gov/news/statement/gensler-statement-private-fund-advisers-proposal-020922.

Global Charts. 2022. "Global Cryptocurrency Market Cap Charts." *Coin Gecko*, November 17. https://www.coingecko.com/en/global-charts.

Goolsbee, Austan. 2020, "Big Sharks Are Starting to Swallow the World." *New York Times*, September 30.

Guyton, John, Patrick Langetieg, Daniel Reck, Max Risch and Gabriel Zucman. 2021. "Tax Evasion at the Top of the Income Distribution: Theory and Evidence." *National Bureau of Economic Research, Working Paper No. 28542*.

Idzelis, Christine. 2019. "Private Equity Changes Everything." *Institutional Investor*, October 16.

Krugman, Paul. 2005. "Is Fiscal Policy Poised for a Comeback? *Oxford Review of Economic Policy*, 21(4).

Langley, Monica. 2015. "Two Activists Put One CEO on the Spot." *Wall Street Journal*, December 16.

Levin, Bess. 2017. "Populist Hero Stephen Schwarzman's Birthday Blowout Included Fireworks, Acrobats, and Live Camel; Let Them Eat "Giant Birthday Cake in the Shape of a Chinese Temple." *Vanity Fair*, February 13.

Livni, Ephrat. 2022. "Gensler Reflects on His First Year as S.E.C. Chairman." *New York Times*, April 18.

Mann, Geoff. 2010. "Hobbes Redoubt? Toward a Geography of Monetary Policy." *Progress in Human Geography*, 34(5).

Merritt, Naomi. 2010. "Cannibalistic Capitalism and Other American Delicacies: A Bataillean Taste of The Texas Chain Saw Massacre." *Film-Philosophy*, 14(1).

Nylen, Leah. 2022. "Lina Khan, Start Your Engine." *Bloomberg Businessweek*, June 20.

Olson, Laura Katz. 2022. *Ethically Challenged: Private Equity Storms US Health Care*. Johns Hopkins University Press.

Palma, José Gabriel. 2009. "The Revenge of the Market on the Rentiers. Why Neo-liberal Reports of the End of History Turn Out to be Premature." *Cambridge Journal of Economics*, 33(4).

Parmar, Herma and Jason Kelly. 2019. "The Returns Are Spectacular. But There Are Catches." *Bloomberg Businessweek*, October 7.

Plotz, David. 1997. "Al Dunlap – The Chainsaw Capitalist." *Slate*, August 31.

Qiu, Linda. 2022. "U.S. Targets Poultry Processors in Labor Case." *New York Times*, July 26.

Rappeport, Alan and Tiffany Hsu. 2022. "Right-Wing Fury at I.R.S. Overhaul." *New York Times*, August 19.

Rennison, Joe and Hannah Kuchler. 2019. "US Healthcare Provider Loans Tumble as Politicians Target Patient Billing; Moves to Shield Patients from Unexpected Treatment Costs Leave Debt Investors Nervous." *Financial Times*, July 29.

Riggs, Taylor. 2022. "BW Talks Luca Zaramella." *Bloomberg Businessweek*, February 11.

Sanger-Katz, Margot, Julie Creswell, and Reed Abelson. 2021. "Mystery Solved: Private-Equity-Backed Firms Are Behind Ad Blitz on 'Surprise Billing." *New York Times*, September 13.

Silver-Greenberg, Jessica and Katie Thomas. 2022. "They Were Entitled to Free Care. Hospitals Hounded Them to Pay." *New York Times*, September 24.

Smith, Yves. 2022. " Eileen Appelbaum and Rosemary Batt Score Important Win Against Private Equity as Surprise Billing Laws Slam KKR Grifter Envision Healthcare." *Naked Capitalism,* March 16.

Stoller, Matt. 2020. "A Land of Monopolists: From Portable Toilets to Mixed Martial Arts." *Big*, July 10.

Stoller, Matt. 2021. "A Simple Thing Biden Can Do to Reset America." *Big*, January 1

Stoller, Matt. 2022a. "Big Tech Tries to Defund the Police." *Big*, February 16.

Stoller, Matt. 2022b. "The Secret Plot to Unleash Corporate Power." *Big*, April 8.

Storm, Servaas. 2018. "Financialization and Economic Development: A Debate on the Social Efficiency of Modern Finance." *Development & Change*, 49(2).

Tabb, William K. 1999. "Marx and the Long Run." In William K. Tabb, ed. *Reconstructing Political Economy: The Great Divide in Economic Thought.* Routledge.

Tracy, Ryan. 2022. "Antitrust Bill Targeting Amazon, Google, Apple Gets Support From DOJ." *Wall Street Journal*, March 28.

Vandevelde, Mark and Eric Platt. 2018. "KKR Agrees to Buy Envision Healthcare in $9.9bn Deal." *Financial Times*, June 11.

Whoriskey, Peter. 2022. "SEC Proposes Basic Rules For Private Equity, Hedge Funds." *Washington Post*, February 9.

Wigglesworth, Robin, Joe Rennison, and Antoine Gara. 2021. "Moody's Warns of 'Systemic Risks' in Private Credit Industry." *Financial Times*, October 26.

Wolf, Martin. 2019. "Why Rigged Capitalism is Damaging Liberal Democracy." *Financial Times*, September 18.

Wursthorn, Michael. 2021. "Black Friday Rout Shows Dangers of Margin Borrowing." *Wall Street Journal*, November 28.

6
THE MAINLINE TRADITION
AND ENDOGENOUS CYCLES

This chapter draws on insights of the transgressive Karl Marx and the widely mis-understood John Maynard Keynes, as well as of Hyman Minsky and contemporary economists who offer a useful alternative to the macroeconomics of mainstream theories and the models that continue to be deployed by the profession. The chapter describes the usefulness of the theory of endogenous crisis which can be contrasted to the incidence of exogenous crisis discussed in the next chapter.

Marx

The deep global financial crises from 2007 to 2008 revived interest in Karl Marx (always a counter-cyclical indicator of an economy in trouble). His conceptual categories and their deployment – fictitious capital, falling rate of profit, dispropor-tionality, and overaccumulation – provide insight into the contemporary conjunc-ture. Marx understood the role of finance in the capitalism of his time in ways that anticipate the current period. He explained,

> With the development of interest-bearing capital and the credit system, all capital seems to double itself, and sometimes treble itself, by the various modes in which the same capital, or perhaps even the same claim on a debt, appears in different forms in different hands. The greater portion of this 'money-capital' is purely fictitious.
>
> *(Marx 1894: Volume III, Part V, chapter 29)*

The concept of fictitious capital offers an antecedent to Keynes' understanding of the reason for the collapse of asset bubbles.

In an inquiry into the theory of crisis, which Marx developed in Volume II of *Capital*, Joan Robinson commented on the close affinities between Marx and

DOI: 10.4324/9781003385240-6

Keynes. A similar point was made by Joseph Schumpeter in his obituary of Keynes where he proposed that "though Keynes' 'breakdown theory' is quite different from Marx's . . . in both theories, the breakdown is motivated by causes inherent to the working of the economic engine, not by the action of factors external to it" (Schumpeter 1954: 284).

Howard Sherman explains that

> it was Marx, not Keynes, who first systematically dissected Say's law by showing that lack of effective demand can cause mass unemployment in capitalism. It was Marx, not Keynes, who first demonstrated in his famous reproduction schema that dynamic equilibrium is possible in capitalism if, and only if, effective demand grows, at a certain rate consistent with supply creation. It was Marx, not Keynes, who first showed that capitalists face not one, but two problems: (1) the problem of producing profit and (2) the problem of realizing profit.
>
> *(1991: 197)*

As the Great Depression produced a crisis, with the profession unable to explain what was going on, Say's Law reigned supreme – though as it should have been clear that it was hardly the case that the production process generates the income necessary for the demand for these products to be purchased. It should also have been apparent that such assumptions offered no explanation for the collapse of output and commensurate rise in unemployment. The same was the case, as Carolina Alves writes introducing a discussion of Joan Robinson's relation to Marx, that the microeconomic claim that each of the factors of production was paid the marginal value of its output was equally dubious, something made clear in the earlier discussion of market concentration and the power it gives the employer class to limit the wages of workers who use their incomes to consume. Marx had seen the advantage to the employer class advantage in the lack of options for those who did not own capital. In the next chapter when inflation is discussed, the class struggle will come into view even for moderate economists who typically regard labor and capital as factors of production that in a competitive economy are paid in relation to how much they contribute to output. That exploitation is not seen in the actual capitalist economy is a tribute to the victory of a marginalist thinking that obscures the absent center of economic relations.

Robinson was inspired by Marx's conviction that capitalism was run by capitalists and not the consumer presumed to be the sovereign in the marketplace. Profit-making and accumulation were central goals for the capitalist who "isn't at all interested in the full employment of workers" (Alves 2022: 248 citing Harcourt and King 1995: 34). Marx critically followed the step of classical political economists by looking into production and trade to understand the creation and distribution of wealth, with great attention to distributional conflicts. Some of his economic concepts may look as alien to a modern academic economist as they looked to Robinson in the late 1930s, but this did not dissuade Robinson (and should not put us off today) (Alves 2022: 250).

Addressing contemporary economists who are perhaps ignorant of Marx, Alves points out that in the Marxian schema, "capitalist and worker can be viewed as different agents with different interests, and their relationship is mediated by power," and that the monetary amount obtained by paying workers less than the amount they produce is called "surplus value." At the center of Marx's analysis is the absent center of contemporary mainstream economics: this relationship of power. Yet it is an understanding that is coming back into acceptance as the causes of growing inequality are better understood.

Robinson went beyond Keynes in recognizing the centrality of class power in determining economic outcomes. For economists unwilling to engage with Marx, reading Robinson allows them to grasp the essentials of his model, the origin of profit in the appropriation of surplus value. She sees that the Keynesian theory of unemployment as the failure of effective demand can be complemented by Marx's idea of non-employment: as the supply of labor grows faster than the number of jobs offered by the capitalist economy, an available and desperate pool of potential employees emerges. Robinson also highlights that this reserve army is one of the mechanisms behind the determination of real wage in the sense that the bargaining strength between capitalist and workers is key in determining the changes in the level of wages. Thus, when labor-saving technical progress reduces the need for workers, it tends to lower the wage rate while raising the rate of exploitation. As has been discussed, contemporary researchers understand that this is the case.

She reminds us that for Marx, if the rate of exploitation rises because costs fall due to labor-saving technical progress while money-wages remain constant, capitalists levy a restriction upon the purchasing power of workers, so that effective demand fails to expand with productive capacity. The labor share of output falls. Robinson seemed to embrace this notion of crisis, shared of course by the Keynesians, though based on a different logic (Alves 2022: 255). A second concern raised by Marx about the balance between the investment and consumer goods departments begins with the insight that the private profit of the capitalist is the sole motivation for production. In the same manner as Keynes, Marx divides all spending between consumption and investment (initially leaving aside government and foreign investment), but with a distinction between wage and profit income and the assumption that all wages are spent on consumption. If part of previous income is saved or if capitalists hoard money from their profits, total spending declines and overproduction results, in which case the value of goods supplied exceeds the planned spending. Overproduction, then, results in capitalists laying off workers and reducing investments.

Finance was not Marx's main interest in *Capital*. Rather, he focused on the exploitation of labor by capital, the relation between the two departments he distinguished in a capitalist economy: one that produces capital goods or means of production and one that produces consumer goods. The anarchy of production, the failure to realize profit, and the overaccumulation of capital are moments in the accumulation process that can produce crisis.

But Marx was also critical of the appropriations of financial capital (Harvey 1982 [1999], chapter 9). It is these insights that are considered here. While rooted in the specifics of his time and place, they are indicative of the continuing importance of finance and its contribution to crises in our time. Marx's discussion in Volume III of *Capital* certainly fits the events of 2007–2008:

> The chain of payment obligations due at specific dates is broken in a hundred places. The confusion is augmented by the attendant collapse of the credit system, which . . . leads to violent and acute crises, to sudden and forcible depreciations, to the actual stagnation and disruption of the process of reproduction, and thus to a real falling off in reproduction.

This pattern is the consequence of the incentives of those who, having enriched themselves through finance, can refuse to renew loans, causing businesses that are unable to repay to default, allowing their assets to be purchased at discount prices.

> The credit system, which has as its focus the so-called national banks and the big money lenders and usurers surrounding them, constitutes enormous centralization, and gives this class of parasites the fabulous power, not only to periodically despoil industrial capitalists but also to interfere in actual production in a most dangerous manner – and this gang knows nothing about production and has nothing to do with it.
>
> *(Marx, Capital Volume III, chapter 33)*

This too is a not inaccurate description of more recent events. And surely the key point Marx makes about fictitious capital is well taken. It is that claims to future income need not be as a bubble inflates be related to an actual realization of profit in production, and this can lead to a crisis. This phenomenon has occurred at other times and in other places not in his purview, in which financialization moved inexorably toward dominating the capitalism of a given conjuncture – for example that of Hilferding's *Finance Capital* a century ago (1981 [1910]). It occurs in our own time as well.

Fictitious capital does not have a material basis in commodities or productive activity. Instead, it relies on the anticipated future value that will be created to justify its paper valuation. According to Marx, when the extent of fictitious capital so exceeds the potential output that people begin to doubt the plausibility of market valuations, the price of assets can suddenly and dramatically fall. In his theory, an overaccumulation of capital results when capital cannot realize the expected rate of profit and financial assets can only be sold at a loss. When a critical mass of investors realizes this growing divergence, the price of assets laden with fictitious capital will drop precipitously. Financial capital, in short, exacerbates both upswings and downswings in economic cycles, with capitalist classes and their allies benefitting disproportionately.

The plural capitalist "classes" identifying those professionals who serve them is consistent with Marx's distinguishing numerous class fractions beyond the two dominant classes of an epoch, as in *The Communist Manifesto* when discussing contemporary or historical period political and economic struggles, which is perhaps confusing to readers (Ollman 1978).

To Marx's way of thinking, the contradiction between the use value and the exchange value of commodities that cannot be sold at the expected profit requires that assets be written down and losses taken. It is only at some lower price that markets will clear. Marxists, along with Austrian free-market economists, see this forcible reassertion of price to reflect value as the function of economic crises. Both schools of thought reject the notion of neoclassical growth models of steady-state growth from one equilibrium to the next with smooth, speedy adjustments. It was Marx's argument that the growth of fictitious capital increases faster than the ability of the economy to support its inflated valuations, resulting in a crisis in which the price of assets returns to realistic levels reflective of the real value created. In the current stage of financialized capitalism, we have seen fictitious capital production, supported by central banks and governments, allowing stocks and bonds to be sold for the previously expected valuations or for even greater valuations than had been foreseen before the downturn.

The speculative activity which inflated the asset bubble in the years leading to the Global Financial Crisis created paper valuations that were only tenuously connected to the productive output of the economy, instead being increasingly influenced by expected capital gains. Much of this speculative activity appears on the balance sheets of special investment vehicles, hedge funds, and private equity. Marx would explain that financialization (not a term he used, although he did write of "unproductive finance capital") is parasitic of the productive forces rather than developing them. Financiers who are unqualified to run an enterprise can restructure its assets in anticipation of financial returns. While financial bubbles and the appropriation of surplus depend on the creation of value in production, if the "parasites," a term he did use, feed off their host to the point of endangering it, the system itself can go into crisis.

The degree to which the appropriations of finance have been as extensive as they have is in itself unhealthy; Marx described the corruption of bankers who evaded punishment after their reckless behavior and swindles. (He would no doubt have taken pleasure in citing Charles Prince as a case in point.) He grasped the essential aspects of this phenomenon; analyzing the credit crises of his day, he argued that a banking system "subordinated" to capital accumulation would produce financial expansions that are inherently unstable, often overshooting due to "over-speculation" and "credit swindles." He recognized that a "large part of the social capital is employed by people who do not own it and who consequently tackle things quite differently than the owner." They would overreach, taking excessive risks with the money of the rentier class. Credit growth would stop, debt would come due, and nervous bankers would scramble, mostly unsuccessfully, for liquidity (Krause 2018). The sudden repricing of assets used in overnight repurchase agreements in the contemporary era is reflected in Marx's description of an abrupt collapse of price "acting like a feather which when added to the weight of the scales, suffices to tip the oscillating balance definitively." This concept of fictitious capital helps explain the Keynes-Minsky reading of business cycles.

Money Matters

One of the most influential ideas of the 1970s and 1980s was that policy did not matter. Based on rational expectations, this pronouncement by the new classical economists of the policy ineffectiveness hypothesis posits that monetary policy cannot systematically manage the levels of output, and employment in the economy further distanced the profession from Keynes (Sargent and Wallace 1975). But when crises strike, strong action works to impact the economy – as Paul Volker's dramatic intervention did and subsequent Fed actions have demonstrated. They do not however produce sustained stability and are often implicated in new crises. In what promises to be the classic treatment of monetary and fiscal policy over the sixty-year period from 1961, Alan Blinder (2022) finds that there has been little progress in managing the economy so as to produce economic stability.

"Despite the importance of enterprises and money in our actual economy, and despite the numerous and complex problems they raise," Milton Friedman (1962: 14) wrote in support of the post-Keynes New Classical Economics, "the central characteristic of the market technique of achieving coordination is fully displayed in the simple exchange economy that contains neither enterprises nor money." His view stands in stark contrast to Keynes' understanding as expressed in his *Essays in Persuasion* (1991 [1932]: 32) regarding the importance of money to the nominal owners of real assets, who "have not infrequently borrowed money in order to become possessed of them. . . . The interposition of this veil of money between the real assets and the wealth owner is a specifically market characteristic of the modern world." (It is a reality that Friedman and others in the present day, with similar assumptions built into their models, exclude from consideration. In the following, the critique of such thinking by Hyman Minsky explains why the continued stress on the money supply under the Fed's direction is a weak reed on which to depend.

Money matters in important ways beyond the simple role to which Friedman assigned it. In this regard, the failure of today's mainstream theory to explain the role of money in destabilizing the economy and its inability to offer practical solutions for financial dangers can be illustrated with a simple witticism. In 2014, commenting on the relationship between what the central bank was doing and what mainstream macroeconomic theory and its models assumed was the way monetary policy worked, Federal Reserve Chair Ben Bernanke offered what he called "the best QE joke ever!" The Fed's bond-buying program "works in practice but it doesn't work in theory" (Berkowitz 2014). This might suggest fault both with the theory and with the consequence of failing to understand that in the new stage of capitalist development the functions of finance require closer examination. Not only does money matter in ways denied by monetarists but institutions matter, and while fiscal policy was abandoned in the 1970s with stagflation and continues to be opposed by conservatives, in the U.S., the Biden administration has employed it effectively to protect American working people. Even Obama used a more conservative fiscal policy in the 2008 economic collapse.

Keynes

In the 1920s, Keynes attempted to establish the significance of stages of economic development along the lines laid out by John R. Commons, the American institutionalist to whom he wrote in 1927, "There seems to me to be no other economist with whose general way of thinking I feel myself in such general accord" (Skidelsky 1992: 229). Keynes' awareness of the importance of institutions never left him; a good deal of the conflict between him and those in the government he advised resulted from establishment figures not understanding when a new conjuncture had come into being in which old ideas no longer sufficed. As a self-defined Platonic guardian, Keynes spent his long career counselling policy makers who reluctantly took his advice, frequently only when they came to see no alternative. When they clung to what he saw as outmoded ideas, he went public, often with results that embarrassed the recalcitrant politicians. Given his recognition that changes in the economy had taken place that required its reform, his task was to rework institutional constraints. Today there is no single figure of Keynes' stature proclaiming heterodox approaches to the changes in the economic policy model that are needed. However, as will be seen in the final chapter, there are a number of increasingly influential economists who have gained attention for views that might be described in the term Keynes used for his own stance – liberal socialism (of which more later).

Keynes asserted that "theorizing starts by assuming a monetary economy with sophisticated financial institutions" and that "changing views about the future are capable of influencing the quantity of employment." In his view, it is "the financial attributes of a capitalist economy," which lead to "the observable unstable behavior" of that economy. On this basis he was able to explain credit crunches when funds are not available, or available only at unacceptable cost and terms, and to argue that unfulfilled expectations in finance often generate business cycles. It is in this crucial regard that pre-Keynes and post-Keynes neoclassical economics is unconnected to the actual world (Bertocco 2017). As a result, Keynes' policy conclusions, it is said, are ignored by most policy makers during every serious modern downturn (Komlos 2021). Better perhaps, they are ignored in theory but not always in practice, to draw on the *bon mot* of the Fed chair. Still, the observational skill and keen judgment of the sort exercised by Keynes as he followed the psychology of markets remain unwelcome, highlighting the extent to which traditional theory continues to ignore key aspects of the economy's functioning. Given the focus here on financialization, it can be noted that there is good reason to argue for the enduring relevance of his theories of the business cycle (Bortz 2021).

Still, basing policy conclusions on observations that are not supported by microeconomic foundations continues to be frowned upon in the precincts of mainstream macroeconomics. "The economist who accommodates reality, by using rules of thumb with no 'microfoundations' – meaning theoretical accounts of actions at the level of every individual – will often be criticized for ad hocery by their peers," Diane Coyle (2022) reminds us. As a result of this thinking, prestige journals are generally not interested in such submissions. Commenting, Simon Torracinta (2022) writes that Coyle contends the field "should abandon its utopia of pure reason and instead embrace the ad hoc nature of all approximations of reality. That means making more room for plausible narratives rather than airtight proofs, and borrowing qualitative methods from neighboring social sciences like sociology and anthropology." This has not widely occurred -- to the detriment of a needed economics that trades rigor for relevance according to Keynes.

The preface and also the first chapter of *The General Theory* begin by emphasizing not that the orthodox economics Keynes was critiquing had not erected a logically consistent model. It had. The fault lay rather in its claim to the generality of its premises. It is on this basis that he considered his to be the general theory, with their limited to conditions that often did not apply (1936: v and 3). His criticism was addressed to "the classical economists," a term he said in a footnote was invented by Karl Marx for the founders of the theory which culminated in Ricardian economics. Keynes also applied it to the group now considered to be the founders of neoclassical economics, most prominently Marshall, Edgeworth, and Pigou. It may also be employed to designate the Chicago School, which emerged to prominence, indeed to dominance, after Keynes' death.

Given his certainty that the economy is not a self-equilibrating system, Keynes opposed such theories. Market processes are unlikely to include the needed requisites for achieving full employment through their intrinsic workings; indeed, their normal functioning is disequilibrating, and if eventually a better situation emerges in the long run, "in the long run we are dead," as Keynes famously asserted in dismissing the eventual return to the satisfactory equilibrium expected by neoclassical economists. A key fault was that the Ricardians and those continuing in that tradition believed that "we can safely neglect aggregate demand." They ignored Malthus on the subject. Keynes (1936: 33) explained that this thesis, so central to his own model, "could only live on furtively, below the surface, in the underworlds of Karl Marx, Silvio Gesell or Major Douglas." The neglect by the dominant economists of the crucial nature of aggregate demand, Keynes argued, resulted in a practice that was of such "apparent cruelty" and so "austere and unpalatable" in its imposition that "the free activity of the individual capitalist, attracted to it the support of the dominant social force behind authority." It may have served powerful interests to force wages and working conditions down. The theorists did no better; "professional economists, after Malthus, were apparently unmoved by the lack of correspondence between the results of their theory and the facts of observation." The neoclassical theory, new classical theory, or as Keynes termed it "the classical theory," which prevailed in his time and again after the Keynesian Revolution, was dismissed. It was simply incorrect.

Unlike the economics modelled on 19th-century physics, which many economists aspired to emulate, Keynes' understanding of the psychology of markets allowed him to recognize that investors tend to believe that the present momentum will continue until a time is reached when they grow worried, at which point the bubble collapses. As long as the "animal spirits" of the investors beget mounting optimism regarding the future prospects of the economy, more money is invested, leading to increases in asset prices, real estate and equities to new and eventually unsustainable heights – until doubts arise. When they do, there is a rush to disinvest. Those who have not liquidated their holdings early enough find they can do so only at greatly decreased prices. The extended downturn, bred by pessimistic expectations, continues until optimism is reborn; eventually there is an upturn and another cycle occurs. This is the process of financial cycles, which have become more prevalent for reasons that have been discussed. The existence of this crisis pattern is supported by a contemporary analysis of IMF data (Beaudry and Willems 2022).

In Chapter 12 of *The General Theory*, Keynes explains that expectations are subject to the uncertainty which exists that is not reducible to mathematical risk calculation. As to the precariousness of the future, while each participant may think his own liquidity assured, there is no such thing as liquidity for the community of investors (speculators) as a whole; "Businessmen play a mixed game of skill and chance, the average results of which to the players are not known by those who have taken a hand" (1936: 150). In a downturn it becomes clear that each punter cannot have a safe way out when a class of assets in which many have invested declines significantly in value.

Keynes' contribution was grasped by John Hicks (1936), who reviewed *The General Theory* on its publication. He noted that from the standpoint of pure theory, its author's treatment of expectations was perhaps its most revolutionary element. His was a complex economy in which the distinction between risk, which involves a knowable probability distribution, and uncertainty, which implies an unknowable (as in uncertainty as first used by Frank Knight [1995 (1921)]), is central to Keynes' perception of financial markets (Dimand 2021).

Key economic decisions depend, Keynes asserted, on "habit, instinct, preference, desire, will, etc." He also believed that institutions matter, that conventional expectations and confidence formation can be understood, and that conditional stability is expected when periods of disorder occur. Keynes importantly rejected a core mainstream belief of economists that decisions are made by totally self-directed individuals. In formulating a Keynesian micromodel, James Crotty (1994: 119) writes that Keynes "assumed that agents are socially and endogenously-constituted human beings, not autonomously constituted, lifeless Walrasian calculating machines." This means that the theory of agent choice "must reflect both the social constitution of the agent (which is contingent on, and changes with, the institutions, values, and practices specific to time and place) as well as the psychological complexity of the human-being-in-society." As crises have occurred with increasing frequency and disturbing impact in recent years, the acceptance of uncertainty and habit is part of the complexity involved in decision-making.

Asset price inflation can become a process of self-levitation in which, as prices of paper claims grow, the assets can be used as collateral to borrow and then to buy still more assets, driving prices yet higher in a seemingly endless spiral. It is endless, that is, until it unceremoniously ceases; what remains are the many players who believed they would be able to sell and decamp before the collapse, with the more naive holding devalued assets and facing severe losses. Animal spirits lead to overextension and thence to fear and to market collapse. The Fed and other central banks have learned to avoid such an outcome, or at least to stop uncontrolled declines by buying assets that would otherwise fall precipitously. This use of monetary tools in place of fiscal policy was defended in the 1970s and 1980s on two bases. One is that fiscal policy takes too long to work; recognition and decision-making lags and unacceptable intervals inevitably occur before fiscal responses can take effect. Monetary policy in contrast, it was asserted, can respond quickly and effectively. The second entails a preference for a smaller role for government, which is accommodated by business cycle concerns being addressed by monetary rather than fiscal policy. Monetary policy slowing the economy, as is seen in the present moment, functions by hurting working families. Fiscal policy under liberal guidance can prioritize tax cuts to the corporations and the wealthy, helping working people survive a crisis.

By the beginning of the 21st century, the use of fiscal policy as a stabilization device had "all but vanished, more or less explicitly in Europe and de facto in the United States. The practical consequences have not been entirely satisfactory, in either place." This produced a questioning of why the eclipse of fiscal policy had occurred and whether it was justified (Solow 2005). The first objection to fiscal policy (as noted earlier) fell into disrepute as monetary policy failed to bring rapid or successful recovery and recessions continued to plague economies. Paul Krugman (2005) argued that economic slumps last for a number of years, offering ample time to implement fiscal expansion: "As a result, the case for fiscal policy made by the first generation of Keynesians has experienced a real revival." His journal article was optimistically titled, "Is Fiscal Policy Poised for a Comeback?" Arguing against what was then the current "new consensus" theoretical framework, a number of other Keynesian economists found the basic proposition of this thinking, that fiscal policy provides at best a limited role, to be unconvincing; they called for a revival of Keynes' approach to economic downturns (Arestis and Sawyer 2003).

The second explanation of why fiscal policy had been rejected continued in force. Yet when the Global Financial Crisis struck, in terms of their actions policy makers appeared as convinced Keynesians, with some economists dusting off their copies of *The General Theory* for review. Keynes' understanding of business cycles, detailed in "Notes on the Trade Cycle," chapter 22 of *The General Theory*, has been more familiar to economists either in the original or for the reminder by Keynesians of what had been explained therein. Keynes had written in *The General Theory*, "The transfer from wage earners to other factors is likely to diminish the propensity to consume." As the economic research detailed earlier reveals, less income for workers slows growth. Keynes (1936: 287) criticized those economists who did not recognize that the decrease in money wages, which they advocated – their policy solution to a depression – ignores the impact of lower aggregate demand. He also saw that for firms and industries with "a relatively low elasticity of employment [such as today's tech firms] a large proportion of it will go to swell the income of entrepreneurs and a smaller proportion to swell the incomes of wage earners and other prime-cost factors." Fiscal policy that supported working-class consumption, such as spending for job creation and government benefits for families, was necessary to raise aggregate demand. Keynes, the Bloomsbury denizen that he was, also endorsed spending on cultural monuments of beauty as well as needed housing for the poor.

Keynes criticized new classical economics for assuming that all other things can be held constant with useful results derived; of course, all other things cannot practically speaking be held constant, as useful as it might be to assume this for mathematical tractability. This struck home for many in times of crisis, in which interdependencies are so obvious and cumulative causation evident. The additive practice of statistical testing can easily miss the nature of the real world. The *ceteris paribus* assumption that led to the precision of neoclassical models was, he judged, misleading in a mutatis mutandis world of evolutionary change and interactive causation. Importantly, in addition these models assume things to be known that cannot be known.

In *The General Theory*, Keynes (1936: 137, 140) offered damning examples of the "pitfalls of a pseudo-mathematical method, which can make no progress except by making everything a function of a single variable and assuming that all the partial differentials vanish." He charged that "[t]oo large a proportion of recent 'mathematical' economics are merely concoctions, as imprecise as the initial assumptions they rest on, which allow the author to lose sight of the complexities and interdependencies of the real world in a maze of pretentious and unhelpful symbols." Much contemporary work has this quality, being part of a conversation among blackboard economists with little connection to the real world – as for instance Jeremy Rudd's critique of 21st-century macroeconomics.

Keynes himself was a superior mathematician (O'Donnell 1990). His objection was to the effort to obscure the fundamental uncertainty regarding the future that could not be reduced to mathematical risk, that is, the disregard for the way expectations are actually formed. The choice of the model used should always fit the circumstances of the real situation faced by policy makers. In a modern depression, 19th-century laissez faire thinking is harmful and in policy discussions should be replaced by what, as noted earlier, Keynes (1925) termed "liberal socialism": "a system where we can act as an organized community for common purposes and to promote economic and social justice, whilst respecting and protecting the individual – his freedom of choice, his faith, his mind and its expression, his enterprise and his property." In Keynes' more detailed explanation of liberal socialism, he emphasized that the overwhelming majority of investment in the economy should be placed under government control or guidance. It may be noted that all of this did not seem very radical in the 1930s, nor does it to many today, especially to young people whose lives have known a loss of faith in capitalism that has robbed them of opportunity and provided poor job prospects.

Keynes was confident that the elite-educated liberals could provide innovative policy proposals that would offer a solution for existing problems, although he was often unable to overcome the prejudices of the very serious people of the British Treasury and Whitehall whose political choices often clashed with the need for radical change that he embraced (Crotty 2019; Fuller 2019). Perhaps this was due to suspicions generated by Keynes' (1933) judgment of the capitalism of his time, that "it is not intelligent, it is not beautiful, it is not just, it is not virtuous – and it doesn't deliver the goods. In short, we dislike it, and we are beginning to despise it. But when we wonder what to put in its place, we are extremely perplexed."

As early as his 1925 essay, "Am I a Liberal?" he wrote, "The transition from economic anarchy to a régime, which deliberately aims at controlling and directing economic forces in the interests of social justice and social stability, will present enormous difficulties both technical and political. I suggest, nevertheless, that the true destiny of New Liberalism is to seek their solution." He concluded *The End of Laissez-Faire* (1926) with the injunction: "We need a new set of convictions which spring naturally from a candid examination of our own inner feelings in relation to the outside facts."

Keynes viewed "the rentier aspect of capitalism as a transitional phase which will disappear when it has done its work. And with the disappearance of its rentier aspect much else in it besides will suffer a sea-change." In advocating a liberal socialism in which most investment would be carried out by the public sector under the direction of a government responsive to the popular will, he declared (1936: chapter 24) that "this state of affairs would be quite compatible with some measure of individualism, yet it would mean the euthanasia of the rentier, and, consequently, the euthanasia of the cumulative oppressive power of the capitalist to exploit the scarcity-value of capital."

Keynes and American Keynesianism

In the 1930s Keynes was attacked by conservative economists, most prominently by Fredrich von Hayek and Ludwig von Mises. The conflict over ideas about freedom, coercion, and democracy between Keynes and Hayek had also occurred between Hayek, John R. Commons, and the philosopher John Dewey. Hayek feared the political power of majorities and legislatures. He proposed limiting the rights of voters and the discretion of legislators. Commons and Dewey, on the other hand, were concerned with the consequences of corporate power. They promoted policies designed to increase the participation, deliberation, inquiry, and intelligence of citizens in public affairs, an important supplement to Keynes' advocacy of innovative economic programs (Chasse 2022). Such broad debates over markets and government have resurfaced in the present period as a consequence of popular economic fears, with public concern evident in the arguments regarding "free enterprise" as opposed to greater government activism. This debate is ongoing, as will be discussed in the concluding chapter. There has also been a renewed effort to restrict the franchise to those deemed worthy, but discussion of this political movement, which features conservative white Christians fearful of the changing complexion of the electorate, would take us too far afield from our focus.

In the 1950s, the counter-Keynes movement in macroeconomic theory again gained momentum. Prominent voices argued for the importance of equilibrium theorizing over what was criticized as "ad hoc factoids." Keynes (1936: 34) had preemptively responded to such attacks when he wrote, "It may well be that the classical theory represents the way in which we should like our economy to behave. But to assume that it actually does so is to assume our difficulties away." However, this is exactly what most "Keynesians" did following his death.

Crotty suggests that there is not a single model in *The General Theory* but rather five overlapping models, only one of which is recognized by so-called Keynesians; as a consequence, they continue to omit consideration of many of his important innovations. There is the short-run IS/LM model, which is taught to every economics student who ventures beyond a first-year introductory course (introduced by Hicks 1937). Typically, no attention is paid to a long-term model of secular stagnation, to a dynamic business cycle model, or to the endogenously generated instability in financial and real markets. Alternative approaches found in Keynes' writings involve disequilibria and instability in asset prices, offering a short-term model of extreme instability originating in financial markets. The first Keynesian model, taken from *The General Theory*, omits the fundamental uncertainty of expectations and the confidence with which they are held, along with the likelihood of a divergence between expectation and realization, the impacts of casino capitalism, and the conditions, which can lead to secular stagnation. Modeling based on Keynes' insights also forms part of the technical literature that has followed close readings of *The General Theory* (Marglin 2021).

The second reason noted earlier for the rejection of Keynes in the early 1950s, a time in which liberal economic ideas were equated with un-Americanism, was due to powerful conservatives having become active in policing what was taught in universities and what ideas were deemed proper for government policy. This had consequences for the development of academic economics.

A year after the death of Keynes, Lorie Tarshis (1947) published a textbook in which his ideas figured prominently. *The Elements of Economics* included a discussion of Joan Robinson's theory of imperfect competition and Edward Chamberlin's of monopolistic competition as well as Keynes' understanding of the macro economy. In contrast the standard principles books of the period dealt only with perfect competition and monopoly with little discussion of macroeconomics beyond the exogenous causes of disequilibrium and the claim that the working of supply and demand in a free market restores full employment and stability. When Tarshis' book was first published it was popular and widely adopted for classroom use. However, it was not long before a nationwide campaign by wealthy conservatives threatened the withdrawal of funding from any university, especially any elite private university, which adopted it. With such threats, its sales fell (Colander and Landreth 1996).

In the conventional works neither the gold standard nor sound finance (balanced budgets) was subject to debate. Conservative criticism of Tarshis' departures from orthodoxy included an attack on his lack of admiration for the market system and the claims of private property. The message conveyed to students by other texts was that unimpeded markets offer the most efficient and just way to organize an economy, since all factors of production receive compensation equal to what they contribute so long as unions and government do not interfere. Any contrary statements, as David Colander and Harry Landreth explain, "were heresy" to most economists (n.d.).

One should not underestimate the impact of the controversies that accompanied followers of Keynes such as Tarshis in the America of the late 1940s and the 1950s. Conservatives identified Keynesianism with the despised New Deal liberalism. The acolytes of Senator Joseph McCarthy condemned such iconoclastic economists as "red agents" (MacIver 1955). Paul Samuelson (1992) wrote decades later that "the McCarthy era, in my judgment, posed a serious threat of American fascism." He observed "at close hand the fears and trembling that the Harvard and MIT authorities experienced and those were the boldest of American institutions."

Why then was Samuelson's 1948 "Keynesian" textbook widely accepted and for decades the standard for the profession? The answer is that Samuelson produced what Joan Robinson termed "Bastardized Keynesianism." He redirected the profession to the so-called Keynes-Neoclassical synthesis, which in his textbook and the wider profession replaced Keynes. Thereafter what was radical in Keynes' theory was not to be found in American Keynesianism. Thus, when Keynesianism was attacked, as it was, what was defended was not Keynes' understanding but a seriously compromised substitute. Among other things, it did not include his views about the misdirection of investment and his conclusion that "the current volume of investment cannot safely be left in private hands" (Keynes 1936: 320–321).

Regarding the textbook dispute, Colander and Landreth remark that:

> the result of this episode was to sanitize economic textbooks from much of the controversy that makes economics exciting. The shift helped create a technicalization of what we teach students, and in doing so has influenced the direction of economics away from the true policy debates which necessarily involve clashes of ideology, and toward a discussion of make-believe policy fights centered around technical aspects of models.
>
> *(1996: 12)*

In the current period, textbooks do include issues of significance but often from a perspective that reflects a fear of being too opinionated, if this means stepping too far from widely accepted mainstream thinking.

From the 1950s and McCarthyism to the present, the rejection of the real Keynes has empowered the conservative economic thinkers more favored by business and university boards (Lawson 2015). Taken together, burying the real Keynes, accepting Samuelson, and condemning Tarshis, have impacted the subsequent development of macroeconomics. What has resulted is a field that demonstrates an incapacity to explain the causes of business cycles and uncontrolled speculation in the presence of uncertainty. The basic point has been made by Robert Skidelsky:

> Whereas Keynes made "underemployment equilibrium" depend on "inescapable uncertainty about the future" . . . leading U.S. Keynesians like Paul Samuelson made it depend on sticky wages and prices. This opened the door to stabilization policy while eliminating the heart of Keynes's theory, which was mathematically intractable.
>
> *(2021)*

Such thinking led to the acceptance of such ideas as rational expectations (that market participants had internalized all relevant information about the future course of markets) and sometimes to overly confident forecasting based on mathematically precise statistical models of expected risk.

If the academic wars resulted in the near disappearance of the intellectual legacy of John Maynard Keynes from Keynesianism, what happened to Marx is hardly surprising (Mattick 1972: 258). In his best-selling text in the mid-1950s at the height of the Cold War and rapid anticommunism, Samuelson (1957) termed Marx "a minor post-Ricardian" and, in a journal article "dissecting" the Marxian economic model, he suggested that "in a perfectly competitive market it really doesn't matter who hires whom; so let labor hire capital." Such a dismissal of Marx may have been a tactic of self-defense, given the conservative hegemony of the 1950s which further insulated Samuelson from criticism. However, as satisfying as such a slight to Marx may have been, to employ such a starting point – as unreasonable as Samuelson's statement presuming the existence of "a free market" in which labor could hire capital. In any way relevant to the real world – this was surely seriously specious and one may wonder why Samuelson put the premise forward.

The Minsky Contribution

In 1985, Hyman Minsky wrote of how the function of money had changed during the previous decades – though this had not altered how economists thought about money. The assumption that the central bank controls "with adequate precision" the quantity of exogenous money was simply wrong, he argued. So also were the claims that "banks still are viewed as passive reactors" which transform high-powered money provided by the Fed into public money, and that profit-maximizing behavior "by business apparently does not extend to banks and bankers." Minsky emphasized the conflict between a central bank's function of controlling the money supply and its role as the lender of last resort.

It is now clear that the Fed wishes to protect the financial system, leading it to bail out overextended banks rather than allow a "too big to fail" institution to bring down the entire financial edifice (Leonard 2022). This creates a moral hazard, argued Minsky (1985). He urged that banks be forced to hold greater reserves, and that the central bank return to the use of the discount window only where banks needing help could apply and could be turned down if submitting impaired collateral. Open-market operations in the contemporary period have produced the expansion of money through the Fed buying below investment grade assets. The latter strategy had replaced the earlier one, undermining the accountability of both the banks and the central bank.

Explaining the causes of financial crises, Minsky (1986) distinguished among what he termed "hedge financing," in which the cash flow from an investment is expected to be more than sufficient to meet contractual payment; speculative financing, where the cash flow is expected to be less than the cash repayment commitment in some, typically near-term periods, but adequate to fund interest on the debt; and Ponzi financing, a situation in which cash flow covers neither principal nor interest, with the borrower wagering that the value of the asset would rise sufficiently to meet the required payment commitment. While hedge finance exposes borrowers to danger if receipts fall short of expectations, speculative and Ponzi financing add additional vulnerability to borrowers in the wake of any changed circumstances in the financial market. The more finance moves from hedge to Ponzi financing, the more unstable the economy becomes. Minsky's (2006 [1977]) financial instability theory describes the process of events that led to the widespread demand to constrain banks and investors from taking unwarranted risks. His model has been found useful for heterodox economists, with better answers to offer for the 2008 and 2020 financial crises.

Speculation in assets and productive capacity tends to move in surges of optimism. Crisis follows when the expected profit is not realized. Mainstream economists ignored even the possibility that a rise in corporate leverage in the 1980s could increase the risk of a sudden economic downturn, having been taught that it did not matter whether corporate investment was funded by stock sales or borrowing (Modigliani and Miller 1958). What looked to mainstream economists like the "Great Moderation" in the years leading up to the 2008 financial crash (because there was little inflation in consumer or wholesale goods) was in fact distinguished by a rising use of credit, pyramiding leveraged buying, and rapid asset valuation inflation, accompanied by rising risk.

Explaining how the neoclassical synthesis and the Keynes theories differ, Minsky (1986: 103, 139–40) wrote that the "focus of the neoclassical synthesis is on how a decentralized market economy achieves coherence and coordination in production and distribution." He explains that "the focus of the Keynesian theory revolves around bankers and businessmen making deals on Wall Street. The neoclassical synthesis ignores the capitalist nature of the economy, a fact that the Keynes theory is always aware of." Because "theory lends legitimacy to policy," the neoclassical synthesis "puts blinders on policy makers by restricting the legitimate options to manipulating government spending and taxation and operating upon the money supply." In the Keynes understanding on the other hand, when animal spirits grow excited, Minsky's speculative finance can quickly turn into Ponzi financing. When debt repayment cannot be maintained, the Minsky moment has arrived and the financial system goes into crisis.

In such a narrative, a Keynes-Minsky overextension leads to a correction, to a fall in asset prices, and thence to bankruptcies, falling wages, and increased unemployment. There is no immediate "efficient market" correction (Minsky 1986: 103, 139–140). Minsky argued for a causal sequence from the creation of bank credit to increased aggregate demand, profits, and inflation. He regarded the globalization of production and the decline in the power of unions as ending any fear of future wage-led inflation, whereas financialization had amplified the business cycle and the movement in asset inflation over the prior forty years. He emphasized the importance of excessive bank lending as the key determinant of greater aggregate spending precipitating profit-led inflation. In his view, financial crises were made likely by attempts, especially by households, to pay off outstanding debt. This dampens aggregate demand, causing a slowdown (Kim 2022). Minsky has been proven correct. But he may have underestimated the willingness of the Fed to continue the extension of credit to investors in order to protect the value of their risky assets, which otherwise would have collapsed. He did not see that central bankers would moderate recessions at the cost of creating ever greater moral hazard and subsidizing the expansion and greater profitability of financial capital. As has been demonstrated, their policies have slowed productivity growth and made income distribution more unequal.

Mainstream economists have much to explain. It is not only that they famously failed to respond meaningfully to the Queen of England, but as James Crotty has written, "It is not likely that deregulation would have been so extreme and the crisis so threatening had most financial economists adopted Keynes-Minsky, which concludes that unregulated financial markets are inherently unstable and dangerous." Instead, he writes,

> they argued that neoclassical efficient financial market theories demonstrate that lightly regulated markets generate optimal security prices and risk levels, and prevent booms and crashes. Efficient market theory became dominant in spite of the fact that it is a fairly-tale theory based on crudely unrealistic assumptions.
> *(2011)*

Forecasting and Macroprudential Regulation

A slowdown in economic activity can be predicted not only by the growth of speculative activity and increasing leverage to the point that asset valuations may collapse but by rising household debt, not only in the U.S. but in other countries where changes in household debt-to-GDP ratios have been found to correlate strongly with a subsequent rise in unemployment (Sufi and Mian 2018). Longer-run data from many countries confirm this relationship. An increase in the household debt-to-GDP ratio has been shown to predict lower GDP growth and higher unemployment in the medium run for thirty countries over roughly the last half century (Mian, Sufi, and Verner 2017). Corporate, bank, and non-bank financial institution debt may provide an even better indicator of impending difficulties.

Drawing on data from seventeen countries over nearly 150 years, Bjorn Richter, Moritz Schularick, and Paul Wachtel offer evidence that policy makers can distinguish between good and bad credit booms with high accuracy and that they can do so in real time. They cite episodes from modern financial history which demonstrate how credit booms that are accompanied by housing price booms and a rising loan-to-deposit ratio is much more likely to end in a systemic banking crisis. They evaluate the predictive accuracy of models which reveal that the characteristics of the credit boom contain valuable information for sorting the data into good and bad booms, and that this information, if made available to policy makers, can guide them in taking action to intervene before an economy crashes (2021). Of course, as the present moment painfully demonstrates, there are factors external to the economy – war, crop failures, and disease – that also produce deep economic disturbances. It is these which are uppermost in the minds not only of economists but of the general public and in the growth of political movements, influencing voting decisions. Under such circumstances, models of endogenous growth and crisis must give way to the power of conjunctural forces, as the next chapter shall discuss.

References

Alves, Carolina. 2022. "Joan Robinson on Karl Marx: His Sense of Reality Is Far Stronger." *Journal of Economic Perspectives*, 36(2).

Arestis, Philip and Malcolm Sawyer. 2003. "Reinventing Fiscal Policy." *Journal of Post Keynesian Economics*, 26(1).

Beaudry, Paul and Tim Willems. 2022. "On the Macroeconomic Consequences of Over-Optimism." *American Economic Journal: Macroeconomics*, 14(1).

Berkowitz, Ben. 2014. "Bernanke Cracks Wise: The Best QE Joke Ever!" *CNBC*, January 16.

Bertocco, Giancarlo. 2017. *Crisis and the Failure of Economic Theory: The Responsibility of Economists*. Edward Elgar.

Bortz, Pablo Gabriel. 2021. "Keynes's Theories of the Business Cycle: Evolution and Contemporary Relevance." *Levy Economics Institute, Working Paper No. 986.*

Chasse, J. Dennis. 2022. "Coercion, Freedom, and Democracy in Hayek, Dewey, and Commons." *Journal of Economic Issues*, 56(1).

Colander, David C. and Harry H. Landreth. 1996. *The Coming of Keynesianism to America: Conversations with the Founders of Keynesian Economics*. Edward Elgar.

Colander, David C. and Harry H. Landreth. n.d. "Political Influence on the Textbook Keynesian Revolution: God, Man, and Laurie Tarshis at Yale." http://articles/Political %20Influence% 20on% 20the%20 Textbook%20Keynesian%20 Revolution.pdf.

Coyle, Diane. 2022. "Rethinking Supply Chains." *Project Syndicate*, June 10.

Crotty, James. 1994. "Are Keynesian Uncertainty and Macrotheory Compatible? Conventional Decision Making, Institutional Structures, and Conditional Stability in Keynesian Macromodels." In Gary Dymski and Robert Pollin eds. *New Perspectives in Monetary Macroeconomics: Explorations in the Tradition of Hyman P. Minsky*. University of Michigan Press.

Crotty, James. 2011. "The Realism of Assumptions Does Matter: Why Keynes-Minsky Theory Must Replace Efficient Market Theory as the Guide to Financial Regulation Policy." https://scholarworks.umass.edu/cgi/viewcontent.cgi?article=1112&context=econ_workingpaper.

Crotty, James. 2019. *Keynes against Capitalism: His Economic Case for Liberal Socialism.* Routledge.

Dimand, Robert W. 2021. "Keynes, Knight and Fundamental Uncertainty: A Double Centenary 1921–2021." *Review of Political Economy*, 33(4).

Friedman, Milton. 1962. *Capitalism and Freedom.* University of Chicago Press.

Fuller, Edward W. 2019. "Was Keynes a Socialist?" *Cambridge Journal of Economics*, 43(6).

Harvey, David. 1982 [1999]. *Limits to Capital.* Verso.

Hicks, J. R. 1936. "Keynes' Theory of Employment, Interest and Money." *Economic Journal*, 46(182).

Hicks, J. R. 1937. "Mr. Keynes and the 'Classics': A Suggested Interpretation." *Econometrica*, 5(2).

Keynes, John M. 1925. "Am I a Liberal?" *The Nation & Athenaeum, Part I August 8, and Part II August 15.*

Keynes, John M. 1933. "National Self-Sufficiency." *The Yale Review*, 22(4).

Keynes, John M. 1936. *The General Theory of Employment, Interest, and Money.* Harcourt, Brace and Company.

Keynes, John M. 1991 [1932]. *Essays in Persuasion.* W.W. Norton & Co.

Kim, Hongkil. 2022. "Minsky's Theory of Inflation and its Theoretical and Empirical Relevance to Credit-Driven Economies." *Journal of Economic Issues*, 56(1).

Knight, Frank Hyneman. 1995 [1921]. *Risk, Uncertainty and Profit.* University of Chicago.

Komlos, John 2021. "Humanistic Economics, a New Paradigm for the 21st Century." In Edward Fullbrook and Jamie Morgan, eds. *Post-Neoliberal Economics.* World Economics Association Books.

Krause, Laurence A. 2018. "Marx on Credit, Agency Problems, and Crises." *World Economics Association Conference "The 2008 Economic Crisis Ten Years On."* https://the2008crisistenyearson.weaconferences.net/papers/marx-on-credit-agency-problems-and-crises/

Krugman, Paul. 2005. "Is Fiscal Policy Poised for a Comeback?" *Oxford Review of Economic Policy*, 21(4).

Lawson, Catherine. 2015. "The 'Textbook Controversy': Lessons for Contemporary Economics." *Journal of Academic Freedom*, 6.

Leonard, Christopher. 2022. *The Lords of Easy Money: How the Federal Reserve Broke the American Economy.* Simon & Schuster.

MacIver, Robert M. 1955. *Academic Freedom in Our Time.* Columbia University Press.

Marglin, Stephen A. 2021. *Raising Keynes. A Twenty-First-Century General Theory.* Harvard University Press.

Marx, Karl. 1894. *Capital.* Edited by Frederick Engels.

Mattick, Paul. 1972. "Samuelson's 'Transformation' of Marxism into Bourgeois Economics." *Science and Society*, 36(3).

Mian, Atif, Amir Sufi, and Emil Verner. 2017. "Household Debt and Business Cycles Worldwide." *Quarterly Journal of Economics*, 132(4).

Minsky, Hyman P. 1985. "Money and the Lender of Last Resort." *Challenge*, March/April.

Minsky, Hyman P. 1986. *Stabilizing an Unstable Economy.* Yale University Press.

Minsky, Hyman P. 2006 [1977]. "The Financial Instability Hypothesis." In Philip Arestis and Malcolm Sawyer, eds. *Handbook of Radical Political Economy.* Edward Elgar.

Modigliani, Franco and Merton Miller. 1958. "The Cost of Capital, Corporate Finance and the Theory of Investment." *American Economic Review*, 48.

O'Donnell, R. M. 1990. "Keynes on Mathematics: Philosophical Foundations and Economic Applications." *Cambridge Journal of Economics*, 14(1).

Ollman, Bertell. 1978. "Marx's Use of 'Class'." In Bertell Ollman ed. *Social and Sexual Revolution: Essays on Marx and Reich*. Black Rose Books.

Samuelson, Paul M. 1957. "Wages and Interest: A Modern Dissection of Marxian Economic Models." *American Economic Review*, 47(12).

Samuelson, Paul M. 1992. "My Life Philosophy: Policy Credos and Working Ways." In Michael Szenberg, ed. *Eminent Economists*. Cambridge University Press.

Sargent, Thomas and Neil Wallace. 1975. " 'Rational' Expectations, the Optimal Monetary Instrument, and the Optimal Money Supply Rule." *Journal of Political Economy*, 83(2).

Schumpeter, Joseph A. 1954. *History of Economic Analysis*. Oxford University Press.

Sherman, Howard J. 1991. *The Business Cycle: Growth and Crisis Under Capitalism*. Princeton University Press.

Skidelsky, Robert. 1992. *John Maynard Keynes: The Economist as Savior, 1920–1937*. Penguin Books.

Skidelsky, Robert. 2021. "What Killed Macroeconomics?" *Project Syndicate*, November 16.

Solow, Robert M. 2005. "Rethinking Fiscal Policy." *Oxford Review of Economic Policy*, 21(4).

Sufi, Amir and Atif Mian. 2018. "The Real Engine of the Business Cycle." *Project Syndicate*, March 5.

Tarshis, Lorie. 1947. *The Elements of Economics*. Houghton, Mifflin.

Torracinta, Simon. 2022. "Bad Economics." *Boston Review*, March 9.

7

INFLATION IN THE CONTEMPORARY CONJUNCTURE

The previous chapter argued that endogenous factors, primarily the oscillation of over-optimism and pessimism in markets can explain financial crises. It stressed that Keynes was correct in his theory, that "animal spirits" promote overconfidence which cannot be maintained, and that when opinion suddenly changes a business cycle downturn occurs that lasts until investors see reason for optimism and a bandwagon builds that will again at some point turn sharply to pessimism and another asset bubble will collapse. This chapter explores the reality that exogenous events too can trigger financial collapse, imposing uncertainty in markets and for policy makers. And while the focus of this book is on the financialization of the American economy, the decisions made in Washington affect the rest of the world and actions of the Federal Reserve conducted to promote employment and control inflation domestically, substantially affect other nations, their banks, businesses, and citizens. This is hardly news.

The Fed's decision to increase U.S. interest rates in the 1980s led to the Latin American financial crisis and to that in Asia in the 1990s. Negative repercussions also occurred from Africa to Eastern Europe and beyond. The greater integration of financial markets by the 2020s made Fed policies even more problematic for the economies of the rest of the world. When interest rates went up in the U.S., policy makers elsewhere had to follow or face devastating capital flight, with the value of their currencies falling, reducing their capacity to pay for needed imports.

Most afflicted by the policy of high interest rates were the poorest nations, who could not afford to import the basic necessities of energy and food without more substantial help from the World Bank and the International Monetary Fund – which extended record loans during this period but minimal debt relief. Even wealthier European nations found their inflation soaring, requiring them to defensively raise interest rates to prevent their currencies from losing value and to combat an inflation

DOI: 10.4324/9781003385240-7

over which they, like the U.S., had little control. One of the most unexpected policy directions was that of the Conservative Party in the U.K. under Prime Minister Liz Truss; it was widely seen as a great mistake, indeed a disaster as will be discussed later in this chapter. First, however, consideration needs to be accorded to the misgivings which prevailed before these events, when the fear concerned the consequence of continued record low interest rates.

Before the Inflation

Noting that bond prices at the time reflected the lowest rates in history, Paul Singer (2021), a successful Wall Street investor and the founder of one of the world's largest activist funds, wrote at the close of 2021 that "across the market landscape, risks are building, many of them hidden from view. Yet, in a surprising twist, a growing number of the largest investors in the world – including socially important institutions such as pension funds, university endowments, charitable foundations and the like – are currently lining up to take on more risk, which could have catastrophic implications for these investors, their clients' capital and the stability of broader public markets." The reason, he explained, was the "radically expansionary" monetary and fiscal policies that had accelerated with the Covid-19 pandemic. Exceptional securities valuations had induced investors to overweigh their portfolios with stocks "even at record-high prices, for fear of missing out on extraordinary gains" He was writing at a moment when correlated risks were perhaps at their highest levels in modern market history.

Singer warned that

> Currently, policies across the developed world are designed to encourage people to believe that risks are limited and that asset prices, not just the overall functioning of the economy, will always and forever be protected by the government. Due to this extraordinary support for asset prices, almost all investment 'strategies' of recent years have made money, are making money and are expected to keep making money. The most successful 'strategy,' of course, has been to buy almost any risk asset, leaning hard on the latest fads, using maximum leverage to enhance buying power.
>
> *(2021)*

The expectation held by investors and speculators alike – with little real distinction between the two – was that there would be another Fed/Treasury bailout should one be necessary. At the same time, Singer offered the view that the ability of governments to protect asset prices from another downturn "has never been more constrained. The global $30tn pile of stocks and bonds that have been purchased by central banks in order to drive up their prices has created a gigantic overhang." Central bankers were "reaching the limits of their ability to support asset prices in a future downturn without further exacerbating inflationary pressures." The result?

"perhaps long-lasting damage when the government-orchestrated music finally stops" Other observers had grown similarly nervous as stock prices continued to rise considerably faster than company profits (Gandel 2021). Eventually, some unforeseen turn of events could trigger a substantial downturn.

Such warnings were soon lost with the arrival of an economic downturn from a very different set of causes. Yet the structural weakness that existed and continues to be present, obscured as it has been by the pandemic and the war in Europe should be noted. It should also be theorized in the context of the response to the Great Recession or Global Financial Crisis.

The extent of the American central bank quantitative easing in response to the 2008 financial crisis had been unprecedented, resulting in part from the Fed chair's research as an academic economist. Ben Bernanke understood that bank failures were responsible for making the Great Recession as deep and long as it had been. His historical explorations of how bank runs had turned an ordinary recession in the 1930s into the worst global economic crisis in history led him to the conclusion, as he demonstrated that bank failures – rather than resulting from the downturn – were responsible for making it so deep and so long. When banks collapsed, valuable information about borrowers disappeared, making it difficult for new institutions to channel savings to productive investments, as the Nobel Committee recounted in awarding him its prize in 2022. The lesson Bernanke drew from this study was that to prevent such a consequence during the 2008 crisis, dropping interest rates to near zero and purchasing assets worth a then-record four trillion dollars could stop the decline of the economy and, he hoped, revive economic activity.

The bailouts necessitated by the new crisis went broadly unquestioned even as they concealed signs of serious weakness in the economy. UBS analysts estimated that in March, 2020 as much as 140 billion dollars of investment grade bonds might fall to junk status and be dumped unceremoniously on the market. As *Bloomberg Businessweek* quoted a financial analyst, "We have to get the markets to function normally so that all these companies that we need to be up and running and paying their employees can borrow" (Boston 2020). There was no discussion of what "normally" meant, although once again it clearly required bailing out finance, as had occurred during similar previous crises. This is the reality of an economic system in which society has been made dependent upon financialization.

The extended period of the record low interest rate policy had consequences that have been discussed. The strategy did prevent a depression that could easily have resulted from both financial collapses, but it produced the debt trap that remains. The extent to which indebted companies, households, and countries were to be endangered when the Fed dramatically raised interest rates to fight inflation tested the determination of the central bankers. If they continued to raise rates in their campaign to bring prices down, they would be doing so by creating a recession. Given the policy lags, the timing of when to ease off on this high interest rate program was difficult to gauge. Pursuing the policy too long could threaten a depression, at least in many countries if not in the U.S. directly, although the blowback from international markets could be very damaging to the American economy.

This does not mean there were not analysts worried about the possible impacts. A record volume of such loans was held in collateralized loan obligations products, in a potential repeat of the 2008 financial collapse meltdown (which had involved mortgage-backed securities). "The optimized economy is full of debt chains," Citigroup's Matt King warned, with an extended lockdown eventually sparking an "exponential" wave of collapses that not even the five trillion dollars at the disposal of the Fed would be able to prevent. Secretary of the Treasury Mnuchin denied this possibility. Like other administration officials, he promised that a reopening was imminent, and that an economic rebound would quickly follow. (White House officials also stressed that scientists would soon develop cures for Covid-19.) As this official optimism was broadcast, about half of U.S. companies would miss their payments, according to the private estimates shown to Gillian Tett (2020) by bankruptcy lawyers. As she thought, "until this medical miracle appears, it will be solvency and not liquidity problems that haunt the economy. Woe betide investors or politicians who confuse the two." Not much came of such warnings.

Heiner Flassbeck and Paul Steinhardt (2018: 780) argue that government deficits will continue to be necessary "forever," or for as long as the net savings of the private sector continue. The point is that while higher public investment would be helpful, "the old notions on prudent public finance are fundamentally obsolete." The common way of thinking, that government should balance budgets and shrink spending, "is now more than obsolete; it is outright stupid." They are not alone in seeing the necessity for government to serve as the engine of growth. The conservative policies of cutting government social spending and giving more to "job creators" place the capitalist system "on a direct road to collapse worldwide," Flassbeck and Steinhardt warn. Such pessimistic fears were widely shared. But conservative ideology blamed government for economic problems and wanted to shrink, not increase, its size and scope. At the same time, without tax increases that conservatives opposed tenaciously, government spending could only come from increased borrowing.

Ruchir Sharma (2021), a chief global strategist for Morgan Stanley Investment Management, views the world to be in a debt trap. He argues that "the debt-soaked and asset-inflated global economy is so sensitive to rate increases that any significant rise is just not sustainable. Surely, if all the standard explanations are falling apart then something deeper must be going on." Asset prices grow, as does the cost of servicing the debt. Both are sensitive to rate increases. Sharma suggests that even mild tightening "could tip many countries into economic trouble. The number of countries in which total debt amounts to more than 300 per cent of GDP has risen over the past two decades from a half dozen to two dozen, including the U.S." Attempting to halt this process by raising interest rates sufficiently would deflate elevated asset prices – but could also produce a new, and perhaps a deeper economic crisis if pursued without great care. Looking at weaknesses in the major economies of the world, Kenneth Rogoff (2022) asked: "Is the global economy flying into a perfect storm, with Europe, China, and the United States all entering downturns at the same time later this year?" His view: "The risks of a global recession trifecta are rising by the day."

Economic uncertainty has deepened with rapid inflation, impeding understanding of the long-term trends in the financialized economy; moreover, the politics created by the strength of the extreme right, for whom anger at a system that was poorly understood but actively hated, has similarly impeded serious economic debate. Nevertheless, the Fed and other central banks saw no alternative to drastically and quickly raising interest rates, which they insisted, was required to prevent a wage/price spiral to become embedded in the economy as the expectation of continued inflation solidified. Michael Hudson's (2021) conclusion stands, that "we face a stark choice: either debt write-downs followed by renewed and more equitable income growth; or continuing wealth concentration, accelerating debt growth, widespread foreclosures and another crash."

Inflation and Quantitative Easing/Tightening

Unlike other recent crises, when the covid pandemic struck, rather than austerity being imposed governments extended significant assistance to citizens. The American Rescue Plan and the Coronavirus Aid, Relief, and Economic Security (CARES) Act were passed while Donald Trump was president. Other programs were legislated after Biden became president. They were understood by economists such as Larry Summers to have overheated the economy, bringing on inflation. Others stressed the positive achievement produced by the desperately needed help that the government had extended through these acts to suffering Americans and their families in the face of the economic dislocations brought on by the covid pandemic. When the Biden administration had first proposed a large relief package, it was defended by the administration as both expansionary and inexpensive (given that the government could then borrow at low cost). But as interest rates rose the U.S. deficit also increased, worrying the Congressional Budget Office among others. While the increased government spending was blamed for the rising inflation, it was a minor aspect compared to the impacts of the pandemic on supply chains and the Russian invasion of the Ukraine which were both far more important in creating the inflation.

Biden economists Jared Bernstein and Ernie Tedeschi (2021) pointed out, although little attention was given to their account, that the administration's Rescue Plan and the investment plans spend resources over different time horizons. The American Rescue Plan offered front-loaded relief – fast-acting direct checks to households, enhanced unemployment insurance benefits, and grants to businesses hit by the pandemic – which was designed to provide funds more expeditiously than the infrastructure and Build Back Better plans were expected to do. White House economists estimated that ARP fiscal support would come to about seven and a half percent of GDP in its first year, 2021. In contrast, in its first year (2022), they expected the infrastructure and BBB plans to disperse just over half of a percent of GDP. This reflects both the longer timeline of infrastructure spending and the fact that the infrastructure and BBB plans would, if passed as designed, be covered through revenue increases.

Closely divided politically, Congress did not pass the ambitious industrial policy plan. But even with only a more modest version of the Biden plan being adopted, the U.S. economy's rebound from the Covid recession had been five times faster than its recovery after the Great Recession. However, this was accompanied by a rate of inflation not seen in four decades. The Federal Reserve responded to rapidly rising prices with a policy of severe economic tightening (ET). What was ignored by those with a single-minded focus on inflation was the potential long-term impact of the administration's progressive, supply-side investment plan. "The transportation, rail, public transit and port investments will reduce efficiency-killing frictions that keep people and goods from getting to markets as quickly as they should," Bernstein and Tedeschi argued (2021). "The child and elder care investments will boost the labor supply of caretakers. The educational investments in pre-K and community college will eventually show up as higher productivity as a result of a better-educated work force." The beneficial impacts of the spending would be felt they argued long after inflation had been brought under control.

Many participants in the policy discussion could not consider the two elements simultaneously; in rejecting Build Back Better it was evidently ignored that the administration in its spending and industrial policy initiatives was working to increase U.S. competitiveness and make the economy more efficient in ways that were at the same time redistributive, increasing jobs and welfare. These elements were not considered in the single-minded attack on inflation that was shaking asset markets.

In the spring of 2022, the Federal Reserve started to raise interest rates and reduce its nine trillion dollar-balance sheet (which had almost doubled during the Covid-19 pandemic, an expanding ninefold since 2008). Asset markets initially accepted this quantitative tightening. They were depressing animal spirits by pulling money out of the economy, suggesting to Gillian Tett (2022) that "it beggars belief that Powell could crush consumer price inflation while leaving asset prices intact."

Chairman Powell's comments that monetary policy would depend on how much inflation dropped were read by many in the investment community that the Fed "put" was history, and that Powell was effectively endorsing the selloff in U.S. equities that had taken the S&P 500 to the edge of a bear market (defined as a twenty percent decline from the market high) at the time he made his remarks. He was clear that the ultimate indicator that would set policy was the consumer price index: "What we need to see is inflation coming down in a clear and convincing way, and we're going to keep pushing until we see that." Krishna Guha and Peter Williams, analysts at the research firm Evercore ISI, concluded that "The immediate significance of Powell's remarks is that he put to bed any idea that the decline in the equity market and wider tightening of financial conditions to date might trigger a 'Fed put'" (Anstey 2022). However, as the corporate profit results came in, demonstrating that the companies had continued to do well (being able to raise prices above the increase in their costs as discussed), the stock indices advanced. But the future remained uncertain, with markets fluctuating unpredictably. It seemed the Fed was "playing chicken" with the markets while it acted to increase unemployment to put downward pressure on wages to cut inflation.

Fed Shock and Demand-Led Versus Supply-Caused Inflation

It is well to remember that the Volker shock of 1979 had raised the Federal Funds rate to their highest level in history (by April 1980 interest rates had climbed above seventeen percent). The consequence of this course of action was that in the second quarter of 1980, the GDP had contracted by almost eight percent. Thousands of businesses and farms went bankrupt and unemployment peaked at almost eleven percent in what was the deepest economic downturn since the Great Depression. Writing two months after Barro expressed the view cited previously, James Galbraith (2022) insisted that "There is no compelling reason to raise interest rates, now or later." He did regard future price pressures to be inevitable but judged a progressive, anti-inflationary strategy both possible and necessary to support job creation and sustain living standards without involving the Fed. It was corporate markups of price over cost rather than wage increases that caused the inflation (Konczal and Lusiani 2022). The contrast between economists on the political right and left was clear.

The debate that ensued concerned how long the inflation was likely to persist and so how extreme the Fed's response should be, and what alternative policy was possible. None of the participants in the discussion could know the answer to the first question. They could not agree as to how much weight to ascribe to the factors contributing to the inflation. Those who viewed it as a supply-side phenomenon pointed to Covid-related supply chain issues. It has been widely noted that supply networks are designed to be fragile, a strategy that lowers cost so long as nothing goes wrong, but that makes them vulnerable to even small disruptions (Elliott, Golub, and Leduc 2022). And Covid's impacts were far from mild (Tooze 2021); nor was the dramatic increase in the cost of energy in Europe as a consequence of the war in Ukraine a minor matter.

Market power allowed corporate profits to rise above their costs, contributing to inflation, although this empirical finding was rejected by many who believed marginal cost pricing to prevail. Those arguing for the former explanation based their conclusion on data, breaking down the three principal components of cost: labor, non-labor inputs, and the "markup" of profits over the first two components. Following this procedure, comparing the pre-covid era with the post-covid inflationary period, Josh Bivens (2022) finds that over half of the increase in prices (54%) could be attributed to larger profit margins, with labor costs contributing less than eight percent. He maintains that "Instead, the already-excessive power of corporations has been channeled into raising prices rather than the more traditional form it has taken in recent decades: suppressing wages."

In contrasting his findings with the demand-side inflation narrative, Bivens (2022) commented that evidence from the past forty years "suggests strongly that profit margins should shrink and the share of corporate sector income going to labor compensation (or the labor share of income) should rise as unemployment falls and the economy heats up. The fact that the exact opposite pattern has happened so far in the recovery should cast much doubt on inflation expectations rooted simply in claims of macroeconomic overheating." His policy recommendation is that an effective way to prevent corporate power from being channeled into inflation, causing higher prices, is an excess profit tax.

"Despite its legal mandate to pursue full employment with price stability, the Fed – in practice – appears to fear tight labor markets even when prices are not going up," James Galbraith (2022) concluded based on research he did with colleagues (Galbraith, Giovannoni, and Russo 2007). "We also found a striking partisan political bias in monetary decisions. During the period we studied, after accounting for both inflation and jobs, interest rates were sharply higher (and yield curves flatter) in presidential election years when the Democrats held the White House. In every model we ran, this bias was substantial." Galbraith suggested that there is nothing surprising about this because

once one discards the myth that the Fed operates like a non-partisan priesthood. America's central bank is dominated by partisan Republicans from the business class – in financial circles, at the regional Federal Reserve Banks, and on the Federal Reserve Board, where Democratic presidents habitually reappoint Republicans.

(2022)

Lawrence Summers, a confirmed inflation hawk who blamed the rapid rise in prices on labor, tweeted that a new era of "populist antitrust policy" could lead to an economy that is "more inflationary and less resilient." Maintaining that the Biden administration was dangerously returning to failed policies of the past, he contended that its policy statements "better reflect legal doctrines of the 1960s than economic understandings of the last two decades." "There are real risks," Mr. Summers tweeted (May 22, 2022). "Policies that attack bigness can easily be inflationary if they prevent the exploitation of economies of scale or limit superstar firms." He dismissed the idea that market power itself was causing inflation.

In reality, the temptation offered by concentrated market power to extort customers is substantial – because it pays to do so. In contradistinction to Wall Street Democrats, the puffery of business-oriented think tanks and anti-government right-wing media is the reality that widespread collusion extracts from consumers an average of twenty percent in the typical price-fixing agreement (Katsoulacos and Ulph 2013). Rigging prices and market-sharing agreements have thrived, based on both formal and informal understandings. There has been little chance of getting caught and, should companies be charged and found to have taken part in collusive practices, fines are modest.

Supporting findings that market power was heavily responsible for the inflation following the outbreak of the pandemic, Matt Stoller (2021a) compiled some rough numbers. In 2019, just before the pandemic and contra Summers, non-financial corporations made about a trillion dollars in profit. By the end of 2021 these firms were making $1.73 trillion a year. Stoller calculated that for every American man, woman, and child in the U.S., corporate America had made $3,081, which then increased to $5,207, a gain of $2,126 per person. In order to understand the significance of that amount relative to inflation, he calculated what inflation was costing the average American. He then multiplied the GDP by the inflation rate. This amounted to 1.577 trillion dollars, or $4,752 per American. This informal calculation reveals that increased profits for corporate America comprised forty-five percent of the inflationary rise in costs. Thus, corporate profits alone were responsible for a three-percent inflation rate for all goods and services in America, all other factors causing the remainder. In other words, had corporate America kept the same average annual level of profits in 2021 as it had from 2012–2019, passing on the excess to consumers, the inflation rate would have been a little over three percent, or almost half as much. Stoller declared, "that's a big difference. Indeed it is the difference between Americans getting a raise, and seeing real wages decline." It turned out that sixty percent of the increase in inflation was going to corporate profits.

Adding weight to the above calculations, Stoller referred to results from Digital. com, a survey research firm that asks businesses about inflation. Fifty-six percent of retailers told the questioners that "inflation has given them the ability to raise prices beyond what's required to offset higher costs." Such price hikes, Digital.com found, were concentrated among larger retailers, with sixty-three percent of big firms using inflation to more than offset costs, as opposed to fifty-two percent of small and medium-sized businesses; of those which increased their prices, twenty-eight percent of the large enterprises raised prices fifty percent or more, compared to only six percent of small and medium-sized enterprises. Size and market power matter. Supply chain disruptions have worked to the advantage of Amazon and Walmart compared to independent retailers. They obtain supplies at existing prices, with costs covered by raising what small businesses are charged (Adams 2022). As Stoller (2021b) concluded, "one person's profits are another person's costs, because firms buy and sell to each other. So when firms raise prices to increase profits, then this increases costs for those who buy from those firms, and accelerates the expectation of more inflation elsewhere. Profits, in other words, are also driving inflation."

Supply chain costs include transporting goods. These have also increased. Shipping lines have been consolidated and capacity pulled offline with the goal of increasing pricing power. The container shipping industry enjoyed 190 billion dollars in profits in 2021, five times its entire profit from 2010–2020. Whereas before deregulation, loose cooperatives with many different shipping lines set prices publicly, today a small number of alliances who use ultra-large container ships that can only fit in a small number of ports do so secretly, explains Stoller. He drew on sources suggesting that fifteen to twenty percent of the total increase in inflation comes from higher shipping costs, which has allowed a great expansion of profit for companies involved in the business.

Others continued to attribute inflation to wage gains. They assert that tight labor markets had increased the bargaining power of workers. A survey conducted for The Wall Street Journal in 2022 found that job-switchers were often reaping double-digit pay raises: "About 64% of job-switchers said their current job provides more pay than their previous job. . . . Nearly 9% are now making at least 50% more." These findings suggested that such wage hikes cause inflation to rise. Workers who change jobs and receive large pay increases incentivize employers to raise wages in order to retain existing workers. Those worried about wage inflation point out that the annual wage growth for the typical worker rose to six percent in March, 2022, averaged over three months, according to the Federal Reserve Bank of Atlanta's wage tracker. However, the consumer-price index had risen eight and a half percent in March from a year earlier.

As inflation continued to rise, wages lagged and the labor share of income fell; inflation was reflected more in corporate profits than it was for labor costs. The concentration in markets allowed nonfinancial corporate profits as a percent of GDP to reach record levels. Firms that already had higher pre-pandemic markups – the difference between profits and costs – increased even more during the pandemic. Konczal and Lusiani (2022: 41) found that between 1960 and 1980 markups averaged twenty-six percent above marginal costs and have been on a consistent rise ever since. The average markup charged in 2021 was seventy-two percent above marginal cost. Moreover, eighty-one percent of the average increase in markups from 1980 to 2019 came from increases within industries, "pointing," they wrote, "to a generalized increase in market power."

Joseph Stiglitz and Ira Regmi (2022: 41) concluded in a review of the available data that the inflation is largely driven by supply shocks and sectoral demand shifts and not by excess aggregate demand, it was clear that "such increases in interest rates will not substantially lower inflation unless they induce a major contraction in the economy, which is a cure worse than the disease." They asserted that "Most importantly, an economic downturn like that is likely to have long-lasting adverse effects, and the most marginalized in society will bear the brunt."

As to the social spending extended due to Covid: "We got a lot more growth, we got less child poverty, we got better household balance sheets, we have the strongest labor market by some metrics I've ever seen," declared Jared Bernstein, an economic adviser to President Biden, defending the decision. "Were all of those accomplishments accompanied by heat on the price side? Yes, but some degree of that heat showed up in every advanced economy, and we wouldn't trade that back for the historic recovery we helped to generate" (Smialek and Casselman 2022).

Lawrence Summers and others who continued to blame government spending call for austerity measures; but the Covid-induced increase in spending only had a statistically small impact. The evidence however, suggests that returning corporate profits to more historical levels, with the labor share recovering to values associated with the pre-pandemic or even earlier decades, would mean inflation could fall more rapidly and higher wage growth could be sustained. If profits fall, it could mean lower inflation for any level of wage growth (Brainard 2023). This could be achieved, as it had been during World War II by price controls.

After the war according to Gallup polls, more than three quarters of the public favored extending controls. Meg Jacobs (2021) recounts that President Harry Truman lost a fight in Congress to do so, and that in the absence of an immediate postwar conversion to a civilian economy, supply shortages led to rapid inflation. In the next election the Democrats lost control of Congress for the first time since 1932. While Truman condemned the "do-nothing" Republicans who placed blame for rising prices on union power, the problem was actually, the president maintained, corporate power. He declared that "The Republicans don't want any price control for one simple reason: the higher prices go up, the bigger the profits for the corporations." More recent Democratic presidents, from Jimmy Carter on, accepted Republican tokenism and policies that allowed the working class to suffer the burden of countering inflation. Joe Biden has been the exception, endorsing trade unionism, wage increases, better working conditions, and higher taxes on the wealthy. However, although executive branch actions were supportive of workers, he did not have the necessary votes to achieve the pro-labor legislation he had advanced.

The Inadequacy of Central Bank Tools and Thinking

As to monetary policy, what can work are the policies central banks reject: specific credit policy that encourages and discourages different kinds of loans and encourage sand discourages too rapid credit in the aggregate. Economists have shown that allowing the expansion of credit greatly in excess of economic growth has triggered financial crises, the pattern both Marx and Keynes among others understood and that the research cited in the previous chapter shows to be relevant – that changes in household debt-to-GDP ratios have been found to correlate strongly with a subsequent increase in unemployment (Sufi and Mian 2018; Mian, Sufi, and Verner 2017). Corporate debt held by vampire companies, banks, and by non-bank financial institutions with their extremely high leverage has been shown to be dangerous and intermittently damaging, as demonstrated in the earlier chapters of this study.

The Fed engaged in a balancing act, fighting inflation while worrying about the unwanted impact of higher interest rates. Expressing what was widely believed but rarely verbalized, writing in the *Financial Times,* Brendan Greeley (2022) notes that every Federal Reserve press conference follows the same pattern: when reporters ask when the Fed will be satisfied that its tools are working, the Fed chair replies that the central bank is watching carefully, informing the media in one formulation or another, that monetary policy has a "long and variable lag." Greeley explained that the "exquisite phrase 'long and variable lag' is a technical-sounding way of saying 'we don't know and we don't know when we will know'." How long will it take for higher interest rates to stop the inflation? Will it do so by producing a recession forcing the Fed to lower interest rates again? And how long will the lags be before lower interest rates stimulate the economy, assuming they have that impact given the loss of confidence? Are the unanswerable questions that are asked. The point Greeley makes is that "central bankers remain forever in lag."

But perhaps more important is the lack of effective fiscal policy to fight inflation – imposing taxes to claw back price markups that were causing inflation. Congress was not interested in passing windfall profit taxes and increasing personal tax rates on the wealthy back to the levels that had governed to hold down inflation during World War II when it was an ever-present danger "and we were all in it together." In 1944–1945, couples making more than $200,000 faced a tax rate of ninety-four percent.

As economists debate whether the lags that accompany economic tightening, allowing high interest rates to prevail so long that the effort to stop the inflation brings on a serious recession or even a global depression, it is useful to remember the elements that characterize contemporary capitalism, as discussed earlier. While the immediate issue is the inflation/growth trade-off, the slow growth that has characterized the global economy has structural roots in the new stage of financialized capitalism, globalization, and the monopolization of intellectual property that together characterize the extended present of capitalism, especially American capitalism.

Greater global savings that have exceeded demand for investment in productive capacity and production of non-financial goods and services have kept global interest rates low, even as some governments, having used deficit financing to a dangerous extent have been forced to pay more to borrow. The extended period of low interest rates for decades prior to the 2020 financial crisis has been termed the Great Moderation, for which the Fed took particular credit for sound management. But it was actually part of a damaging strategy of holding interest rates down in an unsuccessful effort to increase the rate of economic growth.

The Global Picture

As inflation picked up in 2022, International Monetary Fund Managing Director Kristalina Georgieva declared that supply chain disruptions, inflation, and tighter monetary policy were "throwing cold water on the recovery everywhere." IMF economists raised their forecast for what the Covid-19 pandemic would cost the global economy to $12.5 trillion through 2024, she reported (Shalal 2022). Attention focused on Russia as a supplier of oil and natural gas to Western Europe. But Russia and the Ukraine also accounted for thirty percent of the world's wheat exports, seventeen percent of corn, thirty-two percent of barley, and seventy-five percent of sunflower seed oil. Russia exported about fifteen percent of the world's fertilizer. Consequently, a month into the 2022 invasion, wheat prices had increased by twenty-one percent, barley by thirty-three percent, and some fertilizers by forty percent. China revealed that severe flooding the previous year had delayed the planting of a third of the country's wheat crop; the upcoming harvest looked bleak.

Poorer countries would be competing for limited food supplies (Nicas 2022). Global financial crises have a different impact on the countries of the periphery in which a credit crunch gives rise to a sharper spike in interest rates and a deeper recession; a credit flight to the core alleviates the adverse consequences in these money center countries (Farboodi and Kondor 2022). The lack of purchasing power among the world's poor, always a problem, intensified. The price system would "work"; given shortages those who could afford to pay more would. The poor would starve.

What The *Wall Street Journal* described as the U.S. dollar "experiencing a once-in-a-generation rally" has had idespread impacts. "In a worrying sign, attempts from policy makers in China, Japan and Europe to defend their currencies are largely failing in the face of the dollar's unrelenting rise," the paper reported. Along with from the dramatic fall of the British pound, there were damaging declines for the yen and the yuan. The Egyptian pound lost eighteen percent of its value against the dollar, the Hungarian forint quickly fell by twenty percent, and the South African rand was down by over nine percent (Dulaney, Fujikawa, and Feng 2022). Food costs in domestic currencies soared.

Such changes made all of those countries' imports significantly more expensive and their dollar-denominated borrowing and that of local companies heavier burdens. Global investors withdrew money from these and other nations to invest in higher-yielding U.S. assets. And because economic data suggested that U.S. inflation would remain stubbornly high, strengthening the case for more Fed rate increases and an even stronger dollar, the troubles the rest of the world suffered would increase. Fed officials stressed that their mandate was to reduce U.S. inflation. It did not include concern for the rest of the world. As John Connally, President Nixon's secretary of the Treasury had famously remarked to his overseas counterparts, "the dollar is our currency, but it's your problem." It would only be if, or when, there was blowback from difficulties elsewhere that U.S. officials would become concerned.

The World Bank warned that the global economy was heading toward recession and "a string of financial crises in emerging market and developing economies that would do them lasting harm" (Duehren 2022). Forced cuts in education and health spending would result even as the price of food and fuel imports soared. Raising their own interest rates was a defensive, if inadequate, step. As the *Journal* reported, Argentina increased its interest rates to seventy-five percent to curb spiraling inflation and defend the peso, which had lost nearly thirty percent against the dollar before the close of 2022. Ghana lifted rates to twenty-two percent but could not stop the decline in the value of its currency. These currencies and many others continued to fall against the dollar. At the European Central Bank's September 2022 meeting, President Christine Lagarde expressed concern about the euro's twelve percent drop since the start of the year, saying it had "added to the buildup of inflationary pressures." The European Central Bank also raised interest rates, but that measure did little to help the value of the euro. "The ECB is powerless against the dollar's strength," argued Frederik Ducrozet, head of macroeconomic research at Pictet Wealth Management. "Whether the ECB turns more hawkish, whether there's some improvement on the economic outlook, whatever happens, it's generally offset by further dollar strength" (Dulaney, Fujikawa, and Feng 2022).

UK Prime Minister Liz Truss during her record short period in that office declared that tax cuts for high-income households would promote growth and the benefits would "trickle down" to the rest of the economy. The data did not support her. Days after U.K. chancellor of the exchequer Kwasi Kwarteng delivered his "mini" Budget calling for inflationary tax cuts to the rich in a Reagan-like move designed to stimulate the country's economy, the fiscal package was described by the International Monetary Fund as "untargeted" and working "at cross purposes" to the efforts of the Bank of England to counter soaring inflation. The IMF statement "raised eyebrows" (Smith and Politi 2022). Minouche Shafik (2022), director of the London School of Economics and Political Science and a former deputy governor of the Bank of England, declared that the government's recent fiscal plan failed to respond to the UK's twin economic crises of inflation and slow growth "in a manner that takes into account either evidence or experience." Such criticism was widely shared – and often stated in sharper, less diplomatic language. The result would be inflation, not growth. In a cross-country comparison study, economists found that there has been no relationship between changes in top marginal tax rates and the growth between 1960 and 2010 (Piketty, Saez, and Stantcheva 2014). William Gale (2016) summarizes other evidence: "Decades of experience make that claim impossible to support." He asserts that "the record is clear that deficit-financed tax cuts on high-income households and businesses have failed to boost growth at the federal or state level in the U.S., or in other countries."

What supply-side tax cuts to Occupy's 1% do accomplish is to increase the income and wealth inequalities. This has been a phenomenon starting with President Reagan and running through President Trump. The result of the latter's 2017 tax cuts was that by 2018 the richest 400 families in the U.S. paid an average effective tax rate of twenty-three percent while the bottom half of American households paid a twenty-four percent rate (Saez and Zucman 2019). Regarding the Reagan tax cut, research demonstrates that the 1983–1984 economic recovery was not the result of a consumer boom financed by reductions in the personal income tax. The data offer no support for the assertion that the recovery reflected an increase in the supply of labor resulting from a reduction in personal tax rates. The timing of the expansion and the composition of the real output changes made it clear that the primary cause of increased output was the shift to the more expansionary monetary policy that occurred in 1982. It was the lesson of the last of these conclusions that mattered for policy makers (as opposed to libertarians and politicians beholden to the 1% demanding continuous tax cuts). From that moment forward the Federal Reserve flooded the market with liquidity whenever a downturn threatened the economy. Supply-side economics of the sort proposed by the Tories had long been discredited (Feldstein and Elmendorf 1989). More recent studies of past tax cuts have not found any measurable link between lower taxes and economic or employment growth, leading Anis Chowdhury and Jomo Kwame Sundaram (2022) to conclude that

"Oft-cited U.S. examples of Reagan, Bush or Trump tax cuts have been shown to be little more than economic sophistry."

This outmoded ideological approach made no economic sense, and the pound plunged against the dollar. The sell-off of British assets that followed the announcement of the government's plan created a crisis in the country's bond market and reduced lending to businesses and households. The Bank of England issued a statement declaring that "Were dysfunction in this market to continue or worsen, there would be a material risk to U.K. financial stability." The Bank, which had begun to reduce its bond holdings accumulated during the worst period of covid, was forced to reverse course: "The purpose of these purchases will be to restore orderly market conditions," it stated. "The purchases will be carried out on whatever scale is necessary to effect this outcome" (Nelson 2022). The announcement prevented a total meltdown. Embarrassed by such criticism (which came as well from leaders in the U.S, France, Germany, and other allies), and when it became clear that rebellion from within the Conservative Party itself made passage impossible, Truss withdrew the tax cut to the rich. It was understood that the plan would have been ineffective as well as inflationary. Trickle-down economics might still be the mantra of free-enterprise oriented politicians but it no longer passes muster. Forty-four days later Truss was no longer prime minister.

Britain's long-standing economic problems of slow growth were intensified by Brexit which cut the country off from Europe, reducing its available workforce as Polish and other workers were repatriated to the Continent and adding to inflation as investment in the country became less attractive with the loss of tariff-free access to the countries of the EU. There had been underinvestment in infrastructure and the workforce that would have made production in the U.K. more desirable. The idea that trickle-down economics would jumpstart the economy lacked credibility. The drop in the market for U.K. assets and the value of the pound forced the Bank of England, which had been attempting to sell off its large bond accrued to fight the last financial crisis, to promise to buy bonds in unlimited amount to pacify markets. In doing so it worried observers, who recognized that in effect governments could follow policies chosen for political reasons, saving them from the downside of their actions. Some saw the promise of continued blackmail as the central banks would have to take actions against their preferred monetary policy – in effect they could be blackmailed by their own government. This did not work in the case of the U.K., but a look at the dramatically increased borrowing engaged in by so many governments suggested that the limits of central bank bond buying in countries with even weaker currencies might be reaching their limits and that still higher interest rates to hold bond buyers were needed.

Market participants on the continent panicked at the actions of the Conservative Party government. They were mollified by the intervention by the Bank of England, as indeed investors had been when the European Central Bank acted in the capacity of buyer of last resort when the virtually bankrupt eurozone members had needed to rely on similar bailouts. Higher interest rates would have been unkind to the heavily indebted French (with their government debt in the fall of 2022 equaling 113 percent of GDP). Greece's national debt stood at 193 percent of its GDP, Italy's at 151 percent, Portugal's 127 percent, and Spain's at 118 percent. With much of the rest of the world being in the grips of a debt trap, strong measures by central banks to fight inflation could create very hard landings. The trap had been decades in the making. It was due to the dismantling of protective regulations and the reliance on debt creation as the growth regime of financialization and global neoliberalism. Restricting the income of the working class had produced overcapacity on a global scale, with finance the outlet for the social surplus producing great wealth at the top of the income distribution.

Central banks face large losses. The Federal Reserve has been the most transparent about the scale of the expected losses in the value of its bond holdings by up to $670 billion by the end of 2022 (Anderson, Marks, Na, Schlusche, and Senyuz 2022). "In hindsight, it is clear that central banks' massive bond-buying programs were a colossal mistake," argues Daniel Gross (2022). Refusing shared growth and global Keynesianism in favor of working-class austerity, it became apparent that central banks had fallen into both a stagflation trap and a debt trap. "Amid negative aggregate supply shocks that reduce growth and increase inflation," Nouriel Roubini (2022) declared, "they are damned if they do and damned if they don't." If the central banks increased interest rates enough to bring inflation to their target rate they would cause a recession or worse. But if they did not, it was feared would de-anchor inflationary expectations that central bankers feared would bring on a wage-price spiral (despite the weak bargaining power of labor). Wages would fall further behind the increase in the cost of living and labor would pay the cost to bring inflation under control with a lower living standard. Further, inflation would reduce the value of household savings even as the cost rose of carrying existing personal and business debt. The Federal Reserve policy makers read the data as it became available, ready to moderate its rate increases on signs that inflation was peaking, not wanting to create the feared downturn though excessive measures.

The Historical Background

The demise of the Bretton Woods system of fixed exchange rates that had lasted from 1946 to 1973 was followed by "a progressive dismantling of barriers to international financial flows motivated by special-interest politics, national economic competition, and ideology – alongside the benign desire for a more efficient international allocation of capital," as Maurice Obstfelt noted. He found this unfortunate; "free cross-border financial capital mobility can compromise governments' capacities to attain domestic economic and social goals." Countries, especially the smaller and poorer ones as well as the so-called emerging economies, had been whipsawed by large, damaging inflows and sudden withdrawals of short-term movements in and out of their markets. Obstfelt (2021: 1) links the dynamics of financial liberalization to the "Teflon-like resilience of finance to backlash so far," suggesting that national governments need "to enhance multilateral cooperation to manage the financial commons." More bluntly, Martin Wolf (2022) declares that "today's fluid global capital markets have generated waves of financial crises, while bringing little evident benefit." That this needs to be argued continually ignores both the cost of the austerity policies imposed on debtor nations and the response to current inflation, which is supply-side in origin; when it is also met with policies to raise interest rates despite the reality that there is no excess demand, working people are punished for factors that are neither their fault nor under their control.

European bankers imposed their will on governments, setting the terms for a discrediting of democracy and instilling anger against the system – anger that would intensify with the rise of an extreme right. Serge Halimi (2011) suggested questions raised by the economic and democratic crises in Europe: "Why were policies that were bound to fail adopted and applied with exceptional ferocity in Ireland, Spain, Portugal and Greece? Are those responsible for pursuing these policies mad, doubling the dose every time their medicine predictably fails to work?" He further asked, "How is it that in a democratic system, the people forced to accept cuts and austerity simply replace one failed government with another just as dedicated to the same shock treatment? Is there any alternative?" The Left has said yes. The powerful financiers of Germany and other centers of finance have said no.

Beggar-thy-neighbor policies in the U.S. during the 1930s rose from exporting a nation's problems to other countries. It was signaled by the 1930 Hawley-Smoot Tariff Act, which raised U.S. tariffs to record levels on over 20,000 imported goods. Other countries followed suit, resulting in a massive decrease in international trade and domestic production in the U.S. as well as elsewhere. Currently, the U.S. effort to fight inflation with higher interest rates exports inflation to other countries, who must raise their own interest rates, thereby damaging their domestic markets. Debts denominated in dollars became more difficult for businesses and governments to pay and refinance, and the Fed policy impoverished other nations in the global economy, near and far. The high leverage encouraged by the long-standing, low interest rate environment described earlier had turned into a costly strategy. There would be blowback on the American economy as the dollar profits of U.S.-based transnationals fell, along with global investment. The lack of sensible collective efforts to address non-payable debt could prove harmful for all. Without global safety nets the Federal Reserve was unleashing punishing austerity on the world, including to a real if lesser but hardly minor degree on the American working class.

Currency fluctuations and the flight to the dollar both reflected awareness that bad debt might not be paid and that the continued scale of central bank and global state governance institutions, the International Monetary Fund and the European Central Bank most prominently, were delaying what was feared likely to be an eventual major global financial crash. This might take more time than worriers envision, but it will be difficult to avoid.

As inflation continued far longer than the Fed had thought it would, dramatic rate hikes began. Its "aggression," as the *Financial Times* termed it, led to a "reverse currency war." Instead of devaluing a currency to increase their exports, countries needed a strong currency to pay for necessary imports in a world in which many nations were exporting far less, with lower prices not helping them cover the high cost of their commodity imports: energy and food. Attempting to fight domestic inflation, the Fed raised interest rates so aggressively that the World Bank warned it risked, in the words of Claire Jones (2022), "sending the global economy into a devastating recession that would leave the world's poorest countries at risk of collapse." Such fears encourage greater academic attention to financialization in so-called developing and emerging economies (Bonizzi, Kaltenbrunner, and Powell 2022). Economists are developing versions of the core-periphery analysis that feature financialization as a central element (Vielma and Dymski 2022). Such work, important as it is for advancing theory by formulating structural relations of spatial financialization, of course cannot capture the immediacy of the pain that is being felt as a consequence of debt relations and financial flows. Again, it is the poorer nations that suffer.

After informing a reporter that prices were rising across the board, Nooruddin Zaker Ahmadi, who runs an Afghan imports company, made the important point that "The United States thinks it has only sanctioned Russia and its banks. But the United States has sanctioned the whole world." The impact has been greatest for those least able to pay for the higher cost of living. Anis Chowdhury and Jomo Kwame Sundaram (2022) have termed such sanctions "weapons of mass starvation," pointing among other examples to the many poor and food-insecure countries which are major wheat importers from Russia and Ukraine; these two countries provided ninety percent of Somalia's imports, eighty percent to the Democratic Republic of Congo, and about forty percent to both Yemen and Ethiopia. In addition, the cost of fertilizer and energy for these as well as other countries rose substantially. Already in debt, they were devastated by the higher global interest rates and the devaluation of their currencies against the dollar.

This judgment was confirmed by the United Nations Development Program, which predicted that the impact of the war on the global food market alone could cause an additional 7.6 to 13.1 million people to go hungry. "We are facing a full-on development collapse on top of humanitarian and economic crises," declared Kanni Wignaraja, UN Assistant Secretary-General and UNDP Director of the Regional Bureau for Asia and the Pacific. Half of the population is already in need of humanitarian support. This analysis suggests that we are on course for rapid, catastrophic deterioration in the lives of Afghanistan's most vulnerable people" (United Nations Development Program 2021). Americans who had experienced anger and disappointment when the Biden administration, adhering to the timetable announced by President Trump, withdrew from Afghanistan, complained about the abandonment of America's supporters. But they did not noticeably react when hunger pervaded the country as the U.S. froze Afghanistan's assets to punish the Taliban, with no foreign aid being offered despite the dire need.

IMF lending was at an all-time high in response to the large rate increases by major market central banks, which had heightened borrowing costs around the world. The *Financial Times* reported that "some analysts say the IMF's lending capacity could soon be stretched to its limits, as poor countries which are locked out of international debt market are forced to turn to the fund for support" (Wheatley 2022). The Fund denied this possibility. Like the central banks of individual nations, because it creates money to maintain market stability it believed it could continue to expand its loan portfolio. The IMF has capital pledged by member states, which it considers to provide backing for its lending.

One reason the U.S. was ready to find the global state economic governance institutions become more understanding of the plight of the world's poorer countries and emerging market economies was that China had established competing lending facilities. It was providing support worth tens of billions of dollars to Argentina, Pakistan, Sri Lanka, and other nations. Some observers regard this as a tactic, lodging the borrowers in a position where China can make demands on them – as if Western powers have not similarly used debt as a weapon to control colonies and dependent countries, part of an imperial system. The International Monetary Fund continues to impose conditions on debtors, only recently admitting that such a strategy has often not been in their interest.

Because many governments that need IMF financing do not seek it due to the stigma that accompanies such an application, Lawrence Summers and Masood Ahmed (2022) suggest developing a new contingent financing facility that provides funding to countries damaged by external developments without insisting on traditional IMF conditionality. Of course, it can be suggested that given the dire condition of public services that such governments are able to provide, all of the usual austerity conditions should be abandoned, a conclusion the global state economic governance institutions have themselves come to recognize. Also, the governments that have agreed to new commitments but have not released the funds can be called out and encouraged to do so quickly. Given that much of the debt due for repayment is unpayable, it certainly makes sense for the large creditor countries of the Group of 20 to suspend debt service for the neediest countries, although what can legally be done regarding the vulture funds that bought up debt at deep discount and demand a full payment of the entire face value is an open question.

There is also the issue of why lenders are not required to share the burden of the overextended, unpayable debt of the poor country borrowers. Raghuram Rajan, the former head of India's central bank, observed that "If a poorer country over borrows in the good times because global interest rates are low, what responsibility does the U.S. have for that? Does it have none? We need to find a middle ground." There is of course no recognition in the halls of power in Washington that the U.S. had pushed neoliberalism and financialization on the Global South as it had on the Global North (Bastos and Young 2022). When asked about the world-wide repercussions of the Fed's actions, chair Jay Powell, while expressing an awareness of the impacts of what they were doing to other countries, argued that the Fed had a mandate to lower domestic inflation and protect domestic jobs (Jones 2022).

As things stand, the global money supply and debt will continue to grow at a rate far exceeding the increase in GDP as additional loans are made to cover both the repayment of old loans and for needed imports to poor nations (which are unlikely ever to be able to repay them). In wealthier European countries, large budget deficits are addressed through austerity measures that lead to increased support for extreme right parties by voters who see their tax dollars being spent to help immigrants rather than to maintain the welfare state from which they have long benefitted – blaming immigrants for the austerity they have not caused.

For three decades investment demand has declined, driven by a combination of demographic and technological stagnation. Technological progress has slowed, the workforce has aged, birth rates have fallen, and new immigration has been politically rejected, not because the economy does not need workers but because the competition they provide and the loathing of foreign "invaders" by conservatives who dislike the impact on the dominance of white Americans. This will have to change. America needs workers and a Green New Deal would require more workers and increased spending, as would a care economy, and there might be technological breakthroughs many associated with combating climate change that would draw investment to new sectors, restructuring demand in an ecologically oriented economy. Davos leaders expect, or at least hope, that technology will rekindle growth and overcoming stagnation and labor shortages.

However, voters decide to make a serious commitment to fight global warming, the cost of retrofitting factories, insulating buildings, and effecting the extensive myriad of other changes will be expensive and require a larger labor force. The changes that are needed must be paid for by progressive taxation and reclaiming the initiative from financialization. The unsustainable creation of fictitious capital and hence ultimately of the crises that result suggest the necessity of analysis by political economists, a heterodox approach to understanding the pernicious role of global finance is essential for the profession (Bhattacharya and Seda-Irizarry 2017: 329–45). This is a topic to which we shall return in the concluding chapter.

The next chapter turns to the most damaging aspects of financialization, focusing on the long-standing mis-measurement of the costs and benefits of investing and producing fossil fuels and other pollutants that destroy nature while heating the planet – along with bringing on the wars and forced migrations that will follow.

References

Adams, Rose. 2022. "Big Business Games the Supply Chain." *The American Prospect*, February.

Anderson, Alyssa, Philippa Marks, Dave Na, Bernd Schlusche, and Zeynep Senyuz. 2022. "An Analysis of the Interest Rate Risk of the Federal Reserve's Balance Sheet, Part 2: Projections under Alternative Interest Rate Paths." *Fed Notes*, July 15.

Anstey, Chris. 2022. "Put Off." New Economy Daily, *Bloomberg*, May 18.

Bastos, Pedro Paulo Zahluth, and Victor Young. 2022. "The Dollar Enablers and Panhandlers: US Capitalist Power and the Origins of the Financialisation at the Periphery." *Cambridge Journal of Economics*, 46(4).

Bernstein, Jared and Ernie Tedeschi. 2021. "President Biden's Infrastructure and Build Back Better Plans: An Antidote for Inflationary Pressure." *The White House*, August 23. https://www.whitehouse.gov/cea/written-materials/2021/08/23/president-bidens-infrastructure-and-build-back-better-plans-an-antidote-for-inflationary-pressure/.

Bhattacharya, Rajesh and Ian J. Seda-Irizarry. 2017. "Problematizing the Global Economy: Financialization and the 'Feudalization' of Capital." In Theodore Burczak, Robert Garnett and Richard McIntyre, eds. *Economics, Knowledge, and Class: Marxism without Guarantees*. Routledge.

Bivens, Josh. 2022. "Corporate Profits Have Contributed Disproportionately to Inflation. How Should Policymakers Respond?" *Economic Policy Institute*, April 21. https://www.epi.org/blog/corporate-profits-have-contributed-disproportionately-to-inflation-how-should-policymakers-respond/

Bonizzi, Bruno, Annina Kaltenbrunner, and Jeff Powell. 2022. "Financialised Capitalism and the Subordination of Emerging Capitalist Economies." Cambridge Journal of Economics, 46(4).

Boston, Claire. 2020. "Credit in the Scariest Market." Bloomberg Businessweek, March 23.

Brainard, Lael. 2023. "Staying the Course to Bring Inflation Down." *Speech at the University of Chicago Booth School of Business, Chicago, Illinois, Board of Governors of the Federal Reserve System*, January 19. https://www.federalreserve.gov/newsevents/speech/brainard20230119a.htm.

Chowdhury, Anis and Jomo Kwame Sundaram. 2022. "Ideology and Dogma Ensure Policy Disaster." *Challenging Development*, October 4.

Duehren, Andrew. 2022. "World Bank Warns of Global Recession Next Year if Central Banks Lift Interest Rates Too High." *Wall Street Journal*, September 15.

Dulaney, Chelsey, Megumi Fujikawa, and Rebecca Feng. 2022. "Dollar's Rise Spells Trouble for Global Economies." *Wall Street Journal*, September 18.

Elliott, Matthew, Benjamin Golub, and Matthew V. Leduc. 2022. "Supply Network Formation and Fragility." *American Economic Review*, 112(8).

Farboodi, Maryam and Péter Kondor. 2022. "Heterogeneous Global Booms and Busts." *American Economic Review*, 112(7).

Feldstein, Martin and Douglas W. Elmendorf. 1989. "Budget Deficits, Tax Incentives, and Inflation: A Surprising Lesson from the 1983–1984 Recovery." In Lawrence H. Summers, ed. *Tax Policy and the Economy, Volume 3, National Bureau of Economic Research*. MIT Press.

Flassbeck, Heiner and Paul Steinhardt. 2018. "Corporate Power and the Self-Destruction of Neoliberalism." *American Affairs*, 2(4).

Galbraith, James K. 2014. *The End of Normal*. Simon & Schuster.

Galbraith, James K. 2022. "Think Again About Persistent Inflation and the Non-Partisan Fed." *Project Syndicate*, November 18.

Gale, William G. 2016. "An Agenda for Inclusive Growth." *Brookings Institution*, November 4. https://www.brookings.edu/opinions/an-agenda-for-inclusive-growth/

Gandel, Stephen. 2021. "Some Watchers Feeling Nervous As Stock Prices Outpace Profits." *New York Times*, December 10.

Greeley, Brendan. 2022. "On Wall Street It's still Ben Bernanke and Milton Friedman's Fed Central Bank Policymakers Do Not Seem to Want to Find New Tools that Work." *Financial Times*, November 5.

Gross, Daniel. 2022. "The Fiscal Cost of Quantitative Easing." *Project Syndicate*, November 9.

Halimi, Serge. 2011. "Europe's Wakeup Call." *Le Monde Diplomatique*, July 20.

Hudson, Michael. 2021. "Rent-Seeking and Asset-Price Inflation: A Total-Returns Profile of Economic Polarization in America." *Review of Keynesian Economics*, 9(4).

Jacobs, Meg. 2021. "Fighting Inflation Means Taking on Corporations." *New York Times*, December 24.

Jones, Claire. 2022. "A Global Backlash Is Brewing against the Fed." *Financial Times*, September 22.

Katsoulacos, Yannis and David Ulph. 2013. "Antitrust Penalties and the Implications of Empirical Evidence on Cartel Overcharges." *Economic Journal*, 123(572).

Konczal, Mike and Niko Lusiani. 2022. "Prices, Profits, and Power: An Analysis of 2021 Firm-Level Markups." *Roosevelt Institute*, June 21. https://rooseveltinstitute.org/publications/prices-profits-and-power/

Mian, Atif, Amir Sufi and Emil Verner. 2017. "Household Debt and Business Cycles Worldwide." *Quarterly Journal of Economics*, 132(4).

Nelson, Eshe. 2022. "To Calm Markets, Bank of England Will Buy Bonds on 'Whatever Scale Is Necessary'." *New York Times*, September 28.

Nicas, Jack. 2022. "Ukraine War Threatens to Cause a Global Food Crisis." *New York Times*, March 20.

Obstfelt, Maurice. 2021. "The Global Capital Market Reconsidered." *Oxford Review of Economic Policy*, 37(4).

Piketty, Thomas, Emanuel Saez, and Stefanie Stantcheva. 2014. "Optimal Taxation of Top Labor Incomes: A Tale of Three Elasticities." *Economic Policy*, 6(1).

Piketty, Thomas, Emmanuel Saez, and Gabriel Zucman. 2016. "Economic Growth in the United States: A tale of two countries." *Equitable Growth*, December 6.

Rogoff, Kenneth. 2022. "The Growing Threat of Global Recession." *Project Syndicate*, April 26.

Roubini, Nouriel. 2022. "We Face the Mother of All Stagflation Crises." *Time*, October 24–31.

Saez, Emmanuel and Gabriel Zucman. 2019. *The Triumph of Injustice: How the Rich Dodge Taxes and How to Make Them Pay*. W. W. Norton.

Shafik, Minouche. 2022. "UK Government's Plan Is Both Bad Economics and a Lost Opportunity." *Financial Times*, September 29.

Shalal, Andrea. 2022. "IMF Sees Cost of COVID Pandemic Rising Beyond $12.5 Trillion Estimate." *Reuters*, January 20.

Sharma, Ruchir. 2021. "There Is No Easy Escape from the Global Debt Trap: No Matter What Happens to Near-Term Inflation and Growth, the World Is Too Indebted for Rates to Rise Much Higher." *Financial Times*, November 22.

Singer, Paul. 2021. "Markets Volatility: Investors Piling on Risk Are Setting Themselves Up for a Fall Central Banks' Asset-Buying Spree Has Created a Huge Overhang, Limiting Their Ability to Support Prices in a Future Downturn." *Financial Times*, December 6.

Smialek, Jeanna and Ben Casselman. 2022. "Rapid Inflation, Lower Employment: How the U.S. Pandemic Response Measures Up." *New York Times*, April 25.

Smith, Colby and James Politi. 2022. "Fiscal Fisticuffs: The Week the IMF Attacked Britain's Tax Cuts." *Financial Times*, September 30.

Stiglitz, Joseph E. and Ira Regmi. 2022. "The Causes of and Responses to Today's Inflation," *Roosevelt Institute*, December 6.

Stoller, Matt. 2021a. "A Simple Thing Biden Can Do to Reset America." *Big*, January 11.

Stoller, Matt. 2021b. "Corporate Profits Drive 60% of Inflation Increases." *Big*, December 29.

Sufi, Amir and Atif Mian. 2018. "The Real Engine of the Business Cycle." *Project Syndicate*, March 5.

Summers, Lawrence and Masood Ahmed. 2022. "IMF-World Bank Meetings Are the Last Stop Before a Coming Economic Storm." *Washington Post*, October 5.

Tett, Gillian. 2020. "Markets Contemplate a Future in Which Stimulus Does Not Work." *Financial Times*, March 13, p. 78.

Tett, Gillian. 2022. "The Fed Owes the American People Some Plain-Speaking; Chair Jay Powell must acknowledge that free money has made asset prices unsustainably high." *Financial Times*, May 5.

Tooze, Adam. 2021. *Shutdown: How Covid Shook the World's Economy*. Viking.

United Nations Development Program. 2021. "97 Percent of Afghans Could Plunge into Poverty by Mid 2022, Says UNDP." *Press Release*, September 9. https://www.undp.org/press-releases/97-percent-afghans-could-plunge-poverty-mid-2022-says-undp.

Vielma, Nicole Cerpa and Gary Dymski. 2022. "A Core–Periphery Framework for Understanding the Place of Latin America in the Global Architecture of Finance." *Cambridge Journal of Economics*, 46(4).

Wheatley, Jonathan. 2022. "IMF Bailouts Hit Record High As Global Economic Outlook Worsens; Fund Hands Out $140bn in Loans as Interest Rate Rises Push Up Countries' Borrowing Costs." *Financial Times*, September 25.

Wolf, Martin. 2022. "The Looming Threat of Long Financial Covid; Necessary Debt Restructurings Will Be Prolonged and Messy While People and Economies Suffer." *Financial Times*, February 15.

8

FINANCE AND THE ENVIRONMENTAL CRISIS

The impact of climate change will become even more significant in the near future, a reality that should guide policy as practiced by financial institutions, investors, and governments (Dietz, Bowen, Dixon, and Gradwell 2016). Yet because of the repercussions on the producers of energy and other corporate interests as well as the perceived self-interest of many voters, elected officials have been slow to acknowledge the economic and social costs of global warming. When the Biden administration, departing from past precedent, was able to increase spending to counter global warming as a major part of its Inflation Reduction Act of 2022, it used incentives rather than directives as the most effective tactic. This was understandable, given the unwillingness of corporations to act in ways that would reduce their profits and to abandon widespread campaigns of greenwashing, pretending to make changes, or promising to do so to convince the public that they were "woke."

Tim Quinson (2021), covering environmental matters for Bloomberg, cites a study by the Sierra Club and the Center for American Progress which demonstrates that eight of the largest U.S. banks and ten of the largest asset managers together financed an estimated two billion tons of carbon dioxide emissions; he concludes that "Wall Street's toxic fossil-fuel investments threaten the future of our planet and the stability of our financial system and put all of us, especially our most vulnerable communities, at risk." He quotes Ben Cushing, manager of the Sierra Club's Fossil-Free Finance campaign: "Regulators can no longer ignore Wall Street's staggering contribution to the climate crisis." But they are also fearful of the power of these interests if they are too demanding.

The conclusion reached by many economists is that the proper policy to meet the climate challenge is carbon taxes, charging users in relation to how much damage they caused by releasing polluting gases into the environment by driving or other uses of carbon-based fuels. To make a significant difference, these taxes would have

DOI: 10.4324/9781003385240-8

to be high and so would likely be politically unpopular. And raising taxes on people who must drive to work every day is regressive in its impact as well. Subsidizing alternative energy development is more effective in potentially reducing harm – even as economists remain committed to carbon taxes, considering subsidies that are likely to be inefficient and wasteful. Moreover, the single-minded cure of carbon taxation ignores the many other costly developments that are destroying nature and wasting non-replenishable resources.

More generally, the calculation of costs and benefits at the margin by economists is not acceptable with regard to events that do not happen at the margin. Economists are responsible for the methodology that relies on present value calculations to reduce the cost of global warming to future generations and the short-term method of calculating expected profit used by corporations that excludes social costs. This chapter discusses the failure of financial economics and of the public policy that is needed.

With the drop in the cost of alternative energy, carbon capture and storage (CCS) also does not make economic sense – even if it were to work as promised. Those who continue to advocate the technology do so for the most part because they favor a continued dependence on fossil fuels. Promotion of CCS slows the transition away from fossil fuel production and use. That the technology continues to receive federal subsidies in the form of substantial tax credits is a tribute to the political power of the industry. Environmentalists point out that the harmful pollutants were already sequestered in the earth before the oil companies removed them.

In studying the effects of climate change on financial institutions, ecological economists use very different models, ones that demonstrate the interactions between global warming and financial stability and estimate the cost of stranded assets and the erosion of the capital of firms; such models predict rates of default on corporate loans and the undermining of the stability of the banking system (Bolton, Depres, Awazu, Da Silva, Samama, and Svartzman 2021; Bolton, Hong, Kacperczyk, and Vives 2021). Then why are investors heavily invested in oil and gas stocks? It is more than the consequence of the higher prices they are receiving due to the boycott of Russia.

Mark Roe (2022) has made the important distinction between (a) short-termism, choosing policies that maximize return in the short-run but have long-term costs to the same entity, and (b) the problems caused by who pays. If a firm pollutes knowing others will bear the cost, this is not a problem of short-term decision-making. Indeed, for them it is not a problem at all. Profit-seeking corporations and their executives "have incentives to pass costs onto outsiders and keep the gains for themselves. It's profit pressure – not short-termism – that pushes firms to pollute and disregard their climate footprints." They profit by passing costs to others. It is not a matter of short-term thinking, as it is so often regarded.

The planet's environment and the sustainability of the life of its many species, including humans, are threatened by the manner in which the expected profitability of investment is mismeasured in social and environmental terms. It is not simply finance's criteria for the desirability of an investment but the widely accepted measure of well-being, GDP, which ignores nature and indeed the true value of everything that the ecosystems provide, from privately valued raw materials to socially desired clean air and the perpetuation of species. As it has been practiced, finance misdirects analysts by privileging private profit calculations over environmental goals. Its measure of cost in dollar terms ignores the heterogeneity of the costs that are not comparable – which may be viewed as infinite, without measure.

The critique of elected officials not choosing to impose costs on major contributors or job losses on constituents has led to the acceptance of a criterion of maximizing GDP (while minimizing the environmental costs to the polluting companies themselves, as will be explained in the subsequent section), even as this index is understood to have major flaws. A typical critique of GDP offered by a group of University of Cambridge researchers is relevant here: "it ignores the social bonds that tie us to employers and communities, and the trust in institutions vital for generating new knowledge and improving productivity. It ignores the health and skills of entire populations" (Bennett Institute for Public Policy 2022).

The Wealth Economy project at the Bennett Institute builds on the groundbreaking work of their Cambridge colleague Partha Dasgupta, who led the development of a statistical economics extending beyond GDP to include nature and human well-being. Dasgupta argues, "Access to education, healthcare, justice, as well as the degree to which people are protected from risks of conflict, destitution or social upheaval – these are all fundamental to prosperity. The public understands this, and it is past time that economics caught up" (University of Cambridge 2022). The current and potential consequences of global warming raise questions of whether human solidarity will take precedence over building walls, which technologies will be privileged, and the criteria that will guide decision-making with regard to goals and the means of achieving them.

In the U.S., a 2022 Supreme Court decision with wide implications struck down an EPA plan to reduce carbon emissions from power plants. The 6–3 majority argued that such agencies are a manifestation of an administrative state that is unconstitutional. The Court declared that the laws creating the agencies do not authorize experts in them to set rules. This decision undermined the long-standing power of agencies created for the purpose of making such determinations. The Court decided that Congress must impose individually specific mandates which cannot be made by the administrative agencies themselves. The mandates they issue must be designated in legislation. Since a polarized, dysfunctional Congress cannot decide on much of anything, this would result in massive deregulation as standing rules are declared to be excessive overreach.

This is what business interests have wanted since the New Deal. It is a preposterous ruling. In her dissent, Justice Kagan declared that the Court had substituted its own policy judgment for that of Congress. She wrote, "Whatever else this court may know about; it does not have a clue about how to address climate change. And let's say the obvious: The stakes here are high. Yet the court today prevents congressionally authorized agency action to curb power plants' carbon dioxide emissions." She continued, "The court appoints itself – instead of Congress or the expert agency – the decision maker on climate policy," and "I cannot think of many things more frightening." Justice Kagan bluntly stated: "Congress knows what it doesn't and can't know when it drafts a statute; and Congress therefore gives an expert agency the power to address issues – even significant ones – as and when they arise." Republicans in Congress cheered the ruling by their fellow Republicans on the Court with the party's leader in the Senate, Mitch McConnell, asserting that the Court's majority had limited the power of "unelected, unaccountable bureaucrats" (Liptak 2022).

There is good news amidst the bad (of which more will be discussed), both because ignorance of the cost of short termism in financial measures is dissipating and because awareness of such costs allows for a focus on what needs to be done. The good news appears in the 2022 report of the Intergovernmental Panel on Climate Change, the United Nations body for assessing the science related to climate change that has offered workable solutions. According to the report, between 2010 and 2019, the cost of solar energy plummeted by eighty-five percent, wind energy by fifty-five percent, and lithium-ion batteries by eighty-five percent. Those supporting carbon-based energy sources are now defending not only polluting products but in market terms increasingly uncompetitive ones. The 3,000-page UN report also contains what one reader terms "an astonishingly frank assessment of the organised efforts used to thwart climate action."

The report notes that "opposition to climate action by carbon-connected industries is broad-based, highly organized, and matched with extensive lobbying." It specifies who must carry the greatest burden of repair by funding the widespread adoption of renewable energy. The average North American is emitting sixteen tons of carbon dioxide each year from fossil fuel use, compared to just two tons for the average African. Consumption by the top ten percent of households comprises over a third of global greenhouse gases compared to fifteen percent of that of the bottom fifty percent of households. In theory, every government now agrees that the climate crisis is driven by the world's wealthy. The question is whether popular movements can prevail in forcing the rich to meet their responsibilities. Unless they do, the consequences will be dire (Lewis 2022). In the U.S., progressive state governments lead the way. The deadline of 2025 set by California as the year after which fossil fuels will not be allowed to power automobiles sold in the state will substantially impact car manufacturers because California is such a large market; as a consequence the sale of electric vehicles will accelerate in South Carolina and elsewhere.

Climate change increases the need for spending on sustainability as well as to repair damage from storms, droughts and fires. The International Monetary Fund and the World Bank stuck to old formulas they had long enforced on client states such as forcing down government spending so that national debt would not exceed sixty percent of the nation's GDP, regardless of the human suffering following natural disasters (events often the responsibility of man-made global warming and so not "natural" at all). This rule of thumb was arbitrary, contrasting with a U.S. national debt-to-GDP ratio of 150 percent. Meeting such a requirement in the poor debtor nations would be accommodated by spending cuts in health, education, and other basic needs. After decades of causing unnecessary suffering to squeeze these countries, finally the IMF came to accept ending the practice as the unpayable nature of the debt became obvious – even if this reality was met with their issuing still more loans that were also unlikely ever to be repaid, as discussed in the last chapter.

When in 2019, the Bulgarian environmental economist Kristalina Georgieva came to head the IMF, the institution began to change, albeit slowly and inadequately. Its initial response to the damage of climate change was to advise countries to build up a climate reserve fund equal to one percent of their GDP to help pay for disaster recovery, as if they were not already strapped by money set aside being demanded by creditors, especially the vulture hedge funds that had bought up debt at discount and then demanded immediate payment in full. There was no recommendation to the wealthy members to allocate what was needed to reverse global warming and to pay reparations. More recently, the IMF has required that the economic shock of a disaster to low-income countries be taken into account in its analysis of debt. However,

> when in late 2020 Eurodad looked for evidence that the climate-change policies were rising to prominence within the I.M.F., it found little change. Researchers examined 80 I.M.F. programs around the world and found that climate was central to the fund's assessment in only one country – Samoa. Critics and insiders both observe that a sense of urgency is still missing.
>
> *(Lustgarten 2022: 47)*

In terms of the bad news of a future that appears all too probable, Jonathan Neale and the Amandla Editorial Collective project write of the likelihood of the prospect of horrible suffering. "Imagine," they write of their home country,

> South Africa where almost no one can make a living on the land. Where tens of millions of desperate ex-farmers from other African countries flood south. Imagine the hatred for the immigrants, the competition for jobs, the killings. Imagine . . . what is already happening. Cities without water, far more people without jobs. Imagine how the rich in South Africa will treat the poor then.
>
> *(2021)*

The U.S. was hardly immune from a range of devastating disruptions caused by the heating of the planet, even if the connection between global warming and extreme weather events was not obvious to many, especially those who had little faith in scientists. Consider the impact of Hurricane Ian on Florida real estate in 2022. It foreshadowed what would be a wider problem for the insurance and real estate components of the FIRE sector. The prospect of a Miami under water had to be denied so that the future of real estate values and property tax collection could be ignored. Yet for the region, privately insured losses from the devastation caused by Ian are expected to reach sixty-seven billion dollars, not including flood insurance, twice the toll of Hurricane Andrew (1992). Andrew had previously been the most expensive hurricane until Katrina in 2005, the most expensive natural disaster in the nation's history. The cost of each disaster led more insurers to discontinue doing business in the state. By 2022 only smaller companies remained. They were dependent on giant reinsurers based outside the U.S. to cover exceptional losses. Having taken large losses these companies substantially raised the premiums they charged. It was forecast that only the rich would be able to purchase insurance or to self-insure without risk, since only they could afford to rebuild.

Without insurance available at reasonable cost or at all, banks would be unable to extend mortgages in Florida. This would make buying vacation homes prohibitive for those who could not pay the full cost in cash. Local housing markets might collapse. While states, including Florida, moved into the insurance business in a large way to fill the breach, they too had trouble buying reinsurance. Raising the taxes and fees to subsidize damage-prone properties was increasingly difficult politically. Flooding and wildfires in other parts of the country also led to jumps in insurance costs, in some areas prohibitively so for farmers and other businesses as well as for home owners.

The effects of global warming are already apparent across the U.S., in the form of more extreme and longer heat waves; unusually severe rainfall events and associated flooding; excessively frequent and intense droughts driving huge wildfires; and higher sea levels creating coastal flooding and worse storm surges. The President's Council of Economic Advisers (2023: 276) well-referenced annual report lists the many events of the prior year in different parts of the U.S. warned that "Even small changes in average climate conditions can produce large changes in the probability of previously rare weather events. Social, financial, and infrastructural systems that manage these risks typically have certain tolerances with steeply increasing costs when these thresholds are exceeded."

The need for major policy change is further suggested by the 2023 report by the Intergovernmental Panel on Climate Change, prepared by experts convened by the United Nations, that offers the most comprehensive understanding of ways in which the planet is changing. The stark differences between an impact of 1.5 degrees of warming and two degrees are likely to that tens of millions more people worldwide experience life-threatening heat waves, water shortages, and coastal flooding. As António Guterres, the United Nations secretary general, declared in response to the report, "The 1.5 degree limit is achievable, but it will take a quantum leap in climate action." He called on countries to stop building new coal plants and to stop approving new oil and gas projects – yet the world's two biggest polluters, China and the United States, continue to approve new fossil fuel projects. In 2022, China issued permits for 168 coal-fired power plants of various sizes, the Centre for Research on Energy and Clean Air in Finland reports. Even as his Counsel of Economic Advisers released its sophisticated, yet accessible, analysis of what needed to be done to halt global warming, the Biden administration approved a major drilling project on formerly protected federal land in Alaska (Plummer 2023).

Ongoing research by the Biden-Harris Administration (Council of Economic Advisers and Office of Management and Budget 2022) regarding the capacity of the Federal Government to integrate the modeling of both the physical and transition risks of climate change into macroeconomic forecasting suggests the way forward. It dramatically challenges current macroeconomic modeling. The need for such a dramatic departure confronts the resistance to members of Congress funded by the coal, oil, and gas producers and consumers of global warming products. The political constraints on adopting sensible climate policy is defined not only by the self-interest of corporations but also real estate interests, and state and local governments that profited from building on high-risk parcels.

Profit-Making, Risk, and Greenwashing

Consider a legal case that calls attention to both the privatization of water and the increasing use of petroleum feedstock to make plastics that are seen by the oil industry as a growth market for their toxic product. It exposes the hypocrisy among those actively destroying the sustainability of the planet, which has rarely been made clearer. In defending itself in litigation over the greenwashing of plastic recycling, the bottled water company BlueTriton declared that its claims to be environmentally friendly are not violations of the law because they are "aspirational." (BlueTriton owns Poland Spring, Pure Life, Splash, Ozarka, Arrowhead, and other brands. It is responsible for adding hundreds of millions of pounds of plastic to U.S. landfills each year.) The company has a history of draining aquifers to procure the water that it places into the polluting plastic to bottle a third of all branded water sold in the U.S. The company's public relations materials market BlueTriton as a solution to the problems of plastic waste and water. "Water is at the very core of our sustainable efforts to meet the needs of future generations," the firm declares on its website, as it promises stewardship over a picture of pine trees, pristine water, and clouds. On its Instagram account it explains the relevance of its logo: "Triton is a god of the sea in classical Greek mythology. Combined with the color blue, representing water, the new name and logo reflect our role as a guardian of sustainable resources and a provider of fresh water."

However, BlueTriton was sued by the Earth Island Institute, which argued that its misleading claims of sustainability violated a local Washington, D.C. law known as the Consumer Protection Procedures Act, which is designed to prevent "deceptive trade practices." In the face of overwhelming evidence that all of its claims to stewardship were fraudulent, the company defended itself by asserting that its pretensions are indeed fraudulent. The company said of course these are lies, explaining that everyone should realize that the claims are meaningless nonsense: "Many of the statements at issue here constitute non-actionable puffery," BlueTriton's attorneys wrote in a motion to dismiss the case. "BlueTriton's representation of itself as 'a guardian of sustainable resources' and 'a company who, at its core, cares about water' is vague and hyperbolic," the attorneys asserted, and "[b]ecause these statements are 'couched in aspirational terms,' they cannot serve as the basis for Plaintiff's CPPA claim" (Lerner 2022). This brazen defense, startling as it may seem, was the best such a company could offer in its efforts to avoid steep fines and court orders to change its behavior of fraudulent self-presentation.

Other blatantly anti-environment actions represent a different path – passaging of legislation to allow corporations to continue to pollute. Through the mediation of the right-wing, Koch-led lobbying group, the American Legislative Exchange Council, polluters pushed ALEC's state affiliates to adopt laws blocking boycotts of the oil industry. The group's strategy, modelled on legislation to punish advocates of divestment from Israel, was intended to protect the role of the fossil fuel industry in the climate crisis. (ALEC-initiated language had been adopted in more than thirty states to block support for the Boycott, Divestment and Sanctions movement against Israel's oppression of the Palestinians.) "Banks are increasingly denying financing to creditworthy fossil energy companies solely for the purpose of decarbonizing their lending portfolios and marketing their environmental credentials," ALEC's draft legislation said, as if these goals were somehow repugnant. Their model bill proposed a strategy in which states would use their economic purchasing power "to counter the rise of politically motivated and discriminatory investing practices" (McGreal 2022).

Texas led in compiling a list of companies to target for refusing to do business with the oil industry after the state passed a version of the ALEC law in 2021. In order to do business with the state government, any business with more than ten employees would have to certify that it was not boycotting fossil fuel companies. As a consequence of the law, state funds, such as those holding its workers' pensions, are obliged to sell investments in corporations that refuse loans to the oil industry.

ALEC was on solid ground in suggesting that the financial industry was anxious to market their environmental credentials. However, beyond their rhetorical claims, major financial institutions have for the most part continued to ignore the damage they are doing. Analysis of thirty-five leading investment banks reveals their financing of at least $2.66 trillion for fossil fuel industries since the 2015 Paris agreement. JPMorgan Chase, whose economists warned that the climate crisis threatens the survival of humanity, was the largest financer of fossil fuels in the four years following the Paris agreement, providing hundreds of billions of dollars in financial services for the extraction of oil, gas, and coal. An alliance of U.S.-based environmental groups (Rainforest Action Network, BankTrack, Indigenous Environmental Network, Oil Change International, Reclaim Finance, and Sierra Club) found that borrowing by the companies most aggressively involved in new fossil fuel extraction since the Paris agreement surged by nearly forty percent in 2019 alone. (JPMorgan Chase, Wells Fargo, Citi, and Bank of America have dominated financing for fossil fuel development.) Alison Kirsch, a researcher at Rainforest Action Network who led the analysis, reported that "[t]he data reveal that global banks are not only ramping up financing of fossil fuels overall, but are also increasing funding for the companies most responsible for fossil fuel expansion" (Greenfield and Makortoff 2020).

The Global Witness campaign group found that in the five years following the Paris agreement, banks and asset managers extended 119 billion dollars in financing to twenty major agribusinesses linked to deforestation. In addition to their direct funding, the 1,500 banks and asset managers tracked in their database held 37.5 billion dollars in shares in the twenty agribusinesses most responsible for deforestation. Johan Frijns, director of BankTrack, an NGO that monitors the activities of major financial institutions, reported that while over a hundred banks have queued up to proclaim their support for the goals of the Paris Agreement and endorse the Principles for Responsible Banking, the data in "Banking on Climate Change 2020" show these laudable pledges making little difference with the bank funding of the fossil fuel industry "continuing to lead us to the climate abyss" (Hodgson and Morris 2021).

BlackRock, Vanguard, and State Street are the largest shareholders in four-fifths of listed U.S. corporations. Together they manage nearly eleven trillion dollars, three times the aggregate worth of even the global hedge funds, and they cast more than twenty-five percent of votes at corporate shareholder meetings. They have also prioritized short-term profits over long-term investment goals, including confronting climate change. Given their power and the re-concentration of finance capital they represent, this is a problem indeed (Fichtner, Heemskerk, and Garcia-Bernardo 2017). A report by Friends of Earth U.S. shows that the Big Three asset managers collectively own more than twenty-seven percent of shares in the fossil fuel giants Chevron, ExxonMobil, and Conoco Phillips, as well as over thirty percent of major agribusiness companies such as Archer-Daniels-Midland. Such assets make them among the largest shareholders in the two industries most responsible for the majority of greenhouse gas emissions.

The climate crisis destroying the world will eventually wreak havoc on asset management portfolio returns, leading Olúfẹ́mi Táíwò (2022) to ask, "so shouldn't the firms managing those portfolios have a direct financial interest moving climate policy forward?" "No," he says.

You could fit an oil tanker in the space between what's good for asset management companies and what's good for the world. Asset management companies are paid fees for each dollar they manage – they profit by managing as much money as possible . . . encouraging companies to chase big short-term returns or face losing ground to competitors.

He therefore concludes,

Unsurprisingly, asset managers have not used their considerable power to promote genuine climate sustainability or justice-promoting responses to the climate crisis. Instead, they have routinely voted against or abstained on shareholder resolutions that would support establishing serious climate targets or delinking supply chains from deforestation to climate targets.

(2022)

Financiers and corporate managers understand the risks of climate change but are primarily interested in the bottom line. This means that in the face of oncoming disasters they may choose to make as much money as they can for as long as they can from existing polluting investments. While doing so, it is in their interest to ward off regulation that might cost them money. Only a strong, educated environmental movement can force the changes that are needed. This requires a different balance of power in Washington as well as establishing environmentalist priorities in the management of economic decisions. To avoid this, capital has considerable incentive to appear "woke." In early 2020, BlackRock's CEO Larry Fink wrote to the CEOs of the world's largest corporations, stating, "I believe we are at the edge of a fundamental reshaping of finance." Fink declared in his annual letter that "No issue ranks higher than climate change on our clients' lists of priorities." Perhaps, but as Tariq Fancy (2021), the former chief investment officer for Sustainable Investing at BlackRock suggests, the financial services industry "is duping" the American public with its claims of sustainable investment practices. "This multitrillion dollar arena of socially conscious investing" is being presented as something it is not: "In essence, Wall Street is greenwashing the economic system and, in the process, creating a deadly distraction." He maintains that "in truth, sustainable investing boils down to little more than marketing hype, PR spin and disingenuous promises from the investment community."

When Texas passed a law barring the state's retirement and investment funds from doing business with companies that the state comptroller says are boycotting fossil fuels, it targeted BlackRock. When it seemed politic, Fink used his annual letter to corporate leaders to implore them to look beyond the bottom line and make a positive contribution to society, saying that there is a sound business rationale for taking up the fight against climate change and imploring other companies to act responsibly. But he told a different story when faced with the prospect of losing business from Texas and other states. "We are perhaps the world's largest investor in fossil fuel companies, and, as a long-term investor in these companies, we want to see these companies succeed and prosper," as BlackRock's head of external affairs, Dalia Blass, wrote in a letter to Texas regulators. BlackRock had ninety-one billion dollars invested in Texas fossil fuel companies, Ms. Blass made clear, listing BlackRock's sizable holdings in the state's energy companies, including Exxon Mobil, ConocoPhillips, and Kinder Morgan. Further, BlackRock said, it supports fewer shareholders calling for climate action because "we do not consider them to be consistent with our clients' long-term financial interests" (Gelles and Tabuchi 2022).

In a similar fashion, social responsibility soon lost priority for banks when future profitability suggested it was not the best policy. After the mass shooting in 2018 at Marjory Stoneman Douglas High School in Parkland, Florida, killing seventeen people and wounding seventeen others in what was the deadliest shooting at a high school in U.S. history, JPMorgan's chief financial officer assured the media that the bank's relationships with gunmakers "have come down significantly and are pretty limited." However, as state governments under Republican control passed laws saying they would not do business with banks that refused to lend to gunmakers, JPMorgan lawyers sent a letter to Texas declaring its "longstanding business relationships" with the industry and that it "anticipated continuing such relationships into the future." JPMorgan did not discriminate in its lending against companies in the gun industry, it made clear, as had BlackRock and others (Gandel 2022).

Under public pressure, major polluters have sold their most environmentally destructive assets to companies that provide little transparency regarding their operations. This has allowed well-known energy companies to appear "green" while the pollution has not been eradicated. In fact, it remains at least as damaging as before. Essentially nothing has changed with this greenwashing practice (Tabuchi 2021). Thus, it is possible to see Fink's concerns as not reflecting a serious intention to do the right thing for people and the planet. Indeed, as he himself has said at what was billed as a climate conference named "Ecoprosperity," if the world is going to move to net-zero emissions, then "we can't just ask these public companies to move forward. There lies the fundamental problem and that's what I'm really worried about. I don't want to be the environmental police." He asserted: "I don't want BlackRock – because we're a large investor – to be telling every company who's not moving forward [that] we're going to divest of all your shares. That's not a good outcome" (Tan 2021). If BlackRock were to assume the role of sheriff, it would have to begin by arresting itself since it is the largest global financier of the oil-and-gas industry.

ESG as Greenwashing

Tim Quinson writes that "in an age of accelerating climate catastrophe and increasing corporate commitment to a green pivot, most investors are still refusing to support environmental and socially minded shareholder resolutions." Moreover, as depressing as this is, it gets worse:

> Money managers who have signed up to the United Nations-backed Principles for Responsible Investment, a network in which membership means you are committing to support ESG [environmental, social, and governmental] values as part of your investment strategy, are nevertheless failing to do so.
>
> *(2021)*

This is an understatement:

> Players on Wall Street have been torpedoing our chances of averting environmental catastrophe for years. A group of billionaire financiers has made sure the companies the government must partner with to fight climate change are focused on one thing only – making these men (they all seem to be men) even richer

argues Lynn Parramore (2021). She adds that "Instead of leading the world in climate change technology, firms like Apple, GE, and Intel have been pressured to become the personal piggy banks of powerful moneymen – known as hedge fund activists – who can't see beyond the next quarterly report." Naming names and detailing actions by these dominant players have exposed complicit individuals and companies (Wright, Olenick, and Westerville 2021).

Trillions of dollars have flowed into ESG funds that Bloomberg Businessweek terms "Wall Street's new profit engine." Investors who have such concerns would like to know that these funds are actually being disbursed in socially responsible ways. The rating industry, which is not regulated, offers an aura of legitimacy to such investment funds. But it turns out that the criteria for mitigating climate change insure only that environmental regulations pose no threat to the company's bottom line. The most important firm that rates corporations on their "environmental, social, and governance" practices is MSCI. A major contributor to global warming such as McDonald's is upgraded by MSCI because, as difficult as this may be to understand, its emissions are eliminated from their consideration in awarding its score. "This wasn't unusual. Almost half of the 155 companies that got MSCI upgrades never took the basic step of fully disclosing their greenhouse gas emissions." As a result, buying stock in such highly rated companies "can unwittingly increase the carbon footprint" of the well-intentioned pension, university, and other investment funds looking to be socially responsible (Simpson, Rathi, and Kishan 2021). Using such evaluations as a guide, sustainable investment funds may be led to purchasing shares in JPMorgan Chase, which is highly rated – even though since the Paris Agreement it has underwritten more bonds of fossil fuel companies and earned more fees from them than any other bank in the world, as noted earlier.

Aware of the growing ESG concerns, the leveraged buyout industry, which following its preferences has come to be called private equity, celebrates its "impact" funds (a reported 132 such funds existed by the end of 2021) as targeting renewable energy, health care, affordable housing, and other presumed do-good investments. This may help them lure pension funds and others interested in socially responsible investing, even as detractors "question whether an industry known for buying companies and then piling on debt, cutting costs, and cashing out in three to five years will leave those businesses better off," as Alyssa Giachino, climate director of the advocacy group Private Equity Stakeholder Project, declares. "There is an urgent need for greater transparency to avoid what we have now, where companies write a narrative with cherry-picked anecdotes" (Willmer 2021). For example, BlackRock advertises its iShares ESG Aware fund as offering exposure to "U.S. stocks with favorable environmental, social, and governance (ESG) practices." It does not inform potential investors what these "favorable practices" entail (Simpson, Rathi, and Kishan 2021). It could mean anything or nothing at all. The latter is likely closer to the truth, although contrary to the usual understanding, high scores may be designed to indicate that ESG issues do not reduce company profits. This is why the environmental movement must be politically powerful enough to direct public policy in place of the guidance and claims of capital.

Most large U.S. corporations express public concern over the climate crisis with many announcing goals to cut greenhouse gases. At the same time, such leaders as Amazon, Apple, Disney, and Microsoft are among the major companies supporting groups fighting landmark climate legislation. Their pledges to combat the climate crisis continue in their announcements of climate-friendly goals, typically for many years into the future. At the same time such business organizations as the U.S. Chamber of Commerce and the Business Roundtable provide conduits for companies wanting to avoid being seen as opposing spending to address the climate emergency (Milman 2021). Wall Street responds to the prospect of firm guidelines and enforcement mechanisms by insisting that regulation increases prices for consumers and produces market inefficiencies. The ability of energy corporations to avoid regulation and to set their legislative agenda in terms of their bottom line has been well documented (Stokes 2020; Witko, Morgan, Kelly, and Enns 2021). It is difficult not to conclude that capitalism and the incentives it imposes on financial sector decision-makers are largely responsible for continued global warming.

Reports in the business press assert that "investors are more than willing to put up the capital to fund GND goals." As to paying higher taxes so that government can carry out the needed measures, it is argued rather that private finance has the requisite money to fund a Green New Deal. There is no reason to raise the national debt (or taxes on the 1%) to pay for it; just offer investors the right incentives that would of course cost the Treasury lost revenues and that could be gamed for profit. Such discussions include ideas for public-private partnerships, joint ventures, and new bond markets (Dmitrieva and Chasan 2019). Lydia DePillis (2019), then at CNN Business, quotes a consultant who advises investors on public-private partnerships with local governments: " 'There are plenty of companies already out there doing it. I don't think it's the federal government's place to compete with them.'"

This attitude changed as the willingness of the federal government to subsidize corporations who invest in pollution-reducing technologies became evident. Corporations came to an accommodation with the Biden administration, which represented their recognition that there was finally the will to act that had not been demonstrated in the presidencies of Ronald Reagan, the Bushes (George W. Bush had questioned the science of climate change and appointed oil and gas executives to high positions in his administration), and Donald Trump, who had withdrawn from the Paris Accords. Nor had Bill Clinton's and Barack Obama's views on climate change differed substantially from those of the corporate Democrats who advised them on economic policy. As will be discussed in the final chapter, the White House has had some success in developing an American industrial policy to compete with that of China, there were limits to such policies that went beyond guidance through subsidizing private interests. The Biden White House did not have the political support to pass even moderate energy taxes or to cap emissions, certainly not in the context of elevated fuel costs as a result of the boycott of Russian oil. But even without this cost pressure, the politics would be difficult.

After three decades of congressional inertia following the Senate's ratification of the UN Framework Convention on Climate Change in 1992, "the rest of the world sees the truth: America's broken and corrupt Congress remains in the pocket of Big Oil and Big Coal. Financing is at the heart of the geopolitical rupture on climate change" (Sachs 2021). However, the Biden Administration and Senator Charles Schumer, the Democratic leader in the Senate, were able to pass an environmental package in 2022, one which allocated sixty billion dolars to the cause of environmental justice, electric vehicle subsidies, and clean energy, the key parts of the Inflation Reduction Act. The spending would put the U.S. within reach of the Biden goal of fifty percent emissions reduction by 2030. Although the Democratic plan gives significant incentives for corporations to reduce emissions, it also subsidizes oil and natural gas production, a painful concession required for passage of the bill.

However, while corporations are willing to accept subsidies, they have also expressed a reluctance to write off existing profitable capacity. DePillis (2019) points out that from "an investor's perspective, meeting the aggressive goal of moving to 100% clean and renewable energy by 2030 will require retiring a lot of existing infrastructure, such as natural gas power plants and polluting factories, before its lifespan runs out." She quotes Jason Grumet, president of the Bipartisan Policy Center, an organization which has worked to "set a united foundation" for the infrastructure debate. Its website proclaims that "[w]e have trillions of dollars of sunk costs in the current economy"; Grumet counseled, "You don't accelerate the future by messing up the present." Wishing to increase the profits of "the bipartisan" energy companies by continuing as long as possible to harm the planet, the center's funders have good reason to fight the demands of the Green New Deal to end the existence of polluting businesses; that is likely what is meant by "messing up the present." DePillis (2019) reports that for many investors the most disappointing part of the GND is what it does not include: "a promise to strip away regulations, such as environmental reviews that can drag out approvals and throw unexpected obstacles in the path of new projects."

The Dangers of Public-Private Partnership

At the 2021 Conference of the Parties (COP26) of the United Nations Framework Convention on Climate Change (UNFCCC) summit in Glasgow, U.S. Treasury Secretary Janet Yellen (2021) spoke of the inadequate resources of governments, given that "what the world needs is large." In order to finance a global energy transition, "the private sector needs to play a bigger role." Yellen declared that the U.S. supports a capital-markets mechanism that "will help attract significant new private climate finance," providing $500 million a year for clean technology programming. This "partnership" amounts to the government (which presumably lacked the resources to accomplish such a goal) foregoing tax income to incentivize profit-making companies that would control how the energy transition is defined and takes place.

President Biden's special envoy for climate, John Kerry, demonstrated the administration's policy of abandoning government mandates, telling the corporations that they could take the lead in the partnership with their government. As he told *Time* magazine, "I am convinced, unless the private sector buys into this, there won't be a sufficient public-sector path created, because the private sector has the power to prevent that." Perhaps reflecting on the corporate veto of Biden's Build Back Better, the elements of which business heartily approved – except for their refusal to accept higher taxes to pay for the program – he acknowledged, "The private sector has enormous power. And our tax code reflects that in this country. And what we need is our environmental policy to reflect this reality" (Worland 2022: 52). This was surely a remarkably forthright statement.

While heading the Bank of England, Mark Carney had addressed the insurance industry, declaring that if the world were serious about limiting global warming to the two-degree increase target, most coal and oil would have to remain in the ground (Partington 2018). Businesses were not acting responsibly, he asserted, given the long-term costs of droughts, floods, rising sea levels, and other extreme weather events caused by warming. Carney argued that the market would not make the needed changes, nor would financial regulators, unless they were forced to do so. As he explained,

> The horizon for monetary policy extends out to 2–3 years. For financial stability it is a bit longer, but typically only to the outer boundaries of the credit cycle – about a decade. In other words, once climate change becomes a defining issue for financial stability, it may already be too late.
>
> *(2015)*

Such is the consequence of leaving environmental matters to market incentives.

Carney was soon to be widely criticized for his new role, however, that of speaking on behalf of the United Nations Glasgow Financial Alliance for Net Zero, when he declared at the COP26 gathering that financial groups with assets of $130 trillion had committed to programs to cut emissions and to restructure themselves to be ecologically responsible citizens. His stance may, like Kerry's, have reflected his acceptance of the reality that it was only by making it worth the while of companies and investors that climate change could possibly be slowed. Carney (2015), who had taken on the role of U.N. Climate Envoy during COP26, stated that venture capitalists, private equity firms, mutual funds, endowments, and other big investors that buy stocks and bonds could shift funds toward investments helping to lower carbon emissions while still earning a profit. Financial regulators, including the Federal Reserve and the Bank of England, along with the global accounting-standards organization, agreed to add their own oversight to the system through reviews and disclosure standards. "These seemingly arcane but essential changes to the plumbing of finance can move and are moving climate changes from the fringes to the forefront and transforming the financial system in the process," he asserted.

David Benoit (2021), a *Guardian* reporter on the Glasgow conference scene, suggested that the private-sector plans

> are far from concrete. Those that signed up don't all subscribe to the same urgency or time frames; they focus on different industries as helpful and harmful;

and they don't plan to follow the same paths. Few banks or investors even have a true understanding of their current environmental impact, as the data from companies they back is inconsistent or nonexistent.

Even as they flouted the measures proposed by environmentalists, they wanted credit for being involved and active in a popular cause.

The Glasgow Financial Alliance for Net Zero (Gfanz), the grouping of banks, asset managers, insurers, pension funds, and other money managers that Carney had launched in April 2021, which had been greeted by some as a fundamental shift away from purely profit-driven capitalism by the financial sector, was nothing of the kind. To reduce the risk of greenwashing, the U.K. government laid down a single red line, according to Ben Caldecott, finance strategy adviser to the government in the run-up to COP26. Gfanz would have to agree to work alongside an existing verification body for corporate and financial sector pledges: the UN's Race to Zero. "Civil society knew that many of the finance sector commitments were rubbish, so we needed to be proactive on integrity," Caldecott, who also leads the University of Oxford's sustainable finance group, explained. Gfanz's governance documents show that Race to Zero was put in charge of vetting new and existing members and helping define the speed at which they decarbonized their portfolios.

"Yet one year on, and just 10 days before COP27, that red line was erased. Gfanz officially relegated the UN-backed body to the status of one adviser among many," Kenza Bryan reported in the *Financial Times*. Only a quarter of the alliance's 240 largest members offered any policy excluding support for companies developing new coal projects, according to evidence submitted to the UK's environmental audit committee by the campaign group ShareAction. And only a very few leading banks demonstrated a material reduction in bond underwriting for carbon-intensive industries (including mining and automobiles) in 2021 as compared to 2019, according to a report of the financial sector research group Autonomous. Gfanz offered a statement declaring its members' legal rights to follow whatever voluntary pledges they chose (Bryan 2022).

The latest pledges without real intent followed on a half century of denial and unworkable schemes. As Katharina Pistor (2021) argues, "the world has wasted decades tinkering with carbon trading and 'green' financial labeling schemes, and the current vogue is merely to devise fancy hedging strategies ('carbon offsets') in defiance of the simple fact that humanity is sitting in the same boat. 'Offsetting' may serve individual asset holders, but it will do little to avert the climate disaster that awaits us all." She is not alone in declaring that the embrace of "green capitalism" looks very much like simply another strategy to avoid doing what is needed while seeming to be woke. "The notion of green capitalism implies that the costs of addressing climate change are too high for governments to shoulder on their own, and that the private sector always has better answers," Pistor observes and that consequentially, "for advocates of green capitalism, public-private partnership will ensure that the transition from brown to green capitalism will be cost-neutral. Efficiently priced investments in new technologies supposedly will prevent humanity from stepping over into the abyss. But this sounds too good to be true, because it is."

Such a radical critique begins with the assumption that "the entire capitalist system is premised on the privatization of gains and the socialization of losses – not in any nefarious fashion, but with the blessing of the law. The law offers licenses to externalize the costs of despoiling the planet to anybody who is smart enough to establish a trust or corporate entity before generating pollution. It encourages the off-loading of accrued environmental liabilities through restructuring in bankruptcy."

Central bankers and other regulators could establish standards that would require the impact of climate change on the value of firm assets to be accurately reported, forcing the owners to take losses to conform to regulations ordering that pollution-producing assets remain in the ground. While speeding the transition to a safer planet, this would also lead to a dramatic drop in the value of many companies. If banks and insurance companies were forced to accurately disclose the climate risks in their loan portfolios, the loans would not necessarily be made because with this information, the regulators could more accurately carry out stress testing of financial institutions. Companies offering alternative, non-carbon-burning sources of energy and production methods would prosper. There could still be subsidies, but investment and licensing would be understood to entitle a return to taxpayers on their investments. Central banks could also be mandated to disclose which parts of their own balance sheets faced climate risk, and how they intended to manage them in order to set an example by accepting losses. Needless to say, none of this was on the agenda; COP27 broke down, with the less-developed countries demanding restitution for the environmental damage the rich countries had done to them and the planet as well as assistance in meeting the high cost of sustainability.

Meaningful change requires not public-private partnerships but rather governments acting to control how businesses are allowed to function: replacing corporate leaders who violate environmental laws, prosecuting those who are found to be responsible, and limiting investor returns by fining corporations for the harm they inflict (and not allowing such fines to be written off as business expenses). Based on the damage done, this could amount to the imposition of fines exceeding the net value of the companies, effectively requiring their nationalization. As politically difficult and extreme as this may seem, the delays in facing the ecological emergency and the limited time left to make far-reaching, essential change compel such action. The need to radically transform industries is no different from those faced by the nation during two world wars. Only now the enemy is their own economic structures that are warming the planet which need to be radically reconfigured.

The Financialization of Nature

At the same time that global banks and asset managers continue to be the principal funders of oil and gas extraction, deforestation, and biodiversity destruction, they and their ideological co-conspirators proceed in the aggressive commodification of nature, incorporating ecosystem services into the economy "by placing capital values on it and selectively integrating it into capital accumulation itself – a process made easier by the fact that capital makes nature scarcer and more marketable by destroying it" (Foster 2022).

In addition to the creation of the Glasgow Financial Alliance for Net Zero bringing together most of global finance capital, Foster notes two other major interrelated developments occurring at that time: establishing unified rules for global carbon trading markets and announcing the launch of a new class of securities associated with natural asset companies. "Net zero" is corporate-speak for offsetting pollution with efforts to remove carbon from the environment elsewhere, overwhelmingly through the "Reducing Emissions from Deforestation and Forest Degradation" market, which has been shown to be associated with the expropriation of indigenous lands and the removal of its peoples (Crook 2018). This market, with its unregulated and inflated claims to preserve the environment, allows the same putative offsets to be sold many times to different purchasers so that they can continue to pollute with impunity (Schwartzkopff 2022).

Foster (2022) recounts the ongoing development of the perverse construct "natural capital," which involves an explosion of initiatives aimed at "the accumulation and financialization of nature as a means of addressing environmental constraints." In 2011, the U.K. Environment Bank, a private institution devoted to the financialization of nature, received £175,000 from the Shell Foundation to aid it in the development of markets for ecosystem services. The following year, the Natural Capital Committee of the U.K. government and the U.K. Department for Environment, Food, and Rural Affairs began promoting an "aggregate rule" based on the notion of net-zero losses in natural capital in terms of economic value. This involved the development of mechanisms for treating various elements of nature as commensurate, not only with each other but also with commodity markets. Thus, a methodology for managing natural capital had been introduced in which the destruction of biodiversity or the climate would be balanced by offsets that would increase (or protect) natural assets by an amount of equal value elsewhere. Of course, treating species and ecosystems as commensurable and substitutable, as commodities is typical of capitalism's indifference to protecting diversity; it can be seen as actually criminal from the perspective of understanding natural diversity (Foster and Burkett 2017).

Applying Marx's understanding of fictitious capital, Guilherme Leite Gonçalves and Bruno H. P. Rosado (2022) suggest that speculators will overvalue future earnings from the exploitation of nature, causing an excessive use of resources that, based on Marx's expectation, will lead to a bubble in financial speculation and further overproduction which will add to greenhouse gases and an intensification of global warming. They saw the likelihood of such a development in the years of the Covid-19 pandemic.

Global speculative finance seeks to acquire real assets in the planet's ecosystem to allow for the creation of new asset products. Already the commodification and privatization of water have led to sharp price increases that burden poor, working-class communities, producing massive opposition. Nonetheless, the financialization of the earth proceeds. A publication of the Corporate EcoForum, a group of twenty-four transnational companies that includes Alcoa, Coca Cola, Dell, and Disney (in conjunction with The Nature Conservancy), titled the New Business Imperative: Valuing Nature Capital, estimated that in 2012, seventy-two trillion dollars of "free" goods and services could be monetized, it declared, "for the purpose of more sustainable growth." By putting a price on nature, the claim was that it could be preserved and would be used "efficiently." The opportunities to leverage "water-quality trading, wetland banking and threatened species banking, and natural carbon sequestration" were celebrated (Foster 2022).

Economists argue that setting a price on natural resources will protect them from overuse since they will no longer appear "free." The claim is that the price system is based on effective demand – demand backed by purchasing power offering the best way forward. However, allocation based on preexisting wealth and level of income rather than on essentials like water and clean air (based on need) permits the future of wetlands, attractive to developers, to be purchased rather than protected by laws.

The privatization of water has proceeded rapidly with the recognition that as it becomes scarce, water will grow more valuable than oil and other commodities. Agricultural lands in Africa and Latin America, now the shared property of indigenous people and providing substance for peasant agriculturalists, are being sold by national governments even as such communities and small holders struggle to retain their traditional right to survive on land that has long belonged to their people. For decades La Via Campesina has led an international campaign for family-based sustainable agriculture, food sovereignty, the rights of peasants, and an ecological alternative to natural-capital colonization. The conflicts between financial speculators and the stewards of the earth are ongoing and intense.

Addressing itself to the events on the main stage of the COP, a *Financial Times* editorial declared in an editorial that the conference "has turned into a PR event, where leaders are giving beautiful speeches and announcing fancy commitments and targets, while behind the curtains governments of the Global North countries are still refusing to take any drastic climate action." The editorial pointed out that claims of a 130 trillion dollar commitment from the private sector were overblown, that it was a measure of the assets of the companies involved, not of the amount which they declared they would commit to reverse climate change. The editorial lambasted those who had signed the initiative for continuing the funding of fossil fuels. Companies could not be relied upon to take action without stringent, strictly enforced directives. "Regulators could consider whether lenders should be penalised through higher capital charges for holding legacy brown assets on their balance sheets," the *Financial Times* editorial urged; otherwise at the next COP, if they had not yet made the pledged changes, countries and corporations would have to explain "why they have not complied with agreements made at this one." The commentary expressed awareness that "it is all too easy to overpromise and underdeliver, as the path of the previous 25 conferences of the parties has demonstrated."

While waiting for a technological fix to climate change, corporations attempt to convince the public that they are "woke." Airlines are making planes lighter, economizing on fuel. Restaurants and movie theaters are switching from paper towels to hand dryers in their restrooms, saving on the cost of paper. Hotels urge people to hang up towels and forego the expected daily sheet changes, saving energy and money. The fleets used by box stores and logistics firms rely on technology to reduce energy while their trucks are idling; similarly, software that creates more efficient routes improves fuel efficiency, further reducing carbon dioxide emissions and saving expenses for the companies (Martin and Dent 2019). But whether such changes that increase profits are sufficient is a question – to which the answer is "no." Marginal steps to reduce carbon footprints do not reflect a commitment to address the basic, necessary transformation that is required, and delaying action is costly. Agriculture, heavy industry, transportation, finance, and electrical generation technologies are not changing profoundly and quickly enough to avoid a rise above 1.5 degrees Celsius in global heating beyond preindustrial times. Indeed, none of the 2021 forty indicators of the watchdog Systems Climate Lab are on track to meet this Paris Agreement target.

There will be two kinds of economic cost. One will result from implementing the innovative changes required. The second quite different cost will result from existing investments becoming unviable. Financial firms in the world's biggest economies currently possess twenty-two trillion dollars in loans and investments that would be directly affected by a transition from carbon-based energy, according to Moody's Investor Service. Other companies too will be impacted beyond these financial firms. The income of most companies will decrease substantially if they are required to meet ecological standards. Taxes in the U.S. and other wealthy nations will have to increase in order to finance essential changes, and most companies will have to be forced to modify what they produce and how they do it.

In towns and cities across the U.S., acknowledging this new reality will be troublesome for local officials. Data-based research reveals that property values are already altered by expected coastal flooding as sea levels rise (Bernstein, Gustafson, and Lewis 2019). The Federal Reserve Bank of San Francisco has published twelve papers by experts on the damage that climate change is doing to businesses and communities, warning local governments and their lenders of the costs of inaction in what the Fed's Ian Galloway terms "the new abnormal" (Flavelle 2019). Yet to acknowledge this would trigger a decline in property values and tax collection at the same time that there would be a need to spend more to protect endangered property and to relocate instead of rebuild. Denialism can seem politically necessary.

The Difficult Road in Washington

In place of the financiers' criteria for evaluating investments, in 2018 Representative Ocasio-Cortez recommended the creation of a House Select Committee with a mandate to use government initiative to promote ideas and policy for the creation of a Green New Deal. It would entail sustainably shared prosperity in energy, transportation, housing, and healthcare. She also called for living wages with job guarantees for all those willing and able to work. The path for the acceptance of this legislation had been pioneered by the work of progressives. In 2020, Elizabeth Warren (2020) proposed a "Green Apollo Program" to invest in clean-energy technology and a "Green Marshall Plan" devoted to encouraging countries to buy U.S.-made, clean-energy technologies, invoking projects which the nation had earlier sponsored. She suggested replacing the Commerce Department with a "Department of Economic Development" mandated to oversee a national jobs strategy as part of a new "economic patriotism" integral to the Green New Deal. "With big and bold investments in American research, American industry, and American workers, we can lead the global effort to combat climate change – and create more than a million good jobs here at home," she explained. (With a price tag of two trillion dollar, the proposals would require a political revolution, to borrow a term from Bernie Sanders, who offered a transitional plan of his own.)

Sanders' version of the Green New Deal was priced even higher – sixteen trillion dollars – far more than competing plans. But this cost would be paid over fifteen years by compelling the fossil fuel industry to compensate for their pollution through litigation, fees, and taxes and by eliminating federal fossil fuel subsidies. Revenue would also be generated by the renewable energy produced by regional Marketing Authorities (an institution to be established as part of his proposal). Other elements of his overall design to increase the needed revenues would include the income taxes collected from those in the twenty million new jobs created by the plan; the reduced need for federal and state safety-net spending as a result of those well-paying, unionized jobs; and the higher taxes imposed on the wealthy and on large corporations. When Sanders released his Green New Deal proposal, critics found it unrealistic. He responded: "If the environment were a bank, it would have been saved already" (Jones 2019). Looking at the numbers in relation to each other, this is a not unreasonable way to consider the existential environmental emergency.

But even if the Sanders Green New Deal were unable to pay for itself – one might quibble over the numbers – the dollar cost of not acting comprehensively is far greater, while the benefits of acting quickly and substantially are significant. A report of the UN Intergovernmental Panel on Climate Change projected the cost of the threatened increases in global temperatures at fifty-four trillion dollars, a moderate estimate. The actual cost, as the report contended, could run far higher. A more likely increase (on the current path) of 3.7 degrees Celsius would amount to $551 trillion in damages, an unimaginable sum in an unendurable world. The panel's 2021 analysis of the science of global warming reported that the world is likely to heat up by 1.5 degrees Celsius within twenty years, even in a best-case scenario of deep cuts in greenhouse gas emissions. And with rapid emission cuts, temperatures would still continue to rise until at least 2050, the scientists projected, leading to further extreme weather events. To be sure, the calculations are not easy and involve uncertainty, but the evidence suggests that for a long time the damage from environmental destruction has been vastly underestimated (Stern and Stiglitz 2021).

Speaker Pelosi initially refused to consider climate change proposals. In early 2019, she referred to the "Green New Dream – or whatever they call it" in an effort to protect the vulnerable Democrats in more conservative districts (who had given her party control of the House) from having to take a stand on the issue. In any case, the party was not in the habit of attempting to lead public opinion with cautious incrementalism being the primary tactic of its leadership. This caution did not, needless to say, prevent the feared criticism from political opponents. Republicans derided as all proposals for inclusive, and sustainable growth as impractical and unacceptably costly.

Calls to upgrade power grids and existing buildings for maximum energy efficiency and to overhaul transportation systems to address climate change and rebuild society were termed "a socialist wish list." Bob Salera, speaking for the National Republican Congressional Committee, proclaimed the ideas to be "zany," maintaining that "[t]he socialist Democrats are off to a great start with the roll out of their ridiculous Green New Deal" (Friedman and Thrush 2019). The Congressional Leadership Fund, a super PAC affiliated with the House GOP management, launched digital ads attacking the Green New Deal along with Democrats from competitive districts. (The targets of the ads had not in fact signed onto the legislation that was being attacked, nor to any actual Green New Deal proposal.)

When Congress discussed how to promote economic activity in the face of the shutdown caused by the coronavirus, Mitch McConnell criticized the Democrats for advancing their spending projects. Undaunted, Ocasio-Cortez and Senator Ed Markey introduced a bill to create that Green New Deal. Its aim was to slow climate change by ending the reliance of the U.S. economy on fossil fuels within ten years. They foresaw the creation of millions of good jobs by building a hundred percent renewable electrical system and a national "smart grid"; retrofitting residential and industrial buildings; and creating a low-emission transportation system. Their policy suggestions made headway against the dismissal of centrists and denunciations by those who opposed an increased role of government in confronting what for some was still termed the environment hoax.

The campaign for substantial climate change action was endorsed by President Biden, although he disavowed the GND label. He supported a series of actions, some quickly implemented, that drew heavily on the plans of Markey, AOC, and others. Speaker Pelosi quickly fell in line to support Biden's proposals. Yet gridlock prevailed in Washington, with the Republicans effectively possessing the fifty-two votes in the Senate to veto needed change and Democrats Manchin and Sinema voting against the designs supported by the President, successfully demanding painful compromises that gutted much of the proposed legislation in Build Back Better, which addressed the issue.

Republicans continue to reject any federal intervention to address global warming as government overreach and as a job-destroying, unwarranted intervention in the market. When Sarah Bloom Raskin, a Biden nominee to the Fed's Board of Governors, suggested that the regulators' supervisory power be used to encourage addressing the financial risks associated with climate change, Pat Toomey, the top Republican on the Senate Banking Committee, held up her nomination, saying, "I don't think there should be a Politburo that gets to allocate capital in America." Citing his previous experience of working in the financial industry, Toomey proclaimed, "My highest political value has been freedom, and that includes economic freedom, or else you are not really free" (Dennis 2022).

President Biden (2021) responded, "When I think of climate change and the answers to it, I think of jobs. These aren't pie-in-the-sky dreams. These are concrete actionable solutions. And we know how to do this." He pledged to create "millions of good-paying, union jobs" by building electric cars, installing solar panels and wind turbines, performing the necessary work to cap abandoned wells, and turning polluted land and industrial sites "into the new hubs of economic growth." In a White House address during his first week in office, the President declared, "Today is 'Climate Day' at the White House and – which means that today is 'Jobs Day' at the White House. We're talking about American innovation, American products, American labor. And we're talking about the health of our families and cleaner water, cleaner air, and cleaner communities. We're talking about national security and America leading the world in a clean energy future." Such pronouncements were sensible politics as a way of selling his proposals, but they did not influence Senate Republicans who, under their leader Mitch McConnell, insisted on denying President Biden a political victory on any issue and of course avoiding disappointing their coal, oil, and gas funders.

The administration's Financial Stability Oversight Council, chaired by the Secretary of the Treasury and containing members from the major financial regulatory agencies, has termed climate change an "emerging threat" to the stability of the American financial system. Their report points to losses for insurance companies from weather-related causes; a drop in the value of assets and companies tied to oil, gas, and coal; and the harm to the planet following from the use of these sources of energy – for which regulated changes would be costly, impinging yet more heavily on the financial system. Defensive measures needed to be put in place that could both secure lower emissions and protect financial stability from any ensuing market fallout (Rappeport and Flavelle 2021). However, with the war in Ukraine leading to escalating gasoline prices that were damaging the president's popularity and the prospects of the Democrats, the administration took a number of steps to increase oil production, abandoning its efforts to prevent greater burning of carbon-based fuels in an effort to satisfy the public.

What Is to Be Done?

Progress in combating global warming must occur on many fronts, requiring a careful consideration of how change can be accommodated so that the inevitable destabilizing impacts are minimized. In the case of electric cars, for instance, the material required to build the vehicles matters, as does the source of the electricity to charge the cars. And attention needs to be paid to what happens to the people employed in the many gas stations destined to close as the transition proceeds. (There are currently 100,000 gas stations in the U.S. employing 900,000 people.) Moreover, the cars will be sold online, reducing the number of employees involved – no salesmen waiting for customers to visit showrooms. With fewer parts and internet updates of software for vehicles there will also be less demand for servicing, and so fewer mechanics. A similar step-by-step examination needs to be pursued for virtually all comparable change in what is produced. Undertaking and supporting the process of such transitions in so many sectors is an immense challenge; it suggests a crucial role for government, one extending well beyond the conventional limits of peacetime capitalism. Planning will need to take account of forward and backward linkages as profit-maximizing considerations are replaced by ecologically driven measures.

At prices prevailing before the pandemic, leaving polluting sources of energy in the ground could result in as much as twenty-eight trillion dollars in lost revenue for oil, gas, and coal companies over the next twenty years. Before the pandemic Adam Tooze (2019) wrote that a third of equity and fixed-income assets issued in global financial markets could be classified as part of the natural resource and extraction sectors, along with carbon-intensive power utilities and chemical, construction, and industrial firms. Few were inclined to grasp the extent of the financial disruption the needed changes would entail.

While consensus now exists that humans are to blame for climate change, there has not yet been sufficient scrutiny of the familiar meme that "we are all to blame" and that we must all pitch in and do our bit to live respecting the earth. This still conventional wisdom mistakes why we have entered the Anthropocene, "the period in which humanity, at a specific point in its history, namely the rise of advanced industrial capitalism following the Second World War, became the principal geological force affecting Earth System change," as argued by John Bellamy Foster, Brett Clark, and Richard York (2010). They suggest a trajectory of the collapse of industrial civilization and the vast die-down of the human species that could rapidly end the Anthropocene if we do not acknowledge what it is in human behavior and the organization of production and consumption that has allowed such a development and what must be done to address it.

Andreas Malm has proposed substituting the Capitalocene for the Anthropocene to emphasize that it is capitalism that is destroying the planet (2016: 391). But as Foster and Clark (2021) respond, while "maintaining the earth as a safe home for humanity and for innumerable other species that live on it, is impossible under a system geared to the exponential accumulation of capital," such a collapse is not inevitable. They suggest the importance of understanding Capitalinian as a phase of the Anthropocene – that if we are to survive, we "will have to give rise to a radically transformed set of socioeconomic relations, and indeed a new mode of sustainable human production, based on a more communal relation of human beings with each other and the earth." They propose that this necessary (but not inevitable) future geological age following the Capitalinian by means of an ecological and social revolution he termed the Communian age, "derived from communal, community, commons." It is not humanity that is the problem, but rather the economic and political system under which humanity currently lives that is their essential target.

A final question for this chapter: "What does it feel like to live on the brink of a vast historical change?" It is one that Kim Stanley Robinson (2021) rhetorically asks, answering, "It feels like now." Robinson continues, "With its atmosphere of dread foreboding, our time more resembles the years preceding the second world war, when everyone lived with a sensation of helplessly sliding down a slippery slope and over a cliff." But such historical analogies are inadequate in the unprecedented Anthropocene. Just two years after publishing his landmark novel describing events taking place in 2030, *The Ministry for the Future*, he wrote. "I see now we are already well begun. My timeline was completely off; events have accelerated yet again." Referring to a passage attributed to both Fredric Jameson and Slavoj Žižek – "Easier to imagine the end of the world than the end of capitalism?" – Robinson answers this question as well:

No. The time has come to admit that we control our economy for the common good. Crucial at all times, this realisation is especially important in our current need to dodge a mass-extinction event. The invisible hand never picks up the cheque; therefore we must govern ourselves.

(2021)

But which "we" will govern in a deeply divided polity has yet to be determined. The fate of the earth rests on the answer to this last question.

References

Bennett Institute for Public Policy. 2022. *Beyond GDP*. University of Cambridge.

Benoit, David. 2021. "COP26 Latest: Sunak and Yellen Urge Private Sector to Drive Clean Economic Transition." *Wall Street Journal*, November 3.

Bernstein, Asif, Matthew T. Gustafson and Ryan Lewis. 2019. "Disaster on the Horizon: The Price Effect of Sea Level Rise." *Journal of Financial Economics*, 134(2).

Biden, Joe. 2021. "Remarks by President Biden Before Signing Executive Actions on Tackling Climate Change, Creating Jobs, and Restoring Scientific Integrity." *The White House*, January 27.

Bolton, Patrick, Morgan Depres, Luiz Awazu, Pereira Da Silva, Frédéric Samama and Romain Svartzman. 2021. "The Green Swan: Central Banking and Financial Stability in the Age of Climate Change." *Bank for International Settlement and Banque de France*, January. https://www.bis.org/publ/othp31.htm.

Bolton, Patrick, Harrison Hong, Marcin Kacperczyk and Xavier Vives. 2021. *Resilience of the Financial System to Natural Disasters*. CEPR Press.

Bryan, Kenza. 2022. "COP27: Mark Carney Clings to His Dream of a Greener Finance Industry." *Financial Times*, November 9.

Carney, Mark. 2014. "Inclusive capitalism – Creating a Sense of the Systemic." *Conference on Inclusive Capitalism*, London, May 27, Bank for International Settlements. https://www.bis.org/review/r140528b.pdf.

Carney, Mark. 2015. "Breaking the Tragedy of the Horizon – Climate Change and Financial Stability." *Speech Given at Lloyd's of London*, September 29, Bank of England.

Council of Economic Advisers. 2023. Annual Report of the Council of Economic Advisers. https://www.whitehouse.gov/wp-content/uploads/2023/03/ERP-2023.pdf.

Council of Economic Advisers and Office of Management and Budget. 2022. "Climate-Related Macroeconomic Risks and Opportunities." *White House*, April 4.

Crook, Martin. 2018. "Conservation as Genocide: REDD Versus Indigenous Rights in Kenya." *Climate & Capitalism*, March 15.

Dennis, Steven T. 2022. "The Fed Goad in Congress." *Bloomberg Businessweek*, March 14.

DePillis, Lydia. 2019. "Wall Street Wants an Infrastructure Plan, but the Green New Deal Isn't It." *CNN Business*, February 14.

Dietz, Simon, Alex Bowen, Charlie Dixon and Philip Gradwell. 2016. "'Climate Value at Risk' of Global Financial Assets." *Nature, Climate, Change*, 6.

Dmitrieva, Katia and Emily Chasan. 2019. "Wall Street Has Plenty of Green for the New Deal." *Bloomberg Businessweek*, February 19.

Fancy, Tariq. 2021. "Financial World Greenwashing the Public with Deadly Distraction in Sustainable Investing Practices." *USA Today*, March 16.

Fichtner, Jan, Eelke M. Heemskerk and Javier Garcia-Bernardo. 2017. "Hidden Power of the Big Three? Passive Index Funds, Re-concentration of Corporate Ownership, and New Financial Risk." *Business & Politics*, 19(2).

Flavelle, Christopher. 2019. "Government Overhaul of National Flood Insurance Cheered by Climate Resilience Experts." *Insurance Journal*, March 18.

Foster, John Bellamy. 2022. "Defense of Nature: Resisting Financialization of the Earth." *Monthly Review*, 73(11).

Foster, John Bellamy and Paul Burkett. 2017. *Marx and the Earth: An Anti-Critique*. Haymarket Books.

Foster, John Bellamy and Brett Clark. 2021. "The Capitalinian: The First Geological Age of the Anthropocene." *Monthly Review*, 73(4).

Foster, John Bellamy, Brett Clark and Richard York. 2010. *The Ecological Rift*. Monthly Review Press.

Friedman, Lisa and Glenn Thrush. 2019. "Liberal Democrats Formally Call for a 'Green New Deal,' Giving Substance to a Rallying Cry." *New York Times*, February 7.

Gandel, Stephen. 2022. "Law Leads Banks to Vow Not to 'Discriminate' Against Firearm Trade." *New York Times*, May 29.

Gelles, David and Hiroko Tabuchi. 2022. "How an Organized Republican Effort Punishes Companies for Climate Action." *New York Times*, May 27.

Gonçalves, Guilherme Leite and Bruno H. P. Rosado. 2022. "Prediction and Caution after COVID-19 Crisis: The Ecological and Epidemiological Risks of Financial Speculation." *Capital & Class*, 46(4).

Greenfield, Patrick and Kalyeena Makortoff. 2020. "Study: Global banks 'Failing Miserably' on Climate Crisis by Funneling Trillions into Fossil Fuels." *Guardian*, March 18.

Hodgson, Camilla and Stephen Morris. 2021. "Global Finance Industry Sinks $119bn Into Companies Linked to Deforestation." *Financial Times*, October 21.

Jones, Jake. 2019. "'If Environment Were a Bank,' Says Bernie Sanders, 'It Would Have Been Saved Already'." *Common Dreams*, August 30.

Lerner, Sharon. 2022. "Bottled Water Giant BlueTriton Admits Claims of Recycling and Sustainability Are 'Puffery'." *The Intercept*, April 26.

Lewis, Simon. 2022. "Scientists Have Just Told Us How to Solve the Climate Crisis – Will the World Listen?" *Guardian*, April 6.

Liptak, Adam. 2022. "Supreme Court Strips Federal Government of Crucial Tool to Control Pollution." *New York Times*, June 30.

Lustgarten, Abrahm. 2022. "The Barbados Rebellion." *New York Times Magazine*, July 31.

Malm, Andreas. 2016. *Fossil Capital: The Rise of Steam Power and the Roots of Global Warming*. Verso.

Martin, Chris and Millicent Dent. 2019. "Corporate America Has Found a Way to Turn a Profit Off Being Green." *Bloomberg News*, September 20.

McGreal, Chris. 2022. "Rightwing Lobby Group Alec Driving Laws to Blacklist Companies That Boycott the Oil Industry." *Guardian*, February 8.

Milman, Oliver. 2021. "Apple and Disney among Companies Backing Groups Against US Climate Bill." *Guardian*, October 1.

Neale, Jonathan and Amandla Editorial Collective. 2021. "Climate: Rage, Despair and Hope." *Amandla*, 77.

Parramore, Lynn. 2021. "Meet the 'New Koch Brothers' – The Hedge Fund Activists Wrecking America's Green New Deal." *Institute for New Economic Thinking*, March 4.

Partington, Richard. 2018. "Mark Carney Warns of Climate Change Threat to Financial System." *Guardian*, April 6.

Pistor, Katharina. 2021. "The Myth of Green Capitalism." *Project Syndicate*, September 21.

Plummer, Brad. 2023. "World Has Less Than a Decade to Stop Catastrophic Warming, U.N. Panel Says." *New York Times*, March 20.

Quinson, Tim. 2021. "Wall Street Is Close to Triggering a Climate Financial Crisis." *Bloomberg News*, December 14.

Rappeport, Alan and Christopher Flavelle. 2021. "U.S. Warns Climate Change Is 'Emerging Threat' to Financial System." *New York Times*, October 22.

Robinson, Kim Stanley. 2021. "A Climate Plan for a World in Flames; Humanity Stands on the Brink of Disaster. But with Creative Thinking and Collective Will, We May Still Have Time to Avert Catastrophe." *Financial Times*, August 20.

Roe, Mark J. 2022. "Is Stock-Market Short-Termism Really Behind Climate Change?" *Project Syndicate*, June 24.

Sachs, Jeffrey D. 2021. "Fixing Climate Finance." *Project Syndicate*, November 15.

Schwartzkopff, Frances. 2022. "Crazy Carbon Offsets Market Prompts Calls for Regulation." *Bloomberg*, January 6.

Simpson, Cam, Akshat Rathi and Saijel Kishan. 2021. "The ESG Mirage." *Bloomberg Businessweek*, December 13.

Stern, Nicholas and Joseph E. Stiglitz. 2021. "Getting the Social Cost of Carbon Right." *Project Syndicate*, February 15.

Stokes, Leah Cardamore. 2020. *Short Circuiting Policy: Interest Groups and the Battle Over Clean Energy and Climate Policy in the American States*. Oxford University Press.

Tabuchi, Hiroko. 2021. "Obscure Names on a Top 10 List of Big Polluters." *New York Times*, June 2.

Táíwò, Olúfẹ́mi. 2022. "How BlackRock, Vanguard, and UBS Are Screwing the World." *New Republic*, March 7.

Tan, Weizhen. 2021. "BlackRock's Larry Fink Says Big Companies Shouldn't Be the Only 'Climate Police' In the World. *CNBC*, September 28.

Tooze, Adam. 2019. "Why Central Banks Need to Step Up on Global Warming." *Foreign Policy*, July 20.

University of Cambridge. 2022. "Beyond GDP: Time to Measure Inclusive Wealth and Change Economics." *Science Blog*, April 28.

Warren, Elizabeth. 2020. Tackling the Climate Crisis Head On. https://elizabethwarren.com/plans/climate-change.

Willmer, Sabrina. 2021. "Buyout Funds Want to Save the Planet." *Bloomberg Businessweek*, November 8.

Witko, Christopher, Jana Morgan, Nathan J. Kelly and Peter K. Enns. 2021. *Hijacking the Agenda: Economic Power and Political Influence*. Russell Sage Foundation.

Worland, Justin. 2022. "Climate Goes Private; Planet Earth's Future Now Rests in the Hands of Big Business." *Time,* April 25/May 2.

Wright, Georgia, Liat Olenick and Amy Westerville. 2021. "The Dirty Dozen: Meet America's Top Climate Villains." *Guardian*, October 27.

Yellen, Janet. 2021. "Keynote Remarks by Secretary of the Treasury Janet L. Yellen at COP26 in Glasgow, Scotland at the Finance Day Opening Event." *U.S. Treasury Department*, November 3. https://home.treasury.gov/news/press-releases/jy0457.

9
MAKING THE FUTURE
Beyond Financialization

Preceding chapters have argued that financial crises have been brought about by excessive risk-taking that governments and central banks fail to control, and that the costs of the subsequent downturns vastly exceed the capacity of the institutions causing the crisis to compensate the society, assuming they are asked to do so. But they are not asked; restoring and enhancing the existing financial system is the priority of policy makers. It has further been maintained that the growth of financialization has intensified inequality and economic insecurity for most workers while permitting a growing concentration of markets that allows for the increased exploitation of consumers, workers, and suppliers. Tech firms protected by moats provided by increasing returns to scale and intellectual property rights and hedge funds and private equity firms able to leverage their capital with borrowed funds are able to appropriate the economic surplus in their favor in a system of redistributive growth.

A regime of low taxes for presumed job creators, the deregulation of markets, and limited government have been discredited. The reappearance of high inflation, painful to the voters and so the focus of partisan attention, obscures the reality that there is "too much finance" for the good of the economy (Arcand, Berkes, and Panizza 2015). For many this suggested that financialization should be replaced by a democratizing of money (Weber 2018). Because, such a transformation is so profound an undertaking and would be at the expense of so many powerful interests, the creation of an economic democracy, without a political revolution will be rejected for doing the same things in a period of crisis that have not been appropriate in the past. While not inclined to speak of popular control of the economy, respected voices from the regulatory community have become fearful of the economic and political consequences of financialization as a mode of accumulation. They are right to be concerned, as the many warnings of a global "lost decade," to draw on the

DOI: 10.4324/9781003385240-9

characterization by the World Bank, and the warnings of the many economists who have also been cited suggest.

As total debt continues to increase in relation to GDP, financial markets have become more fragile due to the impact of higher interest rates. Solving the problem of unpayable debt by creating still more debt cannot continue indefinitely without engendering a loss of faith in the credit-worthiness of the borrowers. Michael Hudson (2021) is not incorrect when he argues that "we face a stark choice: either debt write-downs followed by renewed and more equitable income growth; or continuing wealth concentration, accelerating debt growth, widespread foreclosures and another crash."

As discussed, a preferable means for controlling the inflation and slow growth that now afflict the world is to address income inequality by taxing the affluent and the corporations that use their profits to purchase their own stock, a policy that would redirect the social surplus that now goes to asset speculation to an alternative growth model which would achieve two goals. The first is to combat global warming and the destruction of nature. The second is to absorb the workers who are currently being displaced by labor-saving technological change, and by doing tasks that pay little, offer no career prospects for advancement, are unpleasant, mindless, and provide no dignity and respect to the worker. Otherwise, tendencies leading to the stagnation prevalent in the contemporary conjuncture will remain, offset only by a series of temporizing expedients, most significantly the policy of the continued creation of greater debt.

There are also the global crises of widespread increasing hunger, the climate crisis, war, and the dysfunctional trade and investment regimes. These combine in a form that is part of what has been termed "the polycrisis," a set of interdependent crises in which "the whole is greater than the sum of its parts," as Adam Tooze tweeted (December 4, 2021). Tooze has offered his own long list of challenges: "War, raising the specter of nuclear conflict, climate change, threatening famine, flood, and fire. Inflation, forcing central banks to crush consumer demand. The pandemic, closing factories and overloading hospitals" (Lowrey 2022). Tooze (2022) believes "a problem becomes a crisis when it challenges our ability to cope and thus threatens our identity," and that "in the polycrisis the shocks are disparate, but they interact. . . . At times one feels as if one is losing one's sense of reality." It certainly seems as though many have done so, at times accepting alternative realities, conspiracy theories, and violent solutions rather than facing the future with an optimism of the will that accepts the pessimism of the intellect as the basis for devising a better future.

The political implications of such stress and disorientation are a subject for another occasion but the route to improvement is clear enough. It involves collective action, cooperation in the common interest. This is difficult in a world of narrow nationalisms and xenophobic hatreds. But the "polycrisis is really unprecedented. And what is very central to all of this is that no one country can solve this crisis on its own. This is the time that you need the world working together. You need global solidarity," World Trade Organization Director-General Ngozi Okonjo-Iweala declares – a sentiment that is widely echoed (Azeez 2022).

Awareness of the polycrisis complicates any consideration of the role of financialization. However, many of these individual crises can be addressed by a single policy: the Green New Deal involves both its social justice elements and social infrastructural investment plans as well as the herculean task of rethinking what is produced, how it is best produced, for whom, and using the inputs and public infrastructure must be designed to produce an ecologically sound economy. The Green New Deal is opposed by conservatives who offer no alternative growth strategy beyond the perpetuation of a petro-based economic order, which is of a piece with their denial of the extent of the devastation that will follow from allowing global warming to continue. The spending that is denounced by conservatives is not only essential; it will also birth new industries, methods of production, and tasks that will increase productivity and promote sustainable growth, in place of the speculative finance driving the current regime.

In an ironical turn, it is the military and economic challenge of China in the face of the diminishing U.S. hegemony that has prompted American politicians to reconsider the country's long-standing commitment to free trade and to follow China's lead in pursuing its own version of state-led industrial policy. With the shock of strained supply chains, reshoring has grown attractive and protecting American producers from foreign competition, especially from China, has become national policy during the Biden administration. It should be said that while it may be useful a political stance to attack China as the new enemy, it makes little sense in a world in which the two superpowers need to cooperate for mutual advantage despite the obvious differences in their systems. It has proven difficult for Washington to forbid investment in China, seen as the country's leading economic competitor and an enemy seeking to replace the U.S. as global hegemon and to punish other nations as the U.S. wishes to isolate China while calling such arm twisting American "leadership." An increasingly multipolar world feels the disadvantage of America's control of the international reserve currency, transfer mechanisms, and the power to veto the investment policies of its allies. More and more nations are refusing to choose sides between the U.S. and a China with which they do a great deal of business.

While there is bipartisan agreement that Washington must help U.S.-based industries to better compete with China, the two political parties differ as to how to achieve this goal. Ambassador Katherine Tai (2022), Biden's U.S. Trade Representative and a presidential cabinet member, offers the view that "Trade has got to be about more than just unfettered liberalization, cheap goods, and maximizing efficiencies. Now, we have not sworn off market opening, liberalization, and efficiency. But it cannot come at the cost of further weakening our supply chains, exacerbating high-risk reliances, decimating our manufacturing communities, and destroying our planet. We need to update the playbook and bring more people in, so that more get pieces of a bigger pie."

Deputy Secretary of the Treasury Wally Adeyemo explains how the Biden administration was accomplishing this: "Using the federal government's scale to unleash the economic potential of communities that have too long faced barriers to their full participation is critical to building sustainable economic growth in this country." He continued, "That's why the CHIPS Act includes workforce and research investments targeted at both underserved geographies and institutions like Historically Black Colleges and Universities that will help broaden opportunity to enter STEM fields" (Tucker 2022).

The approach of the Biden administration has been described as a progressive supply-side policy, involving government working better with market forces and targeting subsidies to pay for what is desired (Klein 2021). Roosevelt Institute economists have read through the extensive studies undertaken by federal government departments, prompted by the Biden White House, on how Washington can provide a groundwork for sustainable growth and a clean energy future, paying for the transition through an equitable tax code. The extent to which some of the reviewed material stresses the need for government planning, ownership, and control, along with the problems with relying on market solutions, suggests how an alternative to financialization as a growth regime can secure the future both of the planet and of a caring society.

Needless to say, programs such as assisting historically black colleges and universities are not a priority for Republican voters, and the detailed targeting and enforcement of "deep state" rules are likely to be opposed by Republicans as restrictive of market freedom. Nor are Republicans likely to support investments targeted at making the U.S. more competitive vis-à-vis China regarding climate change, which they continue to deny to be a problem that government should address. The party has been clear that it regards the Democrats as using climate change as an excuse to pursue a liberal agenda. It is probable that the Republicans in power would favor investment subsidies going to those parts of the country that vote for them, the rural, predominantly white red states, while allowing corporate interests to spend subsidies as they wish with few if any government constraints. Republicans are also likely to favor tax cuts to "job creators," as they have for decades, rather than entering the thicket of industrial policy, and they will spend most of their effort on undoing what Biden has managed to achieve. This suggests continued funds for asset speculation as well as continued financialization of the economy. The need for the American economy to compete better in the global political economy again the rise of China is most salient; however, other countries are becoming more important as well which means that the norms of property rights are open for review in unexpected ways.

A New (or Rather Old) Economic Philosophy

Sanjukta Paul (2020) argues that because antitrust "has effectively established a state monopoly on the allocation of coordination rights, we ought to view coordination rights as a public resource, to be allocated and regulated in the public interest rather than for the pursuit of only private ends." That is, the well-being of companies in the marketplace should not be the main criterion by default. Other interests – those of workers, consumers, and communities – are also relevant;

they should be acknowledged and legally incorporated. The "moral economy" origins of antitrust doctrines, even in the 19th-century restraint of trade doctrine to which the statutory language refers were effectively written out of antitrust history by the Chicago School economists, a procedure that allowed the reverse of the legislative intent of the progressive, populist-driven demand to control the monopolists. Paul argues that this "inversion is not an accident. Judicial primacy in antitrust has been associated with a deflationary view of legislative process and democratic potential." Narrow self-interest became the chief guide to the understanding of law and economics by economists, corporate lawyers, and judges (who are often members of the Federalist Society). They achieved state-sanctioned arrangements that vary from the entitlements and constraints on unions in collective bargaining to publicly set rules and contract enforcement. Once again, the issue involves what alternative forms of regulation and economic coordination are desirable. This discourse is increasingly informed by the consequences of global warming for the economy.

Benjamin Braun argues,

> In a system in which financial return is structurally linked to predation, exercising labor power through capital stewardship is doomed to fail. Unlocking the progressive promise of labor's capital requires a macro-financial regime that strictly regulates finance and that allows for greater economic democracy.
>
> *(2022: 77)*

From the perspective of such critics, economic decisions have political and ethical consequences, a consideration that comprises a central part of what the Scottish moral philosophers who birthed economics, or rather political economy, studied and wrote about – a perspective that may be coming into its own once again (Tabb 1999).

Diane Coyle (2022) points out that the transition to a carbon–neutral economy "will make it impossible for competition authorities to keep operating as they have over the past few decades." For example, because sharing data among firms is essential to reducing waste as the world moves to sustainability, increasing energy efficiency across supply chains in all sectors of the economy "it will be up to competition authorities to decide which data companies may share, which data they must share, and how to monitor their compliance. Regulators must also deepen their understanding of which technologies must be widely shared to enable competition and accelerate the shift to a carbon-neutral economy." Such observations emphasize the need to abandon Chicago School antitrust thinking not only because it inhibits the emergence of new completion from emergent innovative firms, but more substantially because it presumes "an absence of radical structural change. Markets are presumed to be dynamic, but only up to a point. An analysis aiming to understand the impact of, say, 5–10% price increases in clearly defined markets is useless when the prices of some technologies plunge and entirely new markets emerge."

When this survival framework is introduced, a number of other concerns can take on new significance. While self-interest may guide individual choices, many wish to see the needs of all met as part of a strategic order that is intended to preserve the planet in something like its current condition. Since the alternative development model must be global, concern for others in faraway places comes into focus necessarily as a matter of self-interest. This allows support for those who may prefer to live in an economy that treats all of its members as equals regardless of race, gender, and ethnicity, the "another world that is possible," to use the phrase made popular by the World Social Forum: an economy that provides the basics for a good life through meaningful work and chooses to include those unable to participate in the labor force. Such a dramatic widening of the circle of those who are part of an "us" can be mandated by the self-interested desire to avoid massive climate refugee movement.

What is necessary, as Mariana Mazzucato (2022) argues, is to "replace the old, entrenched narrative in which only the private sector plays the leading role, and the state merely fixes market failures along the way." There is an alternative, more constructive to create value for the society: "What is needed is a clear notion of collective investment for the common good, with the public sector as investor of first resort, not just lender of last resort." This is a declaration that conservatives reject on principle and also because the connection she and others want to make between fairness and growth does not follow on economic grounds, only on moral and ethical ones – and these are not the ethics and morality held by conservatives. Those on the right, and even the liberals who propose a very different progressive supply-side approach, do not agree with Mazzucato when she asserts that "we need a Green Deal that emphasizes the 'deal' as much as the 'green.'" This necessitates a new social contract. "Both the risks and rewards associated with public investments in the green transition should be socialized. It is no accident that profits are growing while investment is not. That is simply a reflection of increasing financialization across the Fortune 500."

Mazzucato points to the more than five trillion dollars that have been allotted to buybacks in the U.S. over the previous decade and that have, as discussed earlier, gone to asset speculation. She understands that governments either can simply give money to companies to bail them out, hoping they will invest in socially desirable ways, or that conditions can be placed on assistance, enforcing social priorities over those of the market. Governments can stop outsourcing when the process lowers cost by providing unwarranted profits to companies that cut wages, initiate speed-ups, and reduce the quality of the public services they are mandated to produce. Perhaps the most important aspect of a progressive economic agenda is that it "needs to be inspirational. Progressive economic policies must be accompanied by citizen engagement to forge a clear link with improvements in people's lives." This can mean more than economic security and decent jobs: "Imagine, for example, if the arts were leveraged today as they were in U.S. President Franklin Roosevelt's Works Progress Administration."

We are beginning to see analysis that, in opposition to the rise of a hard-right politics in so many countries, offers a vision of a positive alternative which rejects the anger and thoughtless destruction without regard to what must be built in place of the existing system. It is one that recognizes that society is the collective creator of its own future. In such a perspective, Thomas Piketty maintains that "All wealth is collective by nature in the sense that it relies on the work of hundreds, thousands, millions of engineers, technicians, the accumulation of knowledge." For him this means that private property is a social construction "that we invent in order to organize economic and social relations." And because millionaires and billionaires do not inhabit a world in which it is they who create their vast wealth, which is accumulated rather through the efforts of the collective, "none of these assets are their assets" explains that "we have an institutional setup where you accumulate wealth by using public infrastructure, public education, the health system, and then once you have accumulated the wealth, you push a button and you transfer it somewhere else." Piketty anticipates that a political movement will emerge which will end the ability of the rich to move the collectively produced wealth to some tax haven or into financial speculation, one which will mandate that the social surplus be repurposed for the common good (Marchese 2022).

The individualism that characterizes capitalism as an economic order prevents compassion for those suffering even in their own nation. The calculation of private costs and benefits that preclude a consideration of the social costs that have produced the climate emergency and the destruction of nature, including the growing threat of the extinction of other species which are part of a wider "us," blinds many to the harm being done. We must expand our horizons, nurturing an international and global solidarity that replaces financial calculation as our guiding imperative. Choice is more complicated than mainstream economics suggests and that an artificial separation between economics and politics encourages. As has been argued, choices are made from within legal and regulatory constraints which are in reality mutable. Better choices may be feasible within the context of the alternative norms and institutions that allow them. To simply accept the givens of existing constraints is a decision that members of a society can repudiate. Such a rejection can go beyond redistribution after the fact, or through taxation and government spending, to modify what Piketty terms "the primary distribution," the manner in which legal, fiscal, and educational institutions are designed to provide access either to the select, to the few, or to all.

The Failure of the Existing System

The domain within which capitalism as a system of production "works tolerably well is shrinking," Samuel Bowles and Wendy Carlin (2020) argue. They offer a number of examples beyond finance to support this claim. In their view, it is "imperative on efficiency as well as moral grounds to develop a new paradigm for policies and institutional design" (2020). Such thinking requires an economics that incorporates the important norms and institutions of an era. Such broad-gauged framing is becoming common in a host of discourses. For example, Ingrid Kvangraven and

Carolina Alves (2020) argue that the unpreparedness and inadequate responses by societies to the Covid-19 pandemic exposed weaknesses in the foundations of the dominant economic paradigm. They document the manner in which economics removed itself from broader societal analysis in a vain desire to be more scientific, with less social orientation in its undertakings as a social science, and how this has influenced public policy in problematic ways, leading to the privileging of efficiency over resilience. They view the need for an economics that can regard the economy "as more than just markets and as embedded in society; one that is capable of linking the causes and consequences of the pandemic to our systems of production and distribution." In the wake of the failures of public health systems and supply chains it should be clear that resilience needs to be a priority, one not dismissed by an economics that misunderstands efficiency, seeing it only in market terms and ignoring the demands of social efficiency and the inclusive treatment that has become part of a new awareness of what government needs to be capable of providing.

The theme of the new regime to which many aspire is captured in the term "the care economy," introduced earlier in the discussion of Build Back Better. Anne-Marie Slaughter (2021) maintains that "care is a means to an end, rather than something to be desired and cherished in itself. Care is a duty: we must take care of our planet and our family members." She draws on Hilary Cottam's understanding that the quality and depth of our relationships with others "are essential to our longevity, well-being, and brain development, and to our very humanity." If we expect to repair the earth and ensure the continued sustainability of our interactions with it, "then care – the skills of nurturing and cultivating land, plants, animals, or humans – becomes a central source of value." "Carers," Cottam herself explains, "must be to this technology revolution what engineers were to the last. The work of this century is work of repair: of ourselves and of our wider environments." Slaughter argues that citizens must learn to think of technology as being in the service of "teaching, coaching, mentoring, guiding, nurturing, training, developing, nursing, and many others still to be discovered or rediscovered – that enable human beings to reach their full potential and live in harmony with their environments." This is what others term "the solidarity economy" (Utting, van Dijk, and Matheï 2014; Kawano 2020). It is incompatible with an economic regime in which financialization dominates.

Mainstream economic models have not provided useful answers in their reliance on cost minimization and output maximization from the perspective of private ownership. Reprising the assertions made by Jeremy Rudd offered in Chapter 2, the ideas that "everyone knows to be true" may actually be "arrant nonsense." It will be from mainline or heterodox economics that a new regulatory regime will emerge, one recognizing as Franklin D. Roosevelt declared in his 1937 Second Inaugural Address that "We have always known that heedless self-interest was bad morals; we know now that it is bad economics." Such an orientation calls for a willingness to allow public financing of the provisioning, directly or indirectly, of the services voters say they need and the majority welcome. It is just such a philosophical awareness that informs much respected economic research (Sen, Deaton, and Besley 2020).

Central to relying on a preference for a moral economy as a guide to how research questions are chosen is the rejection of the socially costly asset speculation activities of a regime of financialization that is incapable of producing inclusive, sustainable development. The burden of the weight of all that financialization has been responsible for suggests the urgent need for the replacement of financiers with those who care.

Economists inclined to a liberal socialist orientation (as Keynes used that designation), will welcome pressure from environmental activists – time is growing short to embrace a Green New Deal – and as the threat of financialization and a broader neoliberalism continues to do great damage. Indeed, not only economists and liberal socialists who study finance and macroeconomics have grown increasingly disengaged from traditional approaches as it becomes clear that conventional analysis is responsible to a significant degree for our current predicament. The task is to design better measures and to establish the details of what will have to change in how, where, and what is produced and how it is to be distributed in order to meet social justice and planetary goals – and in doing so to confront the failings of the existing economic system. Such essential criteria can help others see what must be done to confront the polycrisis, key elements of which have been discussed in this volume and that all too frighteningly looms before us.

References

Arcand, Jean, Enrico Berkes and Ugo Panizza. 2015. "Too Much Finance?" *Journal of Economic Growth*, 20(2).

Azeez, Wasilat. 2022. "Okonjo-Iweala Makes Case for Global Solidarity to Alleviate Economic Crises." *The Cable*, May 31.

Bowles, Samuel and Wendy Carlin. 2020. "Shrinking Capitalism." *American Economic Association Papers and Proceedings*, 110.

Braun, Benjamin. 2022. "Fueling Financialization: The Economic Consequences of Funded Pensions." *New Labor Forum*, 31(1).

Coyle, Diane. 2022. "The Double Transformation," *Project Syndicate*, December 9.

Hudson, Michael. 2021. "Rent-Seeking and Asset-Price Inflation: A Total-Returns Profile of Economic Polarization in America." *Review of Keynesian Economics*, 9(4).

Kawano, Emily. 2020. "Solidarity Economy: Building an Economy for People and Planet." In James Gustave Speth and Kathleen Courrier, eds. *The New Systems Reader: Alternatives to a Failed Economy*. Routledge.

Klein, Ezra. 2021. "The Economic Mistake the Left Is Finally Confronting." *New York Times*, September 19.

Kvangraven, Ingrid and Carolina Alves. 2020. "Changing the Narrative: Economics After Covid-19." *Review of Agrarian Studies*, 10(1).

Lowrey, Annie. 2022. "A Crisis Historian Has Some Bad News for Us." *The Atlantic*, July 5.

Marchese, David. 2022. "'All Wealth is Collective by Nature.' Thomas Piketty, the Economist of Economic Inequality, Has Faith in a More Equal American Future." *New York Times*, April 10.

Mazzucato, Mariana. 2022. "Toward a Progressive Economic Agenda." *Project Syndicate*, October 5. https://www.project-syndicate.org/commentary/progressive-economic-policy-agenda-for-2022-by-mariana-mazzucato-2022-10

Paul, Sanjukta. 2020. "Antitrust as Allocator of Coordination Rights." *UCLA Law Review*, 67(2).

Sen, Amartya, Angus Deaton and Tim Besley. 2020. "Economics with a Moral Compass? Welfare Economics: Past, Present, and Future." *Annual Review of Economics*, 12.

Slaughter, Anne-Marie. 2021. "Reimagining Care." *Project Syndicate*, November 29.

Tabb, William K. 1999. "Marx and the Long Run." In William K. Tabb, ed. *Reconstructing Political Economy: The Great Divide in Economic Thought*. Routledge.

Tai, Katherine. 2022. "Remarks by Ambassador Katherine Tai at the Roosevelt Institute's Progressive Industrial Policy Conference." October. https://ustr.gov/about-us/policy-offices/press-office/speeches-and-remarks/2022/october/remarks-ambassador-katherine-tai-roosevelt-institutes-progressive-industrial-policy-conference.

Tooze, Adam. 2022. "Welcome to the World of the Polycrisis. Today Disparate Shocks Interact So that the Whole is Worse than the Sum of the Parts." *Financial Times*, October 28.

Tucker, Todd N. 2022. "Five Takeaways from the Roosevelt Institute's Progressive Industrial Policy Forum." *Roosevelt Institute*, October 13.

Utting, Peter, Nadine van Dijk and Marie-Adélaïde Matheï. 2014. "Social and Solidarity Economy: Is There a New Economy in the Making?" *Occasional Paper 10*, United Nations Research Institute for Social Development.

Weber, Beat. 2018. *Democratizing Money? Debating Legitimacy in Monetary Reform Proposals*. Cambridge University Press.

INDEX

Printed in the United States
by Baker & Taylor Publisher Services